MW01707071

HANDLING PROVINCIAL OFFENCE CASES

IN

ONTARIO

2009

John Pearson Allen

of Allen & Allen

&

The Honourable Justice

Rick Libman

of the Ontario Court of Justice

CARSWELL®

Eleanor Carter

ISSN 1719-8283
ISBN 978-0-7798-1966-9 (2009 edition)

A cataloguing record for this publication is available from Library and Archives Canada.

♾ The acid-free paper used in this publication meets the minimum requirements of American National Standard for Information Sciences - Permanence of Paper for Printed Library Materials, ANSI Z39.48-1984.

Composition: Computer Composition of Canada Inc.

THOMSON REUTERS

CARSWELL, A DIVISION OF THOMSON REUTERS CANADA LIMITED

One Corporate Plaza
2075 Kennedy Road
Toronto, Ontario
M1T 3V4

Customer Relations
Toronto 1-416-609-3800
Elsewhere in Canada/U.S. 1-800-387-5164
Fax: 1-416-298-5082
www.carswell.com
E-mail www.carswell.com/email

Foreword

Here, perhaps for the first time, is a book that speaks equally to all who have dealings with the Ontario *Provincial Offences Act* (POA).

The prosecutor and defence advocate alike will welcome this new publication. Its clear language and logical format make it easily accessible to the lay person as well.

"Handling Provincial Offence Cases in Ontario" is in some ways a very basic book. The authors, the Honourable Justice Rick Libman of the Ontario Court of Justice, and John P. Allen, Barrister and Solicitor, of the law firm Allen & Allen, take the reader step-by-step through the POA process — from the issuance of the "ticket" or the laying of the charge up to the trial and appeal procedures. Along the way, such fundamental concepts as the types of offences prosecuted under the Act, procedural streams, and the roles of the parties in the courtroom are explained.

The guide also addresses more complex topics, such as *Charter* defences, the classification of offences and hearsay evidence. A full chapter is dedicated to the discussion of the rules of professional conduct and the ethical duties of the prosecutor and the defence advocate in what is commonly referred to as the "people's court".

Well-rounded and carefully-considered, this guide will no doubt prove to be an invaluable addition to the literature already in existence on a subject that touches so many of us in our day-to-day lives.

Justice of the Peace Karen R. Walker
Ontario Court of Justice

Summary Table of Contents

For a detailed Table of Contents, see page vii.

Table of Contents

Chapter 4
TYPES OF PROVINCIAL OFFENCES

Chapter 5
PROCEDURAL ISSUES

Chapter 6
MENS REA OFFENCES

Chapter 7
STRICT LIABILITY OFFENCES

Chapter 8
ABSOLUTE LIABILITY OFFENCES

Chapter 9
SPECIAL PROCEEDINGS

Chapter 10
TRIALS

Chapter 11
SENTENCING

Chapter 12
APPEALS

Chapter 13
CHECKLISTS

APPENDICES

Table of Cases

Introduction

This new publication is a joint collaboration between two authors, Mr. Justice Rick Libman of the Ontario Court of Justice, and John P. Allen of the law firm Allen & Allen, both of whom have extensive experience in the area of the Ontario *Provincial Offences Act*. The format followed is that of a practical guide, but one which is especially designed for use by all those who may come before, or have contact with, the provincial offences court, whether as defendants, agents or prosecutors, students or teachers, witnesses or experts, judges or justices. In this way, this practice guide will apply to a broad range of persons, whose contact with the administration of justice in the province of Ontario will most likely be under the provisions of the *Provincial Offences Act*, and the "peoples' court" which it creates.

This is a basic Guide, then, for the defence and prosecution of Ontario provincial offence cases. Provincial offences range from simple parking infractions to highway traffic accidents, to complex occupational health and safety or environmental or securities offence cases, to give but a few examples. Pursuant to the *Contraventions Act* (Canada), certain federal regulatory offences, such as boating, fishing and wildlife cases, are also prosecuted under the *Provincial Offences Act* where the proceedings are commenced by ticket under Part I or Part II under the *Provincial Offences Act*. Factual and legal issues vary greatly among the different offences.

Use this Guide only as a starting point. It contains checklists, with chapters following the successive steps in a case, including the first client interview, how to gather information such as disclosure, pretrial motions, classification of provincial offences, various defences that may apply, trial procedures, sentencing, and reviews and appeals. A new chapter has also been added to this Guide, concerning ethical issues and obligations of the parties who appear before the provincial offences court: the duty of fairness on the prosecutor, which goes beyond the notion of merely "winning" or "losing" the case; the competency requirements imposed on paralegals, so that their clients fully understand the scope of the representation and their rights; and the importance of testimony from defence and prosecution witnesses which respects the process of the court, and accords with the rules of evidence which applies to provincial and federal regulatory offences.

Bill 108, the *Streamlining of Administration of Provincial Offences Act*, 1997, was enacted and received Royal Assent on June 11, 1998, at which time the legislation came into force. This Bill [S.O. 1998, c. 4] amends the *Provincial Offences Act* to allow the Attorney General to make agreements with municipalities permitting them to undertake courts administration and court support functions for the purposes of the Act. Pursuant to Bill 108, a new Part X is enacted which is entitled Agreements with Municipalities Concerning Administration Functions and Prosecutions. Under Part X, the Attorney General can authorize municipalities to conduct prosecutions in proceedings under Parts I and II of the *Provincial Offences Act* and in proceedings under the *Contraventions Act* (Canada) that are commenced by ticket under Part I or II of the *Provincial Offences Act*. Contraventions are federal regulatory offences, other than offences for which an offender may be prosecuted only on indictment, which are enforced in Ontario under the *Provincial Offences Act*.

Commencing in March, 1999, the Attorney General entered into agreements with various municipalities, transferring responsibility for administrative functions and the prosecution of charges under Parts I and II of the *Provincial Offences Act*. As of February, 2002, all municipalities in Ontario have taken over the court administration and prosecution of Parts I and II of the *Provincial Offences Act*. A list of the various provincial offences courts throughout Ontario, including telephone and fax numbers, has been added as an Appendix.

For further reference, an annotation of the *Provincial Offences Act* may be found in the *2008 Annotated Ontario Provincial Offences Act*, Segal and Libman (Carswell, 2008); and for a comprehensive text on regulatory offences, see *Regulatory Offences in Canada*, Swaigen (Carswell, 1992), and more recently, *Libman on Regulatory Offences in Canada* (Earlscourt, 2002).

Recent Developments — 2009 Edition

Legislative Update

Paralegal Professional Conduct Guidelines have been developed by the Law Society to assist paralegals in understanding and complying with the *Paralegal Rules of Conduct*. These Guidelines are to be considered along with the *Rules*, the *Law Society Act*, By-Laws made under the Act, and other relevant case law or legislation. The Guidelines are available in electronic form, and are directly linked to the *Rules* on the Law Society's website. There are 22 separate Guidelines, ranging from the Law Society and its Disciplinary Authority (Guideline 22), to Professionalism – Integrity and Civility (Guideline 1), Undertakings (Guideline 3), Harassment and Discrimination (Guideline 4) and Competence (Guideline 6). A number of amendments have also been made to the *Paralegal Rules of Conduct*, the majority of which deal with matters related to affiliations and multi-discipline practices. Other amendments made in 2008 concern advertising and marketing. The Law Society has also put in place a Practice Management Helpline in the form of a confidential telephone service in order to provide assistance in interpreting the *Paralegal Rules of Conduct* and Law Society By-Laws.

The Law Society has accredited a total of nine paralegal programs at the following institutions: Seneca College, Algonquin College, Sheridan College, Humber College, Durham College, and Westervelt College. These programs meet the standards and competencies for paralegal education program accreditation. They are required to include, at a minimum, certain fundamental courses that cover the essential elements of procedural and substantive practice, as well as ethical and responsible practice. Paralegal applicants who apply for a paralegal licence with the Law Society after 30 June 2010 are required to have graduated from an accredited legal services program. As of the end of January, 2009, almost 2000 paralegal licences have been issued since May, 2008.

Another recent legislative development of interest is By-Law 6.1, approved at September 2008 convocation, respecting the creation of a continuing legal education requirement for newly called *lawyers*. Starting in 2010, all new lawyers called to the Ontario Bar will be required to complete 24 hours of compulsory professional development during their first two years of practice. While no such requirement has been put in place at present for *paralegals*, the Law Society has instituted a series of continuing education programs for paralegals throughout 2008 and 2009.

The amended search warrant provisions under s. 158.1 of the *Provincial Offences Act* have been proclaimed into force and came into effect on 30 June 2008. These new provisions allow for warrants to be issued by fax by designated justices of the peace, and for a report to be made rather than bringing the actual items seized before a justice.

Ont. Reg. 950 which applies to Proceedings Commenced by Certificate of Offence has been recently amended. O. Reg. 259/08, filed 25 July 2008, changes the proscribed form of the Certificate of Offence and Offence Notice. These changes also include Red Light Camera Certificates and Offence Notices. The regulation provides that current Forms 1 (Certificate of Offence), 3 (Offence Notice), 4 (Offence Notice) and 6 (Summons) may continue to be used until 30 June 2009.

In October, 2008, the Government introduced Bill 108, An Act respecting apologies. This legislation provides that an apology made by a person for any matter does not constitute an admission of fault or liability, or affect any insurance or indemnity coverage for any person with respect to that matter. Neither is the apology to be considered when determining fault or liability. Evidence of an apology made by or on behalf of a person for any matter will not be admissible in any civil or administrative proceeding or arbitration as evidence of the fault or liability of any person regarding that matter. This legislation does not affect the admissibility of any evidence in a criminal proceeding or a proceeding under the *Provincial Offences Act*, or the use that may be made of a conviction for a criminal offence or a provincial offence in a civil or administrative proceeding or arbitration.

Another recent piece of legislation of interest is the *Animal Welfare Act*, S.O. 2008, c.16 which went into effect on 1 March 2009. This Act amends the *Ontario Society for the Prevention of Cruelty to Animals Act*, and creates a number of new offences. The search warrant provisions of the *Provincial Offences Act*, specifically ss. 159 and 160 respecting detention of things seized and examination of documents seized, apply with necessary modifications to the *Animal Welfare Act*.

Case Law Update

In *Cochrane v. Ontario (Attorney General)*, [2008] O.J. No. 4165, 2008 CarswellOnt 6229, 92 O.R. (3d) 321, 2008 ONCA 718, 61 C.R. (6th) 374, 242 O.A.C. 192 (Ont. C.A.), the province's legislation banning pit bull dogs was upheld in the face of a number of constitutional challenges under the *Charter*. One issue concerned the admissibility under s. 19(1) of the Act of a document from a veterinarian stating that the dog was a pit bull as proof of that fact, in the absence of evidence to the contrary. In rejecting an attack on this provision as a violation of the presumption of innocence, the court stated that this provision did not amount to a legal prescription which alters the burden of proof. Sections 39 and 46 of the *Provincial Offences Act* give trial judges a discretion to allow for cross-examination of the veterinarian who signed the certificate; it was to be assumed that this discretion would be exercised in a way that is consistent with *Charter* rights. There was no reason to suppose that leave to conduct a cross-examination of the veterinarian, if sought by the defendant, would be improperly denied.

Leave to appeal was granted by the Ontario Court of Appeal in *R. v. Winlow* (April 18, 2008), Doc. M36186 (Ont. C.A. [In Chambers]) where it was held that the matter involving amending the certificate of offence pursuant to s. 34(2) of the *Provincial Offences Act* to increase the speed alleged against the defendant after it had been reduced by the officer at the time of charge, but to vary it according to the officer's evidence at trial, involves an issue of law and the lower courts require some guidance. It was necessary for the proper administration of justice that the issue goes before a panel of the court, in the Court's view. The trial judge's refusal to grant the amendment was upheld by the provincial offences appeal court: *R. v. Winlow*, 2008 CarswellOnt 3031, 2008 ONCJ 240, [2008] O.J. No. 2085 (Ont. C.J.). The case was argued before the Ontario Court of Appeal in January, 2009, and judgment has been reserved.

In *Thibaudeau v. Ontario (Justice of the Peace)*, 2008 CarswellOnt 5935, 2008 ONCA 702, [2008] O.J. No. 3966 (Ont. C.A.), the Court of Appeal affirmed the ruling of the Superior Court of Justice, reported at (2007), 2007 CarswellOnt 7550, (sub nom. *Thibaudeau v. Stafford*) 88 O.R. (3d) 113 (Ont. S.C.J.), holding that the trial justice of the peace has jurisdiction to conduct an inquiry and bar an agent from appearing before him or her at a future time, following the completion of the trial. The decision of the trial judge in this case was rendered prior to s. 50(3) being amended due to the paralegal practitioner licensing regime now in place in Ontario. Under the current s. 50(3), the justice may only bar representatives who are not licensed under the *Law Society Act*.

No regular avenue of appeal is provided where a proceeding is quashed under s. 9(1) of the *Provincial Offences Act*. If the prosecuting authority or the Attorney General believe a justice has misconstrued what constitutes an error going to the regularity or completeness of the certificate, a prerogative remedy can be sought: *London (City) v. Young*, 2008 CarswellOnt 3091, [2008] O.J. No. 2118, 2008 ONCA 429, 237 O.A.C. 357, 233 C.C.C. (3d) 10, 75 Admin. L.R. (4th) 280, 91 O.R. (3d) 215, 65 M.V.R. (5th) 208 (Ont. C.A.).

A *Charter* violation was found in a provincial offences appeal case where the trial transcripts took from 15 and one-half months to 27 months to produce. The four appellants had been convicted under Part I Certificate of Offence proceedings. The court ruled that the appellants' fairness of trial rights were compromised due to the delays occasioned in the preparation of the trial transcripts, and resulted in an abuse of process, contrary to s. 7 of the *Charter*. A stay of proceedings was imposed on appeal, and costs were ordered against the prosecutor: *R. v. Ovided*, 2008 ONCJ 317, 91 O.R. (3d) 593, 174 C.R.R. (2d) 189, 2008 CarswellOnt 4181, [2008] O.J. No. 2780 (Ont. C.J.).

In *R. v. Hale*, 2005 ONCJ 553, 2005 CarswellOnt 10303, [2005] O.J. No. 6368 (Ont. C.J.), the court observed that one of the ways the management of trial workload is accomplished in the provincial offences court is by the holding of judicial pre-trials. The twin goals of the pre-trial process are to resolve matters capable of resolution, or to narrow the issues if no such resolution is possible so that the time required for trial is shortened by agreed statements of fact obviating the need for some witnesses to testify. To suggest that the pre-trial process be abolished at the Ontario Court of Justice level because it is not specifically provided for by legislation is to invite chaos at the province's busiest level of court. In a case where there was a delay of 15 months from the laying of the information for careless driving until the start of the scheduled trial, and 5.5 months of this delay was due to setting up and conducting the judicial pre-trial and finding a date that was available for trial for trial from the perspective of an appropriate justice of the peace, the defendant's s. 11(b) rights were violated.

A justice of the peace is entitled to impose as a condition of probation that the offender not engage directly or indirectly in the business of environmental consulting, under the authority of s. 72(3)(c) of the *Provincial Offences Act* "to prevent similar unlawful conduct": *R. v. Carter*, 2008 CarswellOnt 5301, 39 C.E.L.R. (3d) 1, 2008 ONCA 630, [2008] O.J. No. 3533 (Ont. C.A.), affirming (2008), 2008 CarswellOnt 4339 (Ont. C.J.), varying (2007), 2007 CarswellOnt 9472 (Ont. C.J.).

In a case involving a Crown appeal against a verdict of acquittal where the provincial offences appeal court substituted verdicts of guilt, the Court of Appeal ruled that it was unfair to permit the Crown to raise a new issue on appeal when the defendant had no notice that this was an issue at trial. A Crown appeal is not the time for the prosecution to advance a new theory of liability. As the errors by the appeal judge infected her assessment of the due diligence defence, the Court of Appeal was not convinced that an appeal court would necessarily have reached the same conclusions on liability in the absence of the errors. A re-hearing of the Crown's appeal in the provincial offences appeal court was ordered: *Ontario (Ministry of Labour) v. Modern Niagara Toronto Inc.*, 2008 CarswellOnt 4799, 2008 ONCA 590, 240 O.A.C. 278, 91 O.R. (3d) 774, (sub nom. *R. v. Modern Niagara Toronto Inc.*) 297 D.L.R. (4th) 156, [2008] O.J. No. 3168 (Ont. C.A.).

In a case involving the test for a re-opening under s. 11(1) of the *Provincial Offences Act*, *Thunder Bay (City) v. Kandiah* (2008), 2008 CarswellOnt 2685, [2008] O.J. No. 1863 (Ont. S.C.J.), it was held that the 15-day requirement under s. 11(1) began to run when the defendant had actual knowledge of his conviction. In the instant case, the defendant's agent learned of his client's conviction on January 31, 2008 but was unable to contact his client and inform him of it until February 22, 2008. The defendant's re-opening application on March 4, 2008 was therefore within the time limits prescribed by s. 11(1). While the justice of the peace may have rejected the defendant's explanation that he had lost his ticket, and that the agent, who had been contacted before the conviction was entered, could not obtain information regarding the charge until he received the defendant's authorization, there was evidence in the defendant's affidavit, supplemented by what the justice heard from the defendant and the agent, to support the re-opening decision. The reviewing court was not prepared to say that the exercise of discretion was an error of law. There were no exceptional circumstances to justify an awarding of costs.

In *R. v. Sholtens*, 2008 ONCJ 282, 2008 CarswellOnt 3605, [2008] O.J. No. 2444 (Ont. C.J.), the appeal court held that where a justice of the peace on his own motion adjourns a sentencing hearing to another date for the purposes of providing reasons as to why he cannot accept the guilty plea, and gives reasons for judgment without providing the prosecutor or unrepresented defendant a real opportunity of making submissions, the proceedings take on the appearance of a public lecture rather than an adversarial process before an impartial decision maker. A reasonable person, reasonably informed, would conclude that that the justice's decision had been arrived at before all the evidence and submissions had been heard. The justice of the peace was bound to follow the law on point and enter a conviction, through the application of the doctrine of *stare decisis*; there was a decision of a judge of the Ontario Court of Justice sitting as an appeal court, indicating that it was appropriate to register a finding of guilt in the circumstances of the case. *Stare decisis* is the glue that binds the court system in Ontario together, and gives purposes to the different levels of court and functions so as to prevent injustice. For a similar case, see *R. v. Bellefeuille*, 2008 CarswellOnt 6641, 2008 ONCJ 575, [2008] O.J. No. 4494 (Ont. C.J.) where the justice of the peace rejected the defendant's guilty plea and erroneously dismissed the charges, rather than set a trial date which was the proper course where a guilty plea is rejected.

In a recent case involving the issue as to when a maximum sentence is a fit penalty on sentencing, the Supreme Court of Canada held that the maximum sentence provided for an offence may be appropriate even where the offender is not the worst possible and the offence is not committed in the worst way. If a proper and fit sentence, as determined by the court acting judicially, is at the maximum of the range set by Parliament, then the sentence is fit. The sentencing court must determine the appropriate punishment within the limits established by Parliament: *R. v. Solowan*, 2008 CarswellBC 2396, 2008 CarswellBC 2397, [2008] S.C.J. No. 55, 2008 SCC 62, 299 D.L.R. (4th) 577, 261 B.C.A.C. 27, 440 W.A.C. 27, 70 M.V.R. (5th) 1, (sub nom. *R. v. S. (K.S.T.)*) 237 C.C.C. (3d) 129, 61 C.R. (6th) 268, 381 N.R. 191, [2008] S.C.J. No. 55 (S.C.C.).

The *Highway Traffic Act* offence of "stunt driving" is one of strict liability, there being a strong presumption in favour of classifying an offence as strict liability in nature: *R. v. Bell*, 2008 ONCJ 726, 2008 CarswellOnt 8586, [2008] O.J. No. 5585 (Ont. C.J.), para. 18 [ONCJ]. **Note:** A number of other trial rulings have agreed that this is a strict liability offence, but an appeal court has yet to rule on this issue. See, for example, *R. v. Bond* (2008), 2008 CarswellOnt 8560 (Ont. C.J.).

In *R. v. Fortese* (September 25, 2008), Ferguson J., [2008] O.J. No. 5159 (Ont. S.C.J.), it was held that a police officer has jurisdiction to lay a charge for an offence committed anywhere in Ontario. There is no provision in the *Provincial Offences Act* that requires a proceeding to be commenced in the county, district or regional municipality where the offence occurred. The place of the offence only becomes relevant if the defendant appears and disputes the charge, in which case the court must consider the possible application of s. 29 governing the venue of the proceeding. However, where the defendant fails to appear for trial, the justice was required to proceed in the defendant's absence and enter a conviction and impose sentence pursuant to s. 9.1. If the court does nothing, when it is required to act, the court commits jurisdictional error.

In *R. v. Fuentes*, 2008 ONCJ 598, 2008 CarswellOnt 7068, [2008] O.J. No. 4677 (Ont. C.J.), it was held that it is the client's right to meet with the person who represents him so there will be no misunderstanding as to what occurs in court. It is mandatory that whomever the licensed paralegal hires meets with the client where a paralegal informs the client that another paralegal will represent the client in court. It is not sufficient for the paralegal to merely tell the other agent what the client wants or said. Where the second paralegal pleaded the client guilty without ever speaking to the client, and a licence suspension was imposed, the conviction could not stand.

1

THE PROVINCIAL OFFENCES ACT ("POA")

1.1 PURPOSE OF THE POA

- It was originally enacted in 1979. Before then, provincial offences were prosecuted by reference to the summary conviction procedures in the federal *Criminal Code*, R.S.C. 1985, c. C-46. The POA seeks to simplify provincial prosecutions, eliminate technical defences, and promote speedy and inexpensive decisions without sacrificing justice.

- Provincial offences are "regulatory" — laws passed for the safety, health or well-being of the community. The "wrongs" tend to be specialized breaches of rules in a regulated activity, and the "players" should expect those rules to be enforced in a less formal manner. In contrast, crimes are wrongs of a general nature — obvious affronts to the community. The criminal accused is facing condemnation by society; the stakes are higher and the procedures stricter.

- In *R. v. Jamieson* (1981), 64 C.C.C. (2d) 550, 1981 CarswellOnt 1105 (Ont. C.A.), MacKinnon A.C.J.O. commented that the *Provincial Offences Act* "was intended to establish a speedy, efficient and convenient method of dealing with offences under Acts of the Legislature and under regulations or by-laws made under the authority of an Act of the Legislature" and that "it is not intended as a trap for the unskilled or unwary but rather, as already stated, as an inexpensive and efficient way of dealing with, for the most part, minor offences." In another early case, *R. v. Hill*, cited below, under the *Provincial Offences Act*, the judge stated that the "underlying philosophy" of this Act "is such as to encourage persons to personally represent themselves at trials of provincial offences".

- "In the spirit of the Statute, Judges and Justices presiding in those courts should approach the proceedings with tolerance and understanding towards such unrepresented persons and should permit certain latitudes in matters of procedure and law, provided no offence be done to basic principles of law and evidence": *R. v. Hill* (June 4, 1987), Nadeau Prov. Ct. J., [1987] O.J. No. 1935 (Ont. Prov. Ct.) at 3. In a recent case, *R. v. Zimmerman* (2005), [2005] O.J. No. 1647, 2005 CarswellOnt 1616, 30 C.R. (6th) 360 (Ont. S.C.J.) at para. 20, Trafford J. observed: "The fairness of trials under the POA, and the appearances of fairness of them, is of critical importance to the administration of justice in Ontario and the public confidence in it, given the nature of the cases tried in that Court each year and given the fact that most ordinary, law abiding citizens have some contact with it in the context of alleged traffic violations."

In *R. v. Messina,* (October 28, 2005), Doc. 4860-02-709368, [2005] O.J. No. 4663 (Ont. C.J.), the court set out a number of factors that should be taken into account in most cases when dealing with an "undefended person". If the court concludes that the trial can proceed fairly without representation, it should do the following: (1) determine if the defendant understands the charges and what the case is that he or she has to meet; explain the charge and what the prosecution is required to prove; (2) explain that the prosecution has the onus of proof and that the standard is proof beyond a reasonable doubt; (3) explain briefly the mechanics of the trial, for example, the right of each side to call witnesses, introduce documentary evidence, object to evidence adduced, the choice to testify or not, and that if the person chooses to testify he or she will be cross-examined, and the right to make submissions at the appropriate junctures during the trial; (4) the same should be done if a *voir dire* is held, and if one is held, what a *voir dire* is should be explained; (5) ask if the person needs pen and paper to take notes during the trial; (6) explain the role of the Justice *vis-à-vis* the undefended person, that is, that the Justice is there to ensure that he or she has a fair trial and can offer some guidance regarding the procedures of the trial, but cannot act as the person's advocate; (7) ask if the person has any questions, and tell the person to ask if during the trial there is something that they do not understand; (8) make an order for the exclusion of witnesses.

1.2 OFFENCES PROSECUTED UNDER THE POA

- The POA applies to all offences under any provincial statute, including the prosecution of parking, licensing, employment, health, building code, environmental and securities law offences.

- Pursuant to the *Contraventions Act* (Canada), certain federal regulatory offences are also enforced under the POA where the proceedings are commenced by ticket under Part I or II of the POA. The listing of offences is contained in the schedule of offences under the *Contraventions Act* and includes offences under the *Canadian Environmental Protection Act*, the *Canada Shipping Act* and the *Fisheries Act*.

1.3 PROCEDURAL STREAMS

- There are three procedural "streams" for provincial offences: Part I (Minor Offences), Part II (Parking Infractions), Part III (Serious Offences).

- The Prosecutor chooses which stream to follow depending on the seriousness and complexity of the allegations.

1.4 PART I OF THE POA — MINOR OFFENCES

- Most minor offences (including traffic tickets but not parking tickets) are prosecuted by a certificate of offence.

- The maximum fine is $500 and there is no imprisonment: section 12(1).

- The defendant must be personally served within 30 days of the alleged offence with either a summons or an offence notice: section 3(3).

- If a summons is served, the defendant must appear in court.

- If an offence notice is served, the defendant may plead:
    - Guilty in writing with full payment of the fine: section 8(1);
    - Guilty "with representations" as to penalty, to be made before a justice: section 7(1);
    - Not guilty and have a trial: section 5(1); or
    - Dispute the charges in writing, if the defendant lives outside a designated jurisdiction where the charges were laid: section 6(1).
- If none of the above is plead within 15 days, or if the defendant fails to appear for trial, he or she is deemed not to dispute the charges and, provided the certificate of offence is complete and regular on its face, the defendant can be convicted in his or her absence: sections 9, 9.1.

1.5 PART II OF THE POA — PARKING INFRACTIONS

- Parking tickets can be proceeded by a certificate of parking infraction.
- Parking infractions are usually created by municipalities, carrying a fixed and relatively minor monetary penalty.
- There are special rules for serving the parking infraction notice: section 15.
- The defendant has two options:
    - Pay the fine out-of-court: section 16.
    - Deliver a notice of intention to appear for trial: sections 17, 17.1.
- If the defendant fails to respond within 15 days, the court may send a notice of impending conviction. If the defendant

again fails to respond within 15 days, or fails to appear for trial, provided the certificate of parking infraction is complete and regular on its face, the defendant can be convicted in his or her absence: sections 18, 18.1, 18.2, 18.4.

1.6 PART III OF THE POA — SERIOUS OFFENCES

- Serious provincial offences are prosecuted under Part III.
- The maximum fine is $5,000, unless the charging Act allows for a greater penalty or imprisonment: section 61.
- The complainant must swear the truth of the allegations before a justice in a document called "information": section 23.
- If the justice accepts that the complainant has reasonable and probable grounds for believing that the defendant committed an offence, then the justice will endorse the information: section 24.
- The justice must then decide whether to confirm or issue a summons to appear, or whether to issue a warrant for the arrest of the defendant: section 24.
- The defendant must appear in court, if properly served.

Where a consent to the institution of proceedings is required by statute, but is lacking, the statutory authority to issue process under s. 24(1) is not engaged. Satisfaction of a condition precedent to its exercise is lacking: *R. v. Alrifai*, 2008 ONCA 564, 64 M.V.R. (5th) 159, 2008 CarswellOnt 4338, [2008] O.J. No. 2870, (sub nom. *Alrifai v. Ontario*) 235 C.C.C. (3d) 374 (Ont. C.A.), affirming (2007), 48 M.V.R. (5th) 144, 2007 CarswellOnt 2913, [2007] O.J. No 1805 (Ont. S.C.J.).

2

ROLE OF THE JUSTICE, PROSECUTOR AND DEFENCE ADVOCATE

2.1 THE JUSTICE

- The justice may be a Provincial Court Judge, to be addressed as "Your Honour", "His Honour", or "Her Honour". Serious provincial offence cases are decided by a Provincial Court Judge. Prior to their appointment, a Judge must have been a lawyer for at least ten years, and new appointments are recommended by the Judicial Appointments Advisory Committee. A Judge wears a black robe with a red sash across the front.

- The justice may be a Justice of the Peace, to be addressed as "Your Worship", "His Worship", or "Her Worship". Currently, there are no formal requirements for an appointment. If passed, the *Access to Justice Act* would establish minimum qualifications – a university degree or community college diploma, or an equivalency, including life experience, and at least ten years work experience. A Justice of the Peace wears a black robe with a green sash across the front.

- For a list of the names of the Judges and Justices of the Peace in the Ontario Court of Justice, and the regions across the province in which they preside, see the website of the Ontario Court of Justice: *www.ontariocourts.on.ca/ocj.htm.*

- There is no authority which requires a judge to monitor the progress of a Crown's case and notify the Crown of any deficiencies. This is in contrast to the duty placed on a judge to provide some level of assistance to an unrepresented accused, especially with regard to potential *Charter* defences, for which an unrepresented defendant would be unaware. The court went on to observe that subject to some specific admission made on the record, a defendant is free to bring an application for a directed verdict of acquittal at the conclusion of the Crown's case. If the defendant's application succeeds, the case is over; if unsuccessful the defendant will be given the option as to whether or not to call a defence; if the defendant decides not to call any evidence by way of defence, he/she can argue that the Crown has failed to meet its burden to prove an essential element of the case to the requisite degree of proof. Because a defendant may proceed in this fashion however, does not oblige him/her to do so. A failure to bring a motion for a directed verdict is not an admission of any sufficiency in, or lack of sufficiency thereof, in a Crown's case. See *R. v. Herzog*, 2008 ONCJ 72, 2008 CarswellOnt 1090, [2008] O.J. No. 757 (Ont. C.J.).

2.2 THE PROSECUTOR

- The Prosecutor may be a lawyer with the Ministry of the Attorney General, a lawyer with another branch of the Provincial Government, or an independent agent acting for the Provincial Government.

- Bill 108, the *Streamlining of Administration of Provincial Offences Act, 1997*, was enacted and received Royal Assent on June 11, 1998, at which time the legislation came into force. This Bill [S.O. 1998, c. 4] amends the *Provincial Offences Act* to allow the Attorney General to make agreements with municipalities permitting them to undertake courts' administration and court support functions for the purposes of the Act. Pursuant to Bill 108, a new Part X is enacted which is entitled Agreements With Municipalities Concerning Administration Functions and Prosecutions. Under Part X, the Attorney General can authorize municipalities to conduct prosecutions in proceedings under

Parts I and II of the *Provincial Offences Act* and in proceedings under the *Contraventions Act* (Canada) that are commenced by ticket under Part I or II of the *Provincial Offences Act*. Contraventions are federal regulatory offences, other than offences for which an offender may be prosecuted only on indictment, which are enforced in Ontario under the *Provincial Offences Act*.

- Commencing in March, 1999, the Attorney General entered into agreements with various municipalities, transferring responsibility for administrative functions and the prosecution of charges under Parts I and II of the *Provincial Offences Act*. As of February, 2002, all municipalities in Ontario have taken over the court administration and prosecution of Parts I and II of the *Provincial Offences Act*. A list of the various provincial offences courts throughout Ontario, including telephone and fax numbers, has been added as an Appendix.

In *R. v. Miceli*, 2006 ONCJ 67, [2006] O.J. No. 727, 2006 CarswellOnt 1548 (Ont. C.J.), it was held that it is well recognized that the Crown's prosecutorial discretion is almost absolute. Decisions to prosecute or plea-bargain are a result of professional judgment as to the strength of the evidence, the availability of resources, the visibility of the crime and the likely deterrent effect. Even if it were able to collect, understand and balance all of these factors, a court would find it nearly impossible to lay down guidelines to be followed by prosecutors.

In another recent case, *R. v. Baxter*, 2006 ONCJ 313, [2006] O.J. No. 3512, 2006 CarswellOnt 5294 (Ont. C.J.), the court held that in the absence of any wrong doing or malicious intent, the Crown has the discretion to call the list as he or she sees fit.

2.3 THE DEFENCE

- The defendant may be represented by a lawyer or agent (paralegal). The defendant may also represent himself or herself in person.

- On October 27, 2005, the Attorney General of Ontario unveiled the *Access to Justice Act*. It received Royal Asset on October 19, 2006. Its initiatives include the regulation of paralegals in POA and summary criminal trials. Paralegals are required to complete an approved college program and pass a licensing examination, adhere to a code of conduct, carry insurance and contribute to a compensation fund. There is also a process for receiving and investigating consumer complaints which is similar to the system for lawyers. Paralegals found to have engaged in misconduct are subject to penalties, including the possible loss of their licence.

- Subsection 50(3) of the *Provincial Offences Act*, which provided a justice of the peace with the authority to bar an agent from representing a defendant, has been repealed. The revised section states that a justice of the peace now may not bar a lawyer or a licensed paralegal from representing a defendant, but may bar a person such as a friend or family member who is not a professional licensed under the *Law Society Act*.

Justice Casey rejected a constitutional challenge to the Law Society's authority to regulate non-lawyers in the recent case, *R. v. Toutissani*, 2008 CarswellOnt 1688, [2008] O.J. No. 1174, 2008 ONCJ 139 (Ont. C.J.), leave to appeal refused 2008 CarswellOnt 5424, 2008 CarswellOnt 5425 (S.C.C.). It was argued that since Parliament's criminal law power has granted an agent the right to appear in summary conviction proceedings, the provincial legislature lacks the authority to circumscribe or place limits upon that right through the paralegal licensing regime under the *Law Society Act*. Justice Casey found that both legislative schemes were valid, that is, the *Criminal Code* provisions respecting appearance by agents, and the provincial regulations establishing rules regarding non-lawyers who appear in court. Since a person could, at the same time, comply with both the provisions of the *Criminal Code* and the *Law Society Act*, there was no impermissible conflict between the two pieces of legislation. A person who obtains a licence under the Law Society's by-laws is permitted by both the federal and provincial enactments to represent defendants in summary conviction matters. Parliament's purpose in permitting defendants on summary convictions to be represented by non-lawyers is furthered by the provincial legislation. Since the defendant's representative on the *Immigration Act* charges before the court had not complied with the licensing requirements of the *Law Society Act*, he was not permitted to appear for the defendant.

For cases dealing with the issue of the propriety of an agent appearing on behalf of the defendant, see generally *R. v. Romanowicz* (1999), 26 C.R. (5th) 246, [1999] O.J. No. 3191, 1999 CarswellOnt 2671, 178 D.L.R. (4th) 466, 124 O.A.C. 100, 138 C.C.C. (3d) 225, 45 O.R. (3d) 506, (sub nom. R. c. Romanowicz) 45 O.R. (3d) 532 (Fr.), 45 M.V.R. (3d) 294 (Ont. C.A.), and *R. v. Morden* (2000), [2000] O.J. No. 873, 2000 CarswellOnt 1037 (Ont. C.J.) which considers the appearance of an agent under the *Provincial Offences Act*. These cases hold that the disqualification of the agent who represents the defendant is a serious matter, and should only be considered by the court where it is necessary to protect the proper administration of justice.

In *Thibaudeau v. Ontario (Justice of the Peace)*, 2008 CarswellOnt 5935, 2008 ONCA 702, [2008] O.J. No. 3966 (Ont. C.A.), the Court of Appeal affirmed the ruling of the Superior Court of Justice, reported at (2007), 2007 CarswellOnt 7550, (sub nom. *Thibaudeau v. Stafford*) 88 O.R. (3d) 113 (Ont. S.C.J.), holding that the trial justice of the peace has jurisdiction to conduct an inquiry and bar an agent from appearing before him or her at a future time, following the completion of the trial. The decision of the trial judge in this case was rendered prior to s. 50(3) being amended due to the paralegal practitioner licensing regime now in place in Ontario. Under the current s. 50(3), the justice may only bar representatives who are not licensed under the *Law Society Act*.

In *Hill v. Toronto (City)*, 2007 ONCJ 253, 48 M.V.R. (5th) 55, (sub nom. *Toronto (City) v. Hill*) 221 C.C.C. (3d) 189, 2007 CarswellOnt 3578, [2007] O.J. No. 2232 (Ont. C.J.), it was held that allegations made by a paralegal agent on appeal that a paralegal agent at trial had not acted properly, so as to amount to professional incompetence or to have otherwise contributed to a miscarriage of justice, must be made only after careful consideration. More particularly, such allegations should only be brought forward after the appeal agent has satisfied himself or herself, by means of personal investigations or inquiries, that there is some factual foundation for the allegation, apart from the instructions of the appellant. There must also be afforded to the trial agent a fair opportunity to respond, specifically by providing notice to the trial agent of the allegations being made before the appeal court, and ensuring that a record of this response is placed before the appeal court so that a proper assessment of the allegations may be made by the judge on appeal. Such a procedure or protocol, which places on the paralegal agent on appeal the obligation to investigate and furnish the paralegal trial agent with an opportunity to respond, and thus the appeal court with a proper basis to evaluate such allegations, reflects the need to ensure fairness, openness, and transparency in the provincial offences court, which is so aptly regarded as the "people's court" given the pervasive nature of public welfare/regulatory offences. At the same time, it is in keeping with the new responsibilities of ethical behaviour now mandated by the Law Society of Upper Canada for paralegal practitioners, which includes the required standard of a "competent paralegal", pursuant to the Paralegal Rules of Conduct.

2.4 RULES OF PROFESSIONAL CONDUCT

- The Law Society regulates Ontario's lawyers to ensure a competent and ethical bar. It will also regulate paralegals under proposed Bill 14 – *Access to Justice Act*. The Rules of Professional Conduct must be interpreted and applied with common sense. As stated in section 1.03(1)(f) of the

Rules, they do not address every situation, and should be observed in spirit as well as in the letter.

- This is a brief summary of some of the rules for the courtroom advocate. See the Rules on the Law Society website: *www.lsuc.on.ca.*

- If you have any doubt about what to do in a situation, contact an experienced lawyer and seek guidance.

- The *Paralegal Rules of Conduct* governing paralegal practitioners were approved at the March, 2007 convocation of the Law Society of Upper Canada. These rules impose new responsibilities of ethical behaviour on paralegal practitioners, including the required standard of a "competent paralegal": rule 3.01(1). Other rules of note include rule 2.01 which imposes a requirement of integrity and civility on paralegals in connection with the provision of legal services which are made available to the public. A paralegal is to be "honest and candid" when advising clients (rule 3.02(1)) and is expected to treat tribunals and other licensees with "candour, fairness, courtesy and respect." (rule 4.01(1)). Under rule 6.01(1), paralegals are to "encourage public respect for, and try to improve, the administration of justice". Moreover, according to rule 6.01(2) paralegals are to "take care not to weaken or destroy public confidence in legal institutions or authorities by making irresponsible allegations or comments".

- The effect of these rules is discussed in *Hill v. Toronto (City)*, 2007 ONCJ 253, 48 M.V.R. (5th) 55, (sub nom. *Toronto (City) v. Hill*) 221 C.C.C. (3d) 189, 2007 CarswellOnt 3578, [2007] O.J. No. 2232 (Ont. C.J.). Case law decided before the implementation of the *Paralegal Rules of Conduct* indicates that once a paralegal practitioner undertakes to provide legal services and representation to a client, it is under an obligation to ensure that the client is clearly informed of any limits upon its retainer; it is also obliged to ensure that the client is made aware of the necessity to appear in court for trial. Failure to discharge either obligation results in breach of duty to the client and supports a finding of negligence: see *Hamilton v. X-Copper Legal Services Inc.* (2005), [2005] O.J. No. 2463, 2005 CarswellOnt 3344 (Ont. S.C.J.).

- By-Law 4, effective May 1, 2007, governs licensing requirements for paralegal practitioners. The Class P1 licence authorizes licence holders to provide legal services in Ontario. The scope of activities permitted under the Class P1 licence includes: representing a party, in the case of a proceeding in the Small Claims Court, before the Small Claims Court; in the case of a proceeding under the *Provincial Offences Act,* before the Ontario Court of Justice; and, in the case of a proceeding under the *Criminal Code,* before a summary conviction court: sections 5, 6. It is anticipated that the first licences will be issued in early 2008 following the licensing examination process which is scheduled to commence in January 2008. The ability to appear on summary conviction matters before the Ontario Court of Justice in Ontario is consistent with the practice in other provinces: see, for example, *Law Society (Manitoba) v. Pollock*, 2007 MBQB 51, [2007] 5 W.W.R. 147, 37 C.P.C. (6th) 125, 153 C.R.R. (2d) 131, 2007 CarswellMan 80, [2007] M.J. No. 67, 213 Man. R. (2d) 81 (Man. Q.B.), affirmed 2008 CarswellMan 238, [2008] 7 W.W.R. 493 (Man. C.A.).

- The Law Society of Upper Canada's By-Law 4 was subsequently amended so as to disqualify suspended lawyers from applying for a paralegal licence. This amendment includes lawyers who have been suspended for both disciplinary and administrative (such as non-payment of fees) reasons. However, it does not include layers who have been disbarred.

Justice Casey rejected a constitutional challenge to the Law Society's authority to regulate non-lawyers in the recent case *R. v. Toutissani*, 2008 ONCJ 139, [2008] O.J. No. 1174 (C.J.), leave to appeal refused 2008 CarswellOnt 5424, 2008 CarswellOnt 5425 (S.C.C.). It was argued that since Parliament's criminal law power has granted an agent the right to appear in summary conviction proceedings, the provincial legislature lacks the authority to circumscribe or place limits upon that right through the paralegal licensing regime under the *Law Society Act*. Justice Casey found that both legislative schemes were valid, that is, the *Criminal Code* provisions respecting appearance by agents, and the provincial regulations establishing rules regarding non-lawyers who appear in court. Since a person could, at the same time, comply with both the provisions of the *Criminal Code* and the *Law Society Act*, there was no impermissible conflict between the two pieces of legislation. A person who obtains a licence under the Law Society's by-laws is permitted by both the federal and provincial enactments to represent defendants in summary conviction matters. Parliament's purpose in permitting defendants on summary convictions to be represented by non-lawyers is furthered by the provincial legislation. Since the defendant's representative on the *Immigration Act* charges before the court had not complied with the licensing requirements of the *Law Society Act*, he was not permitted to appear for the defendant.

In *Chancey v. Dharmadi* (2007), 86 O.R. (3d) 612, [2007] O.J. No. 2852, 2007 CarswellOnt 4664, 44 C.P.C. (6th) 158 (Ont. Master), the court considered the issue as to whether a paralegal could be forced to reveal communications and the file in a civil proceeding regarding a collision where the paralegal defended the same party before the provincial offences court. Master Dash ruled that class privilege, such as solicitor-client privilege, is a form of privilege in which there is a *prima facie* presumption that the communications are inadmissible or not subject to disclosure in criminal or civil proceedings. The problem with recognizing a class privilege respecting paralegal-client communications at this time is that a class requires specific identifiable actors. Paralegal licensing is in progress, but as of yet there are no licensed paralegals. There is no principled reason why a class privilege should not be extended to paralegal-client communications, once communications with an identifiable group, namely paralegals licensed by the Law Society, begin. Once licensing of paralegals is in effect, the court may, in an appropriate case, revisit the idea of granting a class privilege to communications between a client and a paralegal licensed by the Law Society to provide legal services, rather than requiring the court to engage in a case by case analysis respecting each such communication. The communications in the instant case between the defence paralegal and the client, including the agent's entire file, were protected by privilege.

- *Paralegal Professional Conduct Guidelines* have been developed by the Law Society to assist paralegals in understanding and complying with the *Paralegal Rules of Conduct*. These Guidelines are to be considered along with the *Rules*, the *Law Society Act*, By-Laws made under the Act, and other relevant case law or legislation. The Guidelines are available in electronic form, and are directly linked to the *Rules* on the law Society's website. There are 22 separate Guidelines, ranging from the Law Society and its Disciplinary Authority (Guideline 22), to Professionalism – Integrity and Civility (Guideline 1), Undertakings (Guideline 3), Harassment and Discrimination (Guideline 4) and Competence (Guideline 6). A number of amendments have also been made to the *Paralegal Rules of Conduct*, the majority of which deal with matters related to affiliations and multi-discipline practices. Other amendments made in 2008 concern advertising and marketing. The Law Society has also put in place a Practice Management Helpline in the form of a confidential telephone service in order to provide assistance in interpreting the *Paralegal Rules of Conduct* and Law Society By-Laws.

- The Law Society has accredited a total of nine paralegal programs at the following institutions: Seneca College, Algonquin College, Sheridan College, Humber College, Durham College, and Westervelt College. These programs meet the standards and competencies for paralegal education program accreditation. They are required to include, at a minimum, certain fundamental courses that cover the essential elements of procedural and substantive practice, as well as ethical and responsible practice. Paralegal applicants who apply for a paralegal licence with the Law Society after 30 June 2010 are required to have graduated from an accredited legal services program. As of the end of January, 2009, almost 2000 paralegal licences have been issued since May, 2008.

In *R. v. Kronshteyn* (2008), 2008 CarswellOnt 4600 (Ont. C.J.), the court set aside a conviction and ordered a new trial where evidence was placed before the court by the trial agent that he misunderstood the defendant's instructions due to a language barrier, and erroneously entered guilty to a lesser charge.

In *R. v. Fuentes*, 2008 ONCJ 598, 2008 CarswellOnt 7068, [2008] O.J. No. 4677 (Ont. C.J.), it was held that it is the client's right to meet with the person who represents him so there will be no misunderstanding as to what occurs in court. It is mandatory that whomever the licensed paralegal hires meets with the client where a paralegal informs the client that another paralegal will represent the client in court. It is not sufficient for the paralegal to merely tell the other agent what the client wants or said. Where the second paralegal pleaded the client guilty without ever speaking to the client, and a licence suspension was imposed, the conviction could not stand.

2.5 DUTIES OF THE PROSECUTION

- Duty to the Truth:
  - As prosecutor, you must fairly present all material facts and law, so the Justice can make the right decision.

  - You are a minister of justice — you neither win nor lose; nor seek false conviction — if the Justice accepts an explanation and acquits the defendant, you have acted with honour.

- Duty to be Fair:

  - You must disclose all potentially relevant evidence and witnesses to the defence, whether tending to show guilt or innocence.
  - If the defendant is unaware of a potential defence (especially if unrepresented), advise the defendant, bring the issue to the attention of the court, and deal with it openly and fairly.
  - Beware of "tunnel vision" — ignoring evidence which may seem peripheral, but which could lead to other reasonable explanations.
  - If there is no reasonable prospect of conviction, or if the prosecution is no longer in the public interest, withdraw the case — it squanders precious time and resources; it causes the defendant unnecessary personal and financial hardship; see section 3.1, "Charge Screening by the Prosecutor" in Chapter 3.

- Advocacy:

  - Be a strong advocate; do not meekly accept any defence or witness assertion; vigorously test the evidence and let the impartial Justice determine the truth at trial.

2.6 DUTIES OF THE DEFENCE ADVOCATE

- Duty to Your Client:

  - You must defend your client's rights.

  - You must advocate your client's personal advantage, as perceived by your client.

  - Your client decides how to plead to the charge; not you.

  - You must accept your client's version of events if, after candidly discussing its credibility, your client insists it is true. If you do not know it is false, let the impartial Justice determine the truth at trial.

  - If you have promised to represent your client, you cannot simply quit — you must give your client reasonable notice so your client can hire another qualified advocate.

  - If you have told the court that you act for your client, you will also need the court's permission to "get off the record"; the court may deny your request if a new advocate would require an adjournment to prepare, and if the delay would unduly inconvenience the court or witnesses.

  - If you are not a lawyer, tell your client and the court. On passage of Bill 14 – *Access to Justice Act*, only lawyers and paralegals licensed by the Law Society will be able to represent defendants under the *Provincial Offences Act*. Bill 14 is consumer protection legislation; your client should know what qualifications you have.

  - Know your client's expectations, how they wish to plead, what they expect to pay, and advise your client how long the trial or resolution will likely take; if possible, get your client's instructions in writing.

  - If your client will not be attending court (and has not been summonsed or ordered to appear), and if you will be appearing as agent or counsel on their behalf, get clear instructions in writing.

- Be Competent:

  - Do not accept a case because you need the "experience" — it is your client's experience that is important; imagine finding out, after an unsuccessful medical procedure, that your surgeon had never performed the operation before, did it without supervision, as a "learning experience".

    - Keep current on changes in the law and procedure; the Law Society mandates continuing legal education for lawyers; on passage of Bill 14 – *Access to Justice Act*, it will also mandate continuing legal education for paralegals.

- Be Prepared:

    - Know the evidence, the inferences likely to be drawn by the Justice, the rules and law that apply, and the likely outcome; advise your client honestly and candidly; do not encourage false hope, but equally, do not discourage a legitimate defence just to enter an easy guilty plea; and consider section 10.2.5 in Chapter 10 regarding credibility evidence.

- Disclose Any Conflict of Interest to Your Client and to the Court:

    - You cannot serve two masters.

    - How can you effectively represent co-defendants, if one could argue that the other is more responsible?

    - How can you fairly cross-examine a witness who is a former client, who earlier provided you with damaging personal information?

- Duty to the Truth:

    - You cannot knowingly obstruct or distort the truth.

    - You cannot misrepresent evidence, facts, law, rulings or precedents, to the court, prosecutor, or authorities.

    - If you know your client is obstructing or distorting the truth, you must persuade them to stop; if they continue, seek permission from the court to withdraw from the case; but give the court minimal reasons; anything more would unnecessarily reveal your client's confidential discussions.

- Confidential Discussions:
  - Everything your client tells you is confidential.
  - But if you have reasonable grounds to believe there is an imminent risk to an identifiable person, or identifiable group of persons, of death or serious bodily harm, including serious psychological harm that substantially interferes with the health or well-being of the person(s), you should disclose enough information to prevent the harm (but no more). If there is time, before doing so, contact an experienced lawyer and request guidance; if there is more time, ask the lawyer to obtain a judicial order for you to disclose the information, presumably on notice to your client.
  - If you have reasonable grounds for believing that a dangerous situation is likely to develop at a court facility, you must inform the local police force and give particulars; if there is time, before doing so, contact an experienced lawyer and request guidance in order to minimize any disclosure of your client's confidential information.
- Right to Silence:
  - If the truth is not your client's friend, remain silent on an issue; what your client has told you is confidential and your client retains the right to remain silent.
  - "Physician, do no harm" is ascribed to Hippocrates; it certainly applies to the advocate; if the prosecution has insufficient evidence to prove an element of its case, do not mention it during trial, but point to the deficiency in summation.
  - Silence only applies to facts and evidence; it does not apply to the law; if you are aware of a law or binding authority, you must disclose it to the Justice.

- Sometimes your client is required to disclose information to the authorities — see section 3.2.5 under "Initial Advice" in Chapter 3.

- A Client who Confesses to You in Private:

  - What if your client voluntarily confesses the elements of the charge to you in private, can you do more than remain silent in court? Yes, as long as you do not obstruct or distort the truth.

  - You may treat your client's "not guilty" plea as a challenge to the prosecution to "prove it", not a proclamation of innocence.

  - You may take objection to the jurisdiction of the court, the constitutionality of the law, the form of charge, the admissibility of evidence, or other so-called "technical" defences.

  - You may test the observation and credibility of prosecution witnesses, to suggest they did not see "it" (which is different than suggesting "it" did not happen).

  - You may argue that the evidence as a whole fails to prove the charge.

  - But you may not set up an affirmative case, or introduce or suggest evidence inconsistent with your client's admissions.

- Beware of Becoming a Witness:

  - An advocate is someone who communicates their client's defence in court; not one who handles evidence outside of court. If you touch, record, gather or handle evidence, just like anyone else, you may become a material witness.

  - For example, if your client leaves evidence or third-party documents in your office, and the history or state of that evidence becomes relevant, you may land in the witness box. Your client's communications are privileged, but the physical or documentary evidence deposited in your office is not.

- You cannot conceal relevant evidence; you cannot retain it for the purpose of suppressing its use by the prosecution.

- If you interview a witness who says something relevant, you could be compelled to testify about the conversation.

- If you do become a material witness, you can no longer act as advocate at trial.

- How can you assist your client by gathering evidence, yet not become a witness? Have someone else from your office, or perhaps an investigator, gather the evidence. Or, if you must be involved, have a credible person also attend, so they can witness the conversation. Or, ask permission of the witness to record or videotape the conversation; hopefully, your testimony won't be necessary.

- Appeals:

  - Should your client be convicted, get written instructions if they do not wish to file an appeal.

  - If you are appeal counsel, and you allege inadequate representation by the trial advocate, give written notice of the alleged deficiencies to the trial advocate (such as a copy of the appeal documents), so the trial advocate can properly address such allegations.

- In seeking to quash a conviction on the basis of ineffective assistance of counsel, an appellant must:

  - Establish the material facts on a balance of probabilities;

- Demonstrate that counsel's acts or omissions were incompetent as measured against a reasonableness standard; and

- Demonstrate that the ineffective representation caused a miscarriage of justice: *R. v. W. (R.)*, (2006), 2006 CarswellOnt 1189, 207 C.C.C. (3d) 137, 207 O.A.C. 280, [2006] O.J. No. 807 (Ont. C.A.), at para. 75, leave to appeal refused (2007), 2007 CarswellOnt 6160, 2007 CarswellOnt 6161 (S.C.C.).

2.7 DUTY OF ALL ADVOCATES

- Duty to the Court:

  - Do not misrepresent evidence, facts, law, rulings or precedents.

  - Do not express your personal views — they are irrelevant and prejudicial.

  - Keep your promises ("undertakings") to the court or opponent.

  - Do not disparage the Justice, the decision, your opponent, the witnesses or other parties outside court; your remedy is an appeal.

- Duty to Witnesses:

  - Do not demean or humiliate a witness; do not suggest a fact without a good faith belief in its truth; do not misrepresent what a witness is saying; do not ask a witness or defendant to comment on the credibility of another witness — credibility is for the Justice to decide.

  - Do not discourage a witness from testifying; do not suggest they change their evidence; do not coach a witness how to testify; do not communicate with your witness when being cross-examined.

  - You may refresh a witness's memory with their earlier statement before trial; but if the witness says there is an error in their earlier statement, do not discourage the witness from changing their evidence (and if you are the prosecutor, disclose the contradictory statements to the defence).

  - Speak to witnesses in the presence of a police officer or appropriate third person; or, with the consent of the witness, record the interview, so the impartial Justice can assess the credibility of the witness at trial.

  - If the defendant or witness is represented, do not communicate with them directly, unless with the consent of their representative.

- Use Common Sense:

  - Does a tactic seem unfair?

  - Does it pass the "smell test"?

  - The Law Society Rules of Professional Conduct must be interpreted and applied with common sense. They do not address every situation, and must be observed in spirit as well as in the letter. Personal ethics cannot be checked at the courtroom door.

  - If you have any doubt about what to do in a situation, immediately seek guidance from an experienced lawyer.

3

PREPARATION FOR TRIAL

3.1 CHARGE SCREENING BY THE PROSECUTOR

- The Province of Ontario, Ministry of Attorney General, Crown Policy Manual (March 21, 2005) requires prosecutors who are conducting criminal prosecutions to screen every charge as soon as practicable after the charge arrives at the Crown's office and prior to setting a date for trial or preliminary hearing. According to the Charge Screening Directive, when considering whether or not to continue the prosecution of a charge, the first step is for the prosecutor to determine whether there is a reasonable prospect of conviction. Where it is determined that there is no reasonable prospect of conviction, at any stage of the proceeding, the prosecution of that charge is to be discontinued.

- Even where there is a reasonable prospect of conviction, the prosecutor is required to go on and consider whether it is in the public interest to discontinue the prosecution, notwithstanding the existence of a reasonable prospect of conviction. The Crown Policy Manual advises that no public interest, however compelling, will warrant prosecuting an individual where there is no reasonable prospect of conviction.

- Provincial offences, of course, are not the same as criminal offences. Indeed, the purpose of the *Provincial Offences Act* is to set out a procedure which reflects this very difference. However, the charge screening process that applies to provincial offences is based on the same principles as those governing criminal offences. As a result, the prosecutor is required to screen provincial offences charges in order to determine the following: whether a *prima facie* case exists, whether there is a reasonable prospect of conviction, and, whether it is in the public interest that the prosecution be continued. (Ministry of Attorney General of Ontario, POA Transfer Project 2001, Handbook for POA Prosecutors, Section 3.2, Charge Screening)

- The requirements of reasonable prospect of conviction and public interest have been discussed above. The requirement of determining whether there is a *prima facie* case requires that the prosecutor should ensure the following:

  - that there is evidence on all the essential elements of the charge which, if believed and answered, would warrant a finding of guilt;

  - that there are no jurisdictional obstacles which would constitute a fatal flaw to the prosecution of the charge; and

  - that where the defendant has been served with an offence notice, ensuring that that the certificate of offence is sufficient on its face, and if not, determining whether the defect can be cured by an amendment. (Handbook for POA Prosecutors, Section 3.2.2(a))

- The obligation to screen charges is on-going. Prosecutors are to discontinue a prosecution if it becomes apparent at any stage of the proceedings that a reasonable prospect of conviction no longer exists, or that it is not in the public interest to continue the prosecution.

- In the case of prosecutions brought on behalf of municipalities, there are "Principles of Transfer" which require that the fundamental tenets of procedural fairness and natural justice be affirmed and upheld. While the municipal partner may establish its own prosecutorial policies, such policies must be consistent with provincial policies and not contrary to the law. As a result, both provincial and municipal prosecutors engage in the practice of charge screening of provincial offences.

3.2 PREPARATION BY THE DEFENCE

3.2.1 CLIENT INTERVIEW

- Gather all information that may be relevant to both trial and sentencing.
- If the client is calling from a police station, ensure privacy, and gather as much information as possible from the officer-in-charge.
- Does the client wish to be interviewed in the presence of a third person?
    - Consider that the solicitor-client privilege may no longer apply and the third person could be forced to testify about the interview.

3.2.2 DOCUMENTS TO OBTAIN

- Obtain copies of the following:
    - Documents served on your client;
    - All relevant correspondence and notes;
    - Employment or business records;
    - Photographs or diagrams.

3.2.3 DETERMINE OFFENCE(S) CHARGED

- The *Provincial Offences Act* is the procedure by which offences under other provincial Acts and certain federal regulatory offences governed by the *Contraventions Act (Canada)* are prosecuted.

- Refer to the charging Act and compare its wording with the charges laid against your client.

- Recognize the illegal "acts" alleged. Later chapters analyze defences that might be available.

3.2.4 SAMPLE QUESTIONS FOR CLIENT

(a) Background Questions

- Obtain and accurately record the following background details from your client.

  1. Name, date of birth, address, and telephone number(s).
  2. First language — would an interpreter be helpful?
  3. Marital status, with names and ages of spouse and any children — does the client support dependants?
  4. Immigration status and residence history.
  5. Education history and plans.
  6. Employment history and source(s) of income.
  7. Ability to pay fine (and your fees).
  8. Mental and/or physical health and treatment.
  9. Criminal and/or provincial record of offences (or other relevant governmental record of misconduct), with explanations, if any.
  10. Bail, probation, or other court or administrative orders or agreements in effect — with contact person to confirm compliance, if necessary.
  11. Charges outstanding.
  12. Character references — does your client want family, friends, or an employer to know of the charge(s)?

(b) The Allegations

- Obtain and accurately record the following details about the allegations against your client.

1. Client's version of the allegations and evidence.
2. Co-defendant? Get details.
3. Steps taken to comply with the law (reasonable care).
4. Steps that could have been taken, with reasons for not doing so.
5. Industry standards for reasonable care.
6. Was the client impaired by alcohol or drugs? Was anyone else impaired?
7. Did the client impede the investigation?
8. Names, phone numbers, and addresses of all potential witnesses, both favourable and unfavourable.
9. Details of all contact with the authorities, and whether rights (such as the right to counsel) were given.
10. Date, time, and place of next court appearance.

(c) Corporate Defendants.

- Both individuals and corporations can be charged under various provincial offences.

- Determine the current directors, officers and shareholders of the corporation. Obtain their names, phone numbers, and addresses.

- Determine the directors and officers in the latest filing at the Companies and Personal Property Security Branch of the Ministry of Consumer and Business Services under the *Corporations Information Act*, R.S.O. 1990, c. C.39. Obtain their names, phone numbers, and addresses.

- Review corporate minutes book.

- Consider corporate by-laws and resolutions.

- Who are the directing minds of the corporation?

3.2.5 INITIAL ADVICE

- Advise your client not to communicate with anyone else about the allegations or to provide samples, documents, or other information. *Even if your client has an explanation demonstrating innocence, it is better to wait and present that evidence before an impartial court bound by the rules of procedural fairness.*

- Advise your client that anything said now can be used *against* him or her at trial (as an admission or to impeach credibility), and nothing said now can be used *for* him or her at trial (prior consistent statements are generally inadmissible).

- In some circumstances, your client may be required to disclose information to the authorities.

  - Under the *Highway Traffic Act*, R.S.O. 1990, c. H.8, s. 199, every person in charge of a motor vehicle who is directly or indirectly involved in an accident shall, if the accident results in personal injuries or in damage apparently in excess of the regulated amount, report the accident forthwith to the nearest police officer with particulars, including: the persons involved, the extent of the injuries or damage, and other necessary information for the police officer's accident report.

  - Under the *Environmental Protection Act*, R.S.O. 1990, c. E.19, ss. 158(7) and 167, every person responsible for a source of contaminant shall furnish such information as a provincial officer requires for the purposes of the Act or Regulations.

  - Under the *Occupational Health and Safety Act*, R.S.O. 1990, c. O.1, ss. 51 *et.seq.* and 62(3), employers must report to the Provincial Director particulars of serious work-site accidents within stipulated times, and no person shall neglect or refuse to provide the inspector with information required in the exercise of his or her duties.

- Nevertheless, advise your client not to disclose any information to anyone until *after* you consider *precisely* what must be disclosed, and when and how to disclose it. Do not be unnecessarily rushed.

- In some circumstances, you might consider disclosing certain information *after receiving full disclosure* of the allegations and evidence against your client.

  - Determine whether, under law, an adverse inference can be drawn from your client's failure to disclose information before trial. *For example, if the defence is alibi, particulars must be disclosed sufficiently before trial to allow the authorities time to investigate. However, during the initial interview, advise your client to remain silent, since the authorities can be advised after you receive full disclosure of the prosecutor's case (and after you, as counsel, privately confirm the truth of the alibis).*

  - Though a defendant provides the police with sufficient notice of an alibi prior to trial to permit the police to investigate the alibi witness, an adverse inference may be drawn where the opportunity for meaningful investigation is lost due to the passage of time and the fading memory of the alibi witness: *R. v. Mearow* (2006), 2006 CarswellOnt 6140 (Ont. C.A.).

- Many regulatory offences provide "due diligence" or "reasonable care" defences (*see Chapter 7 for details*). *For example, in an on-going pollution spill case, your client may appear more diligent if there is full and timely disclosure to the authorities of the contaminant's problems, with requests for professional assistance and follow-up.*

- As to the powers of search warrants and investigations, *see Chapter 10.*

3.2.6 FIRST APPEARANCE

- Arrange for a sufficient retainer before confirming that you are counsel or agent of record to the court.

- Determine whether the client was properly served. (*See Chapter 5 for details.*)

  - If not, consider appearing in court without your client to argue improper service. (But research the law first; by appearing, your client may be taken to have attorned to the jurisdiction of the court.)

3.3 FURTHER DISCLOSURE FOR THE DEFENCE

3.3.1 DISCLOSURE FROM THE PROSECUTION

In *R. v. Stinchcombe* (1991), 68 C.C.C. (3d) 1, [1992] 1 W.W.R. 97, [1991] 3 S.C.R. 326, 83 Alta. L.R. (2d) 193, 8 C.R. (4th) 277 (S.C.C.), the Supreme Court of Canada held that, in an indictable criminal trial, if the defence requests disclosure, the Crown must disclose all information it proposes to use at trial plus all information which *may* assist the defence.

- Initial disclosure must be done as soon as practicable and before trial.

- The request for disclosure must be made in writing to the Prosecutor's Office at the particular court location [See Sample Request Forms in Appendix C].

- The Prosecutor's Office will then make a formal request for disclosure from the police officer in charge [See Request for Disclosure in Appendix C].

- The disclosure material from the Prosecutor's Office will be faxed to the defendant, or to his or her agent, provided they confirm receipt of same [See Disclosure Facsimile Message Form and the Faxing Instruction Sheet in Appendix C]. Alternatively, the disclosure material must be picked up at the Prosecutor's Office at the court location.

- The Crown has the onus of justifying untimely or refusal of disclosure.

- Disclosure is a continuing obligation on the Crown.

- The Crown can refuse to disclose certain information if privileged, but this discretion is reviewable by the trial judge.

In *R. v. Stinchcombe*, Justice Sopinka did not decide whether the same disclosure duties applied to summary conviction or provincial offences. In Ontario, however, the Attorney General's policy is to provide disclosure of provincial offences upon request. See also: *R. v. Fineline Circuits Ltd.* (1991), 10 C.R. (4th) 241 (Ont. Prov. Ct.).

In *Ontario v. 974649 Ontario Inc.*, 2001 CarswellOnt 4251, 47 C.R. (5th) 316 (sub. nom. *R. v. 974649 Ontario Inc.*) [2001] 3 S.C.R. 575, 56 O.R. (3d) 359 (headnote only), 2001 CarswellOnt 4252, (sub nom. *R. v. 974649 Ontario Inc.*) [2001] S.C.J. No. 79, (sub nom. *R. v. 974649 Ontario Inc.*) 2001 SCC 81, (sub nom. *R. v. 974649 Ontario Inc.*) 206 D.L.R. (4th) 444, (sub nom. *R. v. 974649 Ontario Inc.*) 159 C.C.C. (3d) 321, (sub nom. *R. v. 974649 Ontario Inc.*) 88 C.R.R. (2d) 189, (sub nom. *R. v. 974649 Ontario Inc.*) 279 N.R. 345, (sub nom. *R. v. 974649 Ontario Inc.*) 154 O.A.C. 345 (S.C.C.), the Supreme Court of Canada concluded that the justice of the peace acting as a trial justice under the *Provincial Offences Act* possessed the power to order legal costs against the Crown as a remedy for *Charter* breaches arising from untimely disclosure. The costs were awarded on the defendants' disclosure motion which was brought as a result of the Crown's failure to disclose a copy of the Prosecution Approval Form relating to charges laid under the *Occupational Health and Safety Act*. If defendants were deprived of this remedy, a provincial offences court may be confined to two extreme options for relief — a stay of proceedings or a mere adjournment — neither of which may be appropriate and just in the circumstances.

- Consider adjourning the case at the first court appearance for a matter of weeks. This procedure will enable you to:

  - Order and review disclosure with your client before setting a trial date.

  - Assist the court's schedule (and avoid any later adjournments) by advising how long the trial will take and whether you expect any pre-trial motions.

In *Toronto (City) v. Canada Land Corp.*, 2006 ONCJ 421, [2006] O.J. No. 4489, 2006 CarswellOnt 6959 (Ont. C.J.), the court discussed the issue of the Crown's obligation to make give disclosure of "will-say" statements to the defence. It was held that generally, in provincial offences prosecutions commenced under Part I, there would be no need to provide will-says for officers or investigators who have made notes and they are disclosed to the defendant; even in relatively uncomplicated prosecutions commenced under Part III for more serious offences, there would be usually no need for the prosecution to provide a will-say statement for any officers or investigators or civilian witnesses, when the investigating officer has made notes or has taken a statement from a witness and recorded it in his notes, and those notes have been disclosed to the defence. However, even if the prosecution is not obligated to disclose will-says under the present *Stinchcombe* parameters, especially for uncomplicated regulatory prosecutions, the court may still order the prosecution provide such will-says when due to the particular circumstances of a case it is necessary to ensure that the accused or defendant is accorded a fair trial, or that it will provide useful information to the court and is necessary for managing the trial.

While the Crown disclosed the officer's collision reconstruction report prior to the trial, it failed to disclose the amended report. The defence had not completed its cross-examination of the officer, and the Crown's case was not concluded. The appropriate remedy was not a stay of proceedings, but an order for production of the revised report, and an adjournment to allow the defence to review the revised report with leave to recall Crown witnesses. This remedy removed any prejudice to the defence due to non-disclosure: *R. v. Soo*, 2008 ABPC 221, 2008 CarswellAlta 1077, [2008] A.J. No. 881 (Alta. Prov. Ct.).

The Crown's duty to disclose information is relevant to defences that are directly related to one of the elements of the offence, but not a defence that is a constitutional challenge to the validity of legislation or its applicability. A constitutional challenge does not constitute a reasonably possible defence in the context of the duty to disclose: *Tenascon c. Québec (Juge de la Cour du Québec)* (2007), EYB 2007-121464, 2007 CarswellQue 5968, 2007 CarswellQue 13626, [2007] J.Q. No. 6991, 2007 QCCA 946, 2007 QCCA 947, (sub nom. *R. v. Commanda*) [2008] 3 C.N.L.R. 311 (Que. C.A.), leave to appeal refused (2008), 2008 CarswellQue 3557, 2008 CarswellQue 3558, [2007] S.C.C.A. No. 476 (S.C.C).

The Crown cannot be expected to disclose information before trial whose relevance first becomes apparent during the trial itself, and the prosecution cannot be expected to disclose what it does not have. At the same time, the Crown cannot deliberately refrain from making inquiries because of a fear that it may learn about relevant evidence that it would have to disclose: *R. v. Horan*, 2008 CarswellOnt 4801, 2008 ONCA 589, 240 O.A.C. 313, 60 C.R. (6th) 46, 237 C.C.C. (3d) 514 (Ont. C.A.), at para. 27 [ONCA].

3.3.2 REVIEW DISCLOSURE WITH CLIENT

- Fully review the disclosure materials received from the prosecutor with your client.

- There may be explanations for certain conduct.
- Your client may recall evidence or witnesses who were not previously considered relevant.
- Your client may recall evidence which contradicts what the prosecutor's witnesses say.

3.3.3 REQUEST FURTHER DISCLOSURE

- Do you have reason to believe that the prosecutor, or other governmental official, has undisclosed relevant information, physical evidence, or samples?
  - If so, write a letter to the prosecutor detailing the information required before trial. Perhaps you need duplicate samples for independent testing.
  - Where an accused was charged with speeding and sought disclosure of the radar operating manual, the maintenance record of the unit and the officer's training record for the unit, the Crown was ordered to provide sufficient information to answer the relevant information of what the officer would be in a position to testify to: *R. v. Makuch* (1996), 192 A.R. 299 (Alta. Prov. Ct.).

3.3.4 APPLICATION FOR FURTHER DISCLOSURE

The right to disclosure derives from section 7 of the *Charter of Rights*, which states that: "Everyone has the right to life, liberty and security of the person and the right not to be deprived thereof except in accordance with the principles of fundamental justice." It may be that the nature and extent of disclosure depends on the threat to a person's liberty: for example, the Crown may have to investigate and disclose more in a murder case than in a parking infraction case.

- Bring an application to the court for further disclosure, if necessary.
  - Include a notice of application with a supporting affidavit from someone other than the defendant and you (per-

haps your secretary) detailing the correspondence with the prosecutor and the reasons to believe that the authorities have undisclosed relevant material.

- Be prepared to argue that you need full and timely disclosure because a conviction would seriously impair your client's liberty within the meaning of section 7 of the *Charter*.

- Where the defendant has established an infringement of his right to disclosure, on an application to the superior court, the application judge should not order a stay of proceedings as the stay is a drastic remedy unless it is not possible to remedy through reasonable means the prejudice to the defendant's right to make full answer and defence. See: *R. v. Arcand* (2004), [2004] O.J. No. 5017, 2004 CarswellOnt 5160, 10 C.E.L.R. (3d) 161, 125 C.R.R. (2d) 144, 193 O.A.C. 16, 192 C.C.C. (3d) 57, 73 O.R. (3d) 758 (Ont. C.A.).

Trial judge erred in staying proceedings at the outset of the trial based on late disclosure without at least considering adjourning the application to the completion of the trial and without actual evidence of prejudice arising from the late disclosure. (*R. v. Johnson*, [2007] O.J. No. 2228, 2007 CarswellOnt 3583, (sub nom. *R. v. J. (N.)*) 225 O.A.C. 13, 2007 ONCA 419 (Ont. C.A.))

- Book the return date for your application well before trial. That way, should the material be disclosed, you will have time to review or test it.

- Ordinarily, in cases of non-disclosure, a stay of proceedings is only justified if the non-disclosure either irreparably prejudices the defendant's ability to make full answer and defence, or irreparably harms the integrity of the administration of justice: *R. v. Knox* (2006), 2006 CarswellOnt 3042, [2006] O.J. No. 1976, 209 C.C.C. (3d) 76, 80 O.R. (3d) 515, 31 M.V.R. (5th) 60, 211 O.A.C. 164, 142 C.R.R. (2d) 99 (Ont. C.A.).

While it would have been preferable for the Crown to have been more forthcoming with disclosure, the defendant was in possession of all he needed prior to trial and was not prejudiced by the Crown's conduct: *R. v. Arcand*, 2008 CarswellOnt 4971,

[2008] O.J. No. 3294, 2008 ONCA 595, 240 O.A.C. 286, 238 C.C.C. (3d) 204, 92 O.R. (3d) 444, 38 C.E.L.R. (3d) 1 (Ont. C.A.), leave to appeal refused (2008), [2008] S.C.C.A. No. 449, 2008 CarswellOnt 7740, 2008 CarswellOnt 7741 (S.C.C.).

3.3.5 DISCOVERY FROM THIRD PARTIES

- Is there another governmental department or private organization with information which might be relevant?
  - If so, write or phone the organization to find out how to get the information. The information may be public, requiring only a request.
  - The information may be confidential — perhaps the organization cannot even confirm whether they have information. If the information is confidential because of the privacy of a third party, you might:
    - Bring an application to the court for production and release of the organization's records.
      - Include a notice of application and a supporting affidavit in an application record.
      - The affidavit should be sworn by someone other than the defendant or you (perhaps your secretary).
      - It should detail the grounds to believe that the organization has relevant information — "fishing expeditions" are generally not permitted, especially when there are legitimate privacy rights at stake.
- Book a return date for your application well before trial. That way, should the records be disclosed, you will have time to review.
- Serve the application record on the prosecutor, on the third party whose privacy right is at stake, and on any other legally interested party.

- Serve a copy on the organization with the records.
- Serve a summons requiring the keeper of the records (you must find out who this person is) or his or her "designate" to appear in court on the date of your application along with the records.
- At the application, you must persuade the justice there are reasonable grounds to believe that the undisclosed records *may* assist your defence (of course, you won't know for sure because you haven't seen the records).
- The justice may balance your client's right to make full answer and defence (under section 7 of the *Charter*) with other privacy rights.
- The justice may even decide to look at the records in private before releasing them to you.
- Ontario cases are somewhat uncertain on the procedure to utilize, and whether to follow a process analogous to the statutory scheme in the *Criminal Code* for disclosure of third party records which followed the *O'Connor* decision.
- The two-stage test in *R. v. O'Connor* (1995), [1996] 2 W.W.R. 153, 44 C.R. (4th) 1, 103 C.C.C. (3d) 1, [1995] 4 S.C.R. 411 (S.C.C.) was taken regarding business records of the corporate victim: *R. v. Caporicci* (1998), 1998 CarswellOnt 1185, [1998] O.J. No. 1123 (Ont. Prov. Div.).
- The Court of Appeal for Ontario has recently stated that where there are third party records, which the defence wishes to have produced, a written application should be brought using the procedure laid down in *R. v. O'Connor.* See: *R. v. Arcand* (2004), [2004] O.J. No. 5017, 2004 CarswellOnt 5160, 10 C.E.L.R. (3d) 161, 125 C.R.R. (2d) 144, 193 O.A.C. 16, 192 C.C.C. (3d) 57, 73 O.R. (3d) 758 (Ont. C.A.).
- For an example of a provincial offences case where disclosure was ordered of records in the possession of a third

party, see *R. v. Dare Foods Ltd.*, [2004] O.J. No. 3949, 2004 ONCJ 201, 2004 CarswellOnt 3906 (Ont. C.J.); and *R. v. Dare Foods Ltd.*, [2004] O.J. No. 3951, 2004 ONCJ 202, 2004 CarswellOnt 3908 (Ont. C.J.). The case involved a prosecution under the *Occupational Health and Safety Act.* The justice held that there was jurisdiction for the court to order production of a coroner's records respecting the deceased person, following the procedure in *R. v. O'Connor.*

- An *O'Connor*-type application is only necessary where a third party has a reasonable expectation of privacy in the records. See *R. v. McNeil* (2006), 2006 CarswellOnt 7557, [2006] O.J. No. 4746, 43 C.R. (6th) 370, 215 C.C.C. (3d) 22, 218 O.A.C. 1 (Ont. C.A.), leave to appeal allowed (2007), 2007 CarswellOnt 4325, 2007 CarswellOnt 4326, [2007] S.C.C.A. No. 57 (S.C.C.).

The procedure set out in *R. v. O'Connor* (1995), 1995 CarswellBC 1098, 1995 CarswellBC 1151, EYB 1995-67073, [1995] S.C.J. No. 98, [1996] 2 W.W.R. 153, [1995] 4 S.C.R. 411, 44 C.R. (4th) 1, 103 C.C.C. (3d) 1, 130 D.L.R. (4th) 235, 191 N.R. 1, 68 B.C.A.C. 1, 112 W.A.C. 1, 33 C.R.R. (2d) 1 (S.C.C.) provides a general mechanism at common law for ordering production of any record beyond the possession or control of the prosecuting Crown. The procedure is not limited to only those cases where a third party has an expectation of privacy in the targeted documents: *R. v. McNeil*, [2009] S.C.J. No. 3, 2009 CarswellOnt 116, 2009 CarswellOnt 117, 62 C.R. (6th) 1, 238 C.C.C. (3d) 353, 2009 SCC 3 (S.C.C.), at para. 11 [SCC].

3.3.6 INTERVIEW WITNESSES

- Gather evidence from all potential witnesses, both favourable and unfavourable. Even the prosecutor's witnesses, who may be convinced your client is guilty, should be questioned. You may learn new information that was not disclosed.

- If you suspect that witnesses may change their story, and should you wish to "pin them down", follow one of the procedures listed below.

  - Interview them in the presence of an investigator or reliable person from your office.

  - Record the interview, with the witness' consent, if possible.

  - Have the witness sign or swear a statement.

- Consider that if the witness changes his or her story, then you will need evidence to contradict him or her at trial, but do whatever procedure is most comfortable for the witness.

3.3.7 EXPERT ADVICE

- An expert will assist in understanding the issues and where to focus your strategy. And of course, you may want the expert to test samples or testify at trial.

- Hire an investigator, if you can afford to. The investigator should be licensed, reliable, and willing to testify in court if necessary.

- It is also important to consider whether the expert has been qualified by the court to testify before, or if his/her expertise has not been accepted. It is only a properly qualified expert that will be permitted to testify. In *R. v. Mohan*, [1994] 2 S.C.R. 9, 89 C.C.C. (3d) 402, EYB 1994-67655, 1994 CarswellOnt 66, 1994 CarswellOnt 1155, [1994] S.C.J. No. 36, 29 C.R. (4th) 243, 71 O.A.C. 241, 166 N.R. 245, 114 D.L.R. (4th) 419, 18 O.R. (3d) 160 (note) (S.C.C.) at 414 [C.C.C.], the Supreme Court of Canada stated that in order to qualify as an expert, the evidence must be given by a witness who is shown to have acquired "special or peculiar knowledge through study or experience" of the matters on which the witness undertakes to testify. You should also consider whether the expert you are consulting and considering calling as a witness has been called to testify before by the defence, or the prosecutor, or both, as this may be relevant to the issue of bias or independence of the expert.

4

TYPES OF PROVINCIAL OFFENCES

4.1 CLASSIFICATION SCHEME

- In *R. v. Sault Ste. Marie (City)*, [1978] 2 S.C.R. 1299, 7 C.E.L.R. 53, 3 C.R. (3d) 30, 40 C.C.C. (2d) 353, 1978 CarswellOnt 24, 1978 CarswellOnt 594, 85 D.L.R. (3d) 161, 21 N.R. 295 (S.C.C.), the Supreme Court of Canada classified all offences, both regulatory and criminal, as either:

  - *Mens rea* offences,

  - Strict liability offences, or

  - Absolute liability offences.

4.1.1 *MENS REA* OFFENCES

- The prosecution must prove beyond a reasonable doubt that the defendant committed the illegal act(s).

- The prosecution must also prove beyond a reasonable doubt that the defendant had a particular state of mind.

- The state of mind depends on the offence. For example, it might be intent, knowledge, or recklessness.

- The prosecution can prove the defendant's state of mind in two ways:

- Admissions by the defendant as to his or her state of mind; and

- Inferences about the defendant's state of mind based on the common sense principle that people normally intend the natural consequences of their actions.

4.1.2 STRICT LIABILITY OFFENCES

- The prosecution must prove beyond a reasonable doubt that the defendant committed the illegal act(s).

- The defendant must then prove, on a balance of probabilities, that he or she took reasonable care not to commit the illegal act(s), or that he or she made a reasonable mistake of fact which, if true, would have rendered the act(s) lawful.

4.1.3 ABSOLUTE LIABILITY OFFENCES

- The prosecution must prove beyond a reasonable doubt that the defendant committed the illegal act(s).

- The defendant is liable whether or not he or she was at fault.

4.2 CLASSIFICATION OF OFFENCES

- Provincial offences are presumed to be strict liability offences.

- The offence is *mens rea* and not strict liability, however, if the provincial offence clearly requires proof of a particular state of mind. *For example, section 16 of the Discriminatory Business Practices Act, R.S.O. 1990, c. D.12, states that: Every person who, knowingly furnishes false information in an investigation under this Act, fails to comply with any order or assurance of voluntary compliance made or en-*

tered into under this Act; or obstructs a person making an investigation is guilty of a provincial offence. Clearly, the Prosecutor must prove the defendant's knowledge, and so it is a mens rea offence.

- The offence is absolute liability, if the provincial offence clearly excludes the defence of reasonable care and clearly indicates that guilt requires only proof of the illegal act(s). To determine if this is the clear intent of the legislation, courts consider the following: (See John Swaigen, *Regulatory Offences in Canada*, (Carswell, 1992) pp. 38-42):

  - The overall regulatory pattern adopted by the Legislature. *For example, the purpose of the statute, its legislative history, and its relationship with other provincial laws.*

  - The subject-matter of the legislation. *For example, the class of persons protected by the law, the extent of the harm to them if the offence is committed, and the extent to which other remedies are available.*

  - The importance of the penalty. *For example, the harshness of the penalty, and the difficulty of complying with the legislation.*

  - The precision of the language used. *For example, whether the legislation clearly rejects the defence of reasonable care.*

  - The effect on the defendant's *Charter* rights. *See below for further discussion.*

- As Swaigen points out, the categorization process is not consistent and there is a "lack of any rationality" (See John Swaigen, Regulatory Offences in Canada (Carswell, 1992) p. 52. Some statutes employ all three types of offences, as is the case in the *Ontario Highway Traffic Act*: willfully avoiding police while being pursued (*mens rea* offence); failing to yield to pedestrians (strict liability offence); speeding (absolute liability offence). See further *Libman on Reg-*

ulatory Offences in Canada (Earlscourt, 2002) for examples of offences under various provincial, federal and municipal statutes which have been classified as *mens rea* offences (Chapter 4.3), absolute liability offences (Chapter 5.6), and strict liability offences (Chapter 6.5).

- The Supreme Court of Canada has recently confirmed that the issue of classification of the offence has become "a question of statutory interpretation", and that regulatory offences usually fall in the category of strict liability offences. See *Lévis (Ville) c. Tétreault*, 2006 SCC 12, [2006] 1 S.C.R. 420, (sub nom. *Lévis (City) v. Tétreault*) 266 D.L.R. (4th) 165, (sub nom. *Lévis (City) v. Tétreault*) 346 N.R. 331, J.E. 2006-818, 36 C.R. (6th) 215, 31 M.V.R. (5th) 1, 207 C.C.C. (3d) 1, 2006 CarswellQue 2911, 2006 CarswellQue 2912, [2006] S.C.J. No. 12 (S.C.C.).

Another recent example of how the classification of offences analysis is used by the courts is provided by the Ontario Court of Appeal in *Brampton (City) v. Kanda*, 2008 ONCA 22, [2008] O.J. No. 80, 2008 CarswellOnt 79, 41 M.P.L.R. (4th) 199 (Ont. C.A.). In this case, the Court of Appeal determined that the offence of driving while a passenger under 16 years old fails to properly wear a seat belt is a strict liability offence for which the due diligence defence is available. In coming to this conclusion the Court examined the overall regulatory pattern of the legislation, the subject matter, penalty, and precision of the language.

- The classification of strict liability struck an appropriate balance between encouraging drivers to be vigilant about the safety of child passengers and not punishing those who exercise due diligence with respect to children's seatbelts: *Brampton (City) v. Kanda*, 2008 ONCA 22, [2008] O.J. No. 80, 2008 CarswellOnt 79, 41 M.P.L.R. (4th) 199 (Ont. C.A.).

The word "shall" in a traffic offence does not necessarily mean absolute liability: *R. v. Dillman*, 2008 CarswellOnt 1596, [2008] O.J. No. 1120, 68 M.V.R. (5th) 272, 2008 ONCJ 101 (Ont. C.J.).

The *Highway Traffic Act* offence of "stunt driving" is one of strict liability, there being a strong presumption in favour of classifying an offence as strict liability in nature: *R. v. Bell*, 2008 ONCJ 726, 2008 CarswellOnt 8586, [2008] O.J. No. 5585 (Ont. C.J.), para. 18 [ONCJ]. **Note:** A number of other trial rulings have agreed that this is a strict liability offence, but an appeal court has yet to rule on this issue. See, for example, *R. v. Bond* (2008), 2008 CarswellOnt 8560 (Ont. C.J.).

Section 19.2 of the Manitoba *Legislative Assembly and Executive Council Conflict of Interest Act* is an absolute liability offence because it has a stringent code of conduct for senior public servants, and because no relief is given to senior public servants who commit an offence through inadvertence. A similar analysis might be applied in Ontario statutes: *R. v. Kupfer*, [2008] M.J. No. 276, 2008 CarswellMan 405, 232 Man. R. (2d) 98, 2008 MBQB 203 (Man. Q.B.).

Failing to yield at a crosswalk – in Ontario, is an absolute liability offence: *R. v. Kelleher* (2008), 2008 CarswellOnt 8609, 2009 ONCJ 5, [2009] O.J. No. 670 (Ont. C.J.).

4.3 *CHARTER* ISSUES IN CLASSIFYING OFFENCES

Section 7 of the *Charter* states: "Every person has the right to life, liberty and security of the person and the right not to be deprived thereof except in accordance with the principles of fundamental justice".

- It is a principle of fundamental justice that the morally innocent should not be convicted. *An absolute liability offence, which can punish those who did not intend to commit the act, and even those who take all reasonable precautions not to commit the act, can punish the morally innocent.* See: *Reference re s. 94(2) of the Motor Vehicle Act (British Columbia)* (1985), 48 C.R. (3d) 289, 23 C.C.C. (3d) 289, [1985] 2 S.C.R. 486, 69 B.C.L.R. 145, 36 M.V.R. 240, [1986] 1 W.W.R. 481 (S.C.C.).

- An absolute liability offence is only contrary to *Charter* section 7, however, where the defendant's "liberty" is at stake. *Courts generally only see liberty at stake when there is a possibility of imprisonment or probation upon conviction. If punishment for the offence does not include the possibility of imprisonment, then even though a morally innocent defendant may be convicted, his or her section 7 Charter right is likely not breached.*

- If an absolute liability offence breaches section 7 of the *Charter*, and if it is not a reasonable limit under section 1 of the *Charter*, then by virtue of section 52(1), the offence is unconstitutional and of no force or effect.

- However, courts are loathe to render provincial statutes of no force or effect. *More likely, where prison is a possibility, the court will interpret what might otherwise be an absolute liability offence as a strict liability offence, thereby keeping it constitutional. That way, the defendant can still prove (on a balance of probabilities) that he or she is morally innocent (because he or she took reasonable care).* See: *R. v. Rube* (1992), 75 C.C.C. (3d) 575, [1992] 3 S.C.R. 159, 74 B.C.L.R. (2d) 1, [1993] 1 W.W.R. 385 (S.C.C.).

4.4 CONCLUSION

- Research the law on the section of the statute with which your client is charged.
  - Is it a *mens rea* offence?
  - Is it strict liability?
  - Is it absolute liability?
- If the offence is absolute liabilty, and if there is a possibility of prison, consider challenging the law as unconstitutional. However, be prepared for the court to re-interpret the offence as strict liability so that it remains constitutional.
- Note that in some statutes, such as the *Highway Traffic Act* of Ontario, all three types of offences may be charged, such as speeding and failing to stop for a red light or stop sign, which are absolute liability offences; willfully avoiding the police while being pursued, which is a *mens rea* offence; and strict liability offences like careless driving and driving while suspended.
- For a list of offences which have been classified in these various categories, see *Libman on Regulatory Offences in Canada* (Saltspring Island B.C.: Earlscourt Legal Press, 2002): Chapter 4.3 – Examples of *Mens Rea* Offences, Chapter 5.6 – Examples of Absolute Liability Offences, Chapter 6.5 – Examples of Strict Liability Offences.

5

PROCEDURAL ISSUES

5.1 JURISDICTIONAL DEFENCES

5.1.1 TIMING

- Jurisdictional defences should be raised before your client pleads. In effect, you are challenging the right of the court to hear the case.

Where the defendant was served with a notice of trial, but the court house was closed on the trial date due to a power failure, the court regained jurisdiction over the person by mailing out a fresh notice of trial. It is apparent that the legislative intent of the *Provincial Offences Act* was to ensure that technical objections do not impede the arrival of a verdict on the merits, and that it was intended to be a speedy, efficient and convenient way of dealing with provincial offences matters. See: *York (Regional Municipality) v. Scarcello* (2004), (sub nom. *R. v. Scarcello*) [2004] O.J. No. 1002, 2004 CarswellOnt 6077 (Ont. S.C.J.).

5.1.2 TERRITORIAL JURISDICTION

- Proceedings shall be heard in the county or district in which the offence occurred, or in an adjoining county or district if the court's sittings are reasonably close to where the offence occurred (provided that the adjoining place of sitting is named in the summons or offence notice): section 29.

- The court may transfer the proceedings to any other territory upon motion by the defendant or prosecutor, if it is in the interests of justice to do so: section 29(4).

- Some provincial acts allow trials in places other than where the offence occurred. *For example, under section 68 of the*

Occupational Health and Safety Act, R.S.O. 1990, c. O.1, the informant may elect trial in the county or district in which the accused is resident or carries on business.

In *R. v. Fortese* (September 25, 2008), Ferguson J., [2008] O.J. No. 5159 (Ont. S.C.J.), it was held that a police officer has jurisdiction to lay a charge for an offence committed anywhere in Ontario. There is no provision in the *Provincial Offences Act* that requires a proceeding to be commenced in the county, district or regional municipality where the offence occurred. The place of the offence only becomes relevant if the defendant appears and disputes the charge, in which case the court must consider the possible application of s. 29 governing the venue of the proceeding. However, where the defendant fails to appear for trial, the justice was required to proceed in the defendant's absence and enter a conviction and impose sentence pursuant to s. 9.1. If the court does nothing, when it is required to act, the court commits jurisdictional error.

5.1.3 LIMITATION PERIODS

- A limitation period begins to run from the moment that the offence has ceased. If the offence continues over a period of time (for example, an ongoing pollution offence), the limitation period begins from the moment of the last offending behaviour.

- The issue involving the breach or observance of the limitation period for the commencement of proceedings against the defendant, including applying the discoverability rule, is a question of fact which ought to be left to the trial judge. See: *R. v. Windsor Utilities Commission* (2005), [2005] O.J. No. 474, 2005 CarswellOnt 493, 13 C.E.L.R. (3d) 156 (Ont. S.C.J.), affirmed (2005), [2005] O.J. No. 3370, 2005 CarswellOnt 3513 (Ont. C.A.).

(a) In the Charging Act

- Many provincial statutues contain limitation periods, beyond which no charge can be laid. For example,

  - Under the *Occupational Health and Safety Act*, *supra*, section 69 prohibits any prosecution more than one year after the last act or default.

- Under the *Dangerous Goods Transportation Act*, R.S.O. 1990, c. D.1, section 4(3) prohibits any prosecution more than two years after the date of the alleged offence.

- Under the *Ontario Water Resources Act*, R.S.O. 1990, c. O.40, section 94 prohibits any prosecution more than two years after (a) the day on which the offence was committed; and (b) the day on which evidence of the offence first came to the attention of a Director (Provincial Officer) appointed under the Act.

(b) In the POA, Section 76

- Where no limitation period is prescribed in the charging Act, the limitation period is six months after the date of the alleged offence.

- A limitation may be extended by a justice with the consent of the defendant.

- In some cases, the defendant may consider it to be in his/her interests to consent to the extension of a limitation period under section 76 of the *Provincial Offences Act*. An example is where a driving charge under the *Criminal Code* will be withdrawn in exchange for a guilty plea to a driving offence under a provincial statute, such as the *Highway Traffic Act*. The prosecutor's consent is also required in such a situation: see section 45(4) of the *Provincial Offences Act*.

5.1.4 PROPER SERVICE

(a) Part I: Minor Offences

- A youth must be summoned (section 95) within 30 days of the offence (section 3(3)) and a copy must be delivered to the youth's parent(s) (section 96).

- An adult defendant must be served with an offence notice or a summons to appear within 30 days of the offence: section 3(3).

- Proof of service may be:

  - Admitted by the defendant;

  - Certified by the provincial offences officer who issued the certificate of offence; or

  - By affidavit of service in the prescribed form: section 3(4-8).

In *R. v. Singh* (2000), 2000 CarswellOnt 5360, 16 M.V.R. (4th) 141 (Ont. C.J.), where the certificate of offence as filed included no proof of service on the defendant, it was held that the language of section 3(5) is mandatory in requiring the issuing officer, who performed service of the certificate, to certify service on the certificate of offence. In the circumstances, the failure to comply with section 3(5) rendered the certificate incomplete, and irregular on its face for the purpose of section 9(1).

- There may be special rules for service under the particular charging Act.

(b) Part II: Parking Offences

- The provincial offences officer may serve the *owner* of the vehicle in two ways:

  - Affixing the notice in a conspicuous place at the time of the alleged infraction; or

  - Delivering the notice personally to the person having care and control of the vehicle at the time of the alleged infraction: section 15(4).

- The provincial offences officer may serve the *operator* of the vehicle by delivering it to him or her personally at the time of the alleged infraction: section 15(5).

- The provincial offences officer shall certify on the certificate of parking infraction that the notice was served on the person charged with the date and method of service: section 15(6).

- If done so, the certificate is proof of service unless there is evidence to the contrary: section 15(7).

In *Toronto (City) v. Weingust*, 2006 ONCJ 23, 18 M.P.L.R. (4th) 182, 2006 CarswellOnt 461, [2006] O.J. No. 341 (Ont. C.J.), it was held that the provision of parking spaces on city streets is a reasonable and rational use of a service for which the city is permitted to charge a fee.

(c) Part III: Serious Offences

(i) Requirements of the Summons

- The defendant is ordered to appear in court by a summons. The summons shall:
  - Be directed to the defendant;
  - Set out briefly the offence; and
  - "Require the defendant to attend court at a time and place stated therein to attend thereafter as required by the court in order to be dealt with according to law": section 26(1).

(ii) Service of the Summons *Before* an Information is Laid

- A provincial offences officer may serve a person with a summons in the prescribed form before an information is laid where:
  - An offence was committed; and
  - The officer believes, on reasonable and probable grounds, that the person whom the officer finds at or near the place where the offence was committed, committed the offence: section 22.

(iii) Service of the Summons *After* an Information is Laid

- Where an information is laid before serving a summons:
  - The justice shall issue a summons in the prescribed form: section 24(1)(a).
  - The summons shall be served by a provincial offences officer by:
    - Delivering it personally to the person to whom it is directed, or
    - If that person cannot conveniently be found, by leaving it for the person at the person's last known or usual place of abode with an inmate thereof who appears to be at least 16 years of age: section 26(2).

(iv) Additional Means of Service *After* an Information is Laid

- Where the person does not reside in Ontario, the summons shall be deemed to have been duly served seven days after it has been sent by registered mail to the person's last known or usual place of abode: section 26(3).
- Service on a corporation may be effected by delivering the summons personally (section 26(4-6)):
  - In the case of a municipal corporation, to the mayor, warden, reeve or other executive officer of the corporation or person apparently in charge of a branch thereof.
  - In the case of any other corporation, to the manager, secretary or other executive officer of the corporation or person apparently in charge of a branch thereof; or
  - By mailing the summons by registered mail to the corporation at an address held out by the corporation to be its address, in which case the summons shall be deemed

to have been duly served seven days after the day of mailing.

- A justice may, upon motion and upon being satisfied that service cannot be effectively made on a corporation in the above manner, authorize another method of service that has a reasonable likelihood of coming to the attention of the corporation.

- Service of a summons may be proved by statement under oath or affirmation.

- For a youth, a copy of the summons must be delivered to the parent(s): section 96.

5.2 CONSTITUTIONAL DEFENCES

- Under the *Constitution Act* (British North America Act), only the federal government can create criminal offences. If a provincial offence is in pith and substance criminal, then it is unconstitutional and the defendant cannot be convicted.

- Provinces, however, can prohibit conduct which is incidentally criminal if the purpose of the law is to regulate a provincial power. *For example, the Ontario Securities Act, R.S.O. 1990, c. S.5, s. 122, as amended, creates offences regarding the misrepresentation of securities information. These offences may incidentally be criminal fraud, especially where the defendant knowingly or recklessly disseminated false information. However, the purpose of the provincial offences is to regulate the securities industry, which is a provincial power, and so the offences are constitutional.*

- The offence of soliciting a stopped car while on a roadway, pursuant to the *Safe Streets Act* or section 177 of the *Highway Traffic Act*, constitutes valid provincial legislation, regulating the interaction of pedestrians and vehicles on the roadways, in the interests of public safety, efficient circulation, and public enjoyment of public thoroughfares. *R.*

v. Banks, 2007 CarswellOnt 111, 39 M.V.R. (5th) 1, [2007] O.J. No. 99, 220 O.A.C. 211, 150 C.R.R. (2d) 239, 216 C.C.C. (3d) 19, 2007 ONCA 19, 275 D.L.R. (4th) 640, 44 C.R. (6th) 244, 84 O.R. (3d) 1 (Ont. C.A.) (Ont. C.A.), leave to appeal refused (2007), 2007 CarswellOnt 5670, 2007 CarswellOnt 5671, [2007] S.C.C.A. No. 139, 156 C.R.R. (2d) 376 (note) (S.C.C.).

In *R. v. Sibernagel*, 2000 BCCA 251, 2000 CarswellBC 764, 139 B.C.A.C. 7, 227 W.A.C. 7 (B.C. C.A.), leave to appeal refused (2000), 2000 CarswellBC 2171, 2000 CarswellBC 2172, 263 N.R. 396 (note), 151 B.C.A.C. 160 (note), 249 W.A.C. 160 (note) (S.C.C.), the Court of Appeal found that the justice of the peace was not bound as a matter of stare decisis by co-ordinate orders of other justices of local jurisdiction in respect of a constitutional issue. Absent authority from above, a finding as to constitutionality was properly made on a case-by-case basis.

5.2.1 NOTICE OF CONSTITUTIONAL CHALLENGE

- Serve a notice of challenge on the Attorney General, the prosecutors' office, and the court with proof of service, should you wish to challenge the constitutional validity or applicability of a provincial law.

- Do this as soon as practicable, and in any event, no later than 15 days before trial. (See *Courts of Justice Act*, R.S.O. 1990, c. C.43, s. 109, as amended.)

- As the notice requirements under section 109(1) are mandatory, it is inappropriate for the justice of the peace to summarily dispense with service of the notice as he or she lacks jurisdiction to waive these procedural requirements. See: *R. v. Dickson*, [2004] O.J. No. 4710, 2004 CarswellOnt 4794, 2004 ONCJ 279 (Ont. C.J.).

The parties must make sure all the relevant documents are properly before the court, including affidavits which are signed. In one recent case, the trial judge was found to have erred in dismissing the defendant's constitutional challenge on the basis that the defendant's affidavit was not properly executed and signed: *R. v. Bodik* (2008), 2008 CarswellOnt 1948 (Ont. C.J.).

Where the Notice of Constitutional Question was not served properly or within the time limits prescribed by the legislation, the court considered there was no reason to make any rulings on the validity of the specific requests in the order sought, and the defendant's constitutional challenge was denied: *R. v. Harizanov*, 2008 ONCJ 690, 2008 CarswellOnt 8208, [2008] O.J. No. 5430 (Ont. C.J.).

5.2.2 VOID FOR VAGUENESS DEFENCE

- It is a principle of fundamental justice that citizens be able to foresee whether their conduct might be illegal. If an offence is too vague, then it is in effect nothing but governmental discretion cloaked in legal terminology.

However, in *Canada v. Pharmaceutical Society (Nova Scotia)*, 15 C.R. (4th) 1, (sub nom. *R. v. Nova Scotia Pharmaceutical Society*) [1992] 2 S.C.R. 606, (sub nom. *R. v. Nova Scotia Pharmaceutical Society*) 74 C.C.C. (3d) 289 (S.C.C.). Justice Gonthier cautioned against using too rigorous a standard for legislative clarity. In some situations, valid governmental legislation cannot be straight-jacketed "by requiring the law to achieve a degree of precision to which the subject-matter does not lend itself" (at 313). See also: *Reference re ss. 193 and 195(1)(c) of the Criminal Code (Canada)*, 56 C.C.C. (3d) 65, 77 C.R. (3d) 1, [1990] 1 S.C.R. 1123, [1990] 4 W.W.R. 481 (S.C.C.).

- Generally, provided the law delineates an area of risk which can be determined by a reasoned analysis of previous court judgments, the law is sufficiently clear (*Nova Scotia*, *supra*, at 311).

5.2.3 *CHARTER OF RIGHTS* DEFENCES

- The *Charter of Rights* is the supreme law of Canada. Any inconsistent law is, to the extent of the inconsistency, of no force and effect: *Charter*, section 52(1).

- Some of the rights in the *Charter* which may be impinged by a provincial law are:

  - Freedom of conscience and religion: *Charter*, section 2(a).

  - Freedom of thought, belief, opinion and expression, including freedom of the press and other media of communication: *Charter*, section 2(b).

In *R. v. Glad Day Bookshops Inc.* (2004), [2004] O.J. No. 1766, 2004 CarswellOnt 1688, 239 D.L.R. (4th) 119, 118 C.R.R. (2d) 209, 183 C.C.C. (3d) 449, 70 O.R. (3d) 691 (Ont. S.C.J.), the defendant was charged with distributing an adult sex film that was not approved by the Ontario Film Review Board (OFRB) pursuant to the *Theatre Act* and Regulations. The charges were dismissed as the statutory scheme requiring prior approval of the films was overly broad in applying to expressive material, and thereby violated section 2(b) of the *Charter*. In response to this decision, the Regulations under the *Theatres Act* were amended as of July 5, 2004, and narrowed the criteria the OFRB could use to review and approve film.

- Freedom of peaceful assembly: *Charter*, section 2(c).

In *R. v. Behrens*, [2004] O.J. No. 5135, 2004 CarswellOnt 5315, 2004 ONCJ 327, 126 C.R.R. (2d) 50 (Ont. C.J.), the defendants were convicted under the *Trespass to Property Act* for taking part in a demonstration at Queen's Park, after being served with trespass notices following an early demonstration. A recognized category of parliamentary privilege was the ejection of "strangers" from the legislature and its grounds. The issue of trespass notices fell under the Speaker's parliamentary privilege, and the court lacked any jurisdiction to review that action, even on the basis of a *Charter* argument that a conviction would be an infringement of their *Charter* freedom of peaceful assembly right.

- Freedom of association: *Charter*, section 2(d).
- Life, liberty and security of the person and the right not to be deprived thereof except in accordance with the principles of fundamental justice: *Charter*, section 7.
- Equal protection and equal benefit of the law without discrimination, except for laws designed to assist the disadvantaged: *Charter*, section 15.

Where legislation is intended to promote the safe use of public places without the danger or harassment posed by the interaction with those who solicit in an aggressive manner, such provisions do not have the effect of restricting expression within the meaning of section 2(b) of the *Charter*. See *Safe Streets Act, 1999*, S.O. 1999, c. 8.

The prohibition against aggressive solicitation of persons on streets under the *Safe Streets Act, 1999*, and on roadways under subsection 177(2) of the *Highway Traffic Act* was not in violation of freedom of expression under section 2(d) of the *Charter*. See *R. v. Banks* (2005), [2005] O.J. No. 98, 2005 CarswellOnt 115, 17 M.V.R. (5th) 93, 126 C.R.R. (2d) 189, 248 D.L.R. (4th) 118, 192 C.C.C. (3d) 289, 27 C.R. (6th) 296 (Ont. S.C.J.), affirmed, 2007 CarswellOnt 111, 39 M.V.R. (5th) 1, [2007] O.J. No. 99, 220 O.A.C. 211, 150 C.R.R. (2d) 239, 216 C.C.C. (3d) 19, 2007 ONCA 19, 275 D.L.R. (4th) 640, 44 C.R. (6th) 244, 84 O.R. (3d) 1 (Ont. C.A.), leave to appeal refused (2007), 2007 CarswellOnt 5670, 2007 CarswellOnt 5671, [2007] S.C.C.A. No. 139, 156 C.R.R. (2d) 376 (note) (S.C.C.), reversing (2001), 55 O.R. (3d) 374, 2001 CarswellOnt 2757, 45 C.R. (5th) 23, 86 C.R.R. (2d) 104, 205 D.L.R. (4th) 340 (Ont. C.J.).

- *For the right against unreasonable search and seizure, and the right to counsel, see Chapter 10.*

In *Cochrane v. Ontario (Attorney General)*, [2008] O.J. No. 4165, 2008 CarswellOnt 6229, 92 O.R. (3d) 321, 2008 ONCA 718, 61 C.R. (6th) 374, 242 O.A.C. 192 (Ont. C.A.), the province's legislation banning pit bull dogs was upheld in the face of a number of constitutional challenges under the *Charter*. One issue concerned the admissibility under s. 19(1) of the Act of a document from a veterinarian stating that the dog was a pit bull as proof of that fact, in the absence of evidence to the contrary. In rejecting an attack on this provision as a violation of the presumption of innocence, the court stated that this provision did not amount to a legal prescription which alters the burden of proof. Sections 39 and 46 of the *Provincial Offences Act* give trial judges a discretion to allow for cross-examination of the veterinarian who signed the certificate; it was to be assumed that this discretion would be exercised in a way that is consistent with *Charter* rights. There was no reason to suppose that leave to conduct a cross-examination of the veterinarian, if sought by the defendant, would be improperly denied.

5.3 SUFFICIENCY OF THE CHARGES

- Like jurisdictional defences, an objection to an information or certificate for a defect apparent on its face should be made *before* the defendant pleads: section 36(1).

- After the plea, the objection can only be raised with leave of the court: section 36(1).

- The court shall not quash an information or certificate unless an amendment or particulars would fail to satisfy the ends of justice: section 36(2): See Appendix A.

- The requirement to provide sufficient detail in the wording of a charge for a provincial offence is set out in section 25(6), the legislation which governs the prosecution of provincial offences in Ontario. If the wording of a charge for a provincial offence is not sufficiently detailed, a court may order the prosecution furnish particulars under section 35 where the court finds that it is necessary for a fair trial. For a recent case considering this issue, see *Toronto (City) v. Canada Land Corp.*, 2006 ONCJ 421, [2006] O.J. No. 4489, 2006 CarswellOnt 6959 (Ont. C.J.).

Where the defendant was charged with discharging effluent into water, contrary to s. 30(1) of the *Ontario Water Resources Act*, the information was not deficient but the prosecutor was required to provide particulars of watercourses that may have been impaired, such that the information was more specific than "any waters in Ontario": *R. v. Inco Ltd.*, 2007 ONCJ 656, 2007 CarswellOnt 8854, [2007] O.J. No. 5212 (Ont. C.J.).

5.3.1 COMMON OBJECTIONS

- Common objections include:
  - That the charging document does not clearly identify the alleged wrong so the defendant can adequately prepare for full answer and defence. Furthermore, whatever the verdict, the defendant must be protected from being charged again for the same wrong — and so the offence must be clearly stated: See *R. v. WIS Development Corp.*, [1984] 1 S.C.R. 485, 31 Alta. L.R. (2d) 289, 40 C.R. (3d) 97, 12 C.C.C. (3d) 129 (S.C.C.).
  - The charging document should indicate the date, time and place of the offence.
  - The charging document shall set out each offence in separate counts.
  - The charging document must comply with the signing rules. For example, an information must be sworn, a certificate must be certified, etc.
- As for general requirements, see section 25 of the POA reproduced in Appendix A.

5.3.2 DIVIDING COUNTS

- Section 33 outlines the power to divide counts: See Appendix A.

5.3.3 AMENDMENTS

- Section 34 outlines the power to amend a charging document: See Appendix A.

- The broad curative powers under section 34 include the ability to amend at any stage of the proceeding, including after the Crown closes its case. See *R. v. Larizza* (2006), 2006 ONCJ 400, 2006 CarswellOnt 6795 (Ont. C.J.). The focus of the amendment analysis can only be the potential of prejudice or injustice to the defendant: *R. v. Vanier* (2005), 2005 ONCJ 318, [2005] O.J. No. 5466, 2005 CarswellOnt 7358 (Ont. C.J.).

- What emerges as a consistent theme in case law relating to amendments is the prejudice that could be occasioned to a defendant in mounting a defence: *R. v. Silverstrone* (2007), [2007] O.J. No. 4855, 2007 CarswellOnt 8006 (Ont. S.C.J.).

The defendant was charged under the *Traffic Safety Act* (Sask.) with speeding in a national park. However, the court determined that the charge should have been brought under the *Canada National Parks Regulations*. An amendment to the charge was not granted on the basis that allowing an amendment at this stage of the proceedings would be unfair to the accused, given the nature of the charge and the proceedings which have been undertaken to this stage: *R. v. Walker*, 2008 CarswellSask 185, 2008 SKPC 31, 62 M.V.R. (5th) 138, 315 Sask. R. 114, [2008] S.J. No. 187 (Sask. Prov. Ct.).

Conversely, in *Ontario (Ministry of Labour) v. Thomas Fuller Construction Co.*, 2008 CarswellOnt 6044, 2008 ONCJ 487, [2008] O.J. No. 4004 (Ont. C.J.), the court permitted an amendment that added the entry "(1958)" so that the correct name of the corporate entity being charged would be set out. Relevant considerations in making the amendment included the fact that no evidence had been taken at trial, the circumstances of the case were serious as a fatality was involved, there was no prejudice to the defendant given the close relationship of the corporate entities, the expiry of any limitation period was not in itself sufficient to prevent an amendment, and there was no injustice since the defendant had been fully apprised of the circumstances of the case since the date of the fatality. There was no evidence that there had been a considered decision to charge Fuller, as opposed to Fuller (1958), and the decision was more likely a product of confusion or mistake that resulted from the complex corporate organization of the Fuller Group.

In *R. v. Winlow*, 2008 CarswellOnt 3031, 2008 ONCJ 240, [2008] O.J. No. 2085 (Ont. C.J.), leave to appeal granted (April 18, 2008), Doc. M36186 (Ont. C.A. [In Chambers]), it was held that the justice of the peace was entitled to exercise her discretion and refuse the amendment sought by the prosecution in a case involving amending the certificate of offence pursuant to s. 34(2) of the *Provincial Offences Act* to increase the speed alleged against the defendant after it had been reduced by the officer at the time of charge, but to vary it according to the officer's evidence at trial. Where the defendant, minutes or moments before the trial, suddenly finds out that he is facing a defence to a speed that has been doubled in terms of the amount over, it does not affect the defence on the merits he is putting forward, but it does affect the risk he is undergoing. An adjournment for the defendant to seek legal advice would require a further delay, and does not promote the expeditious dealing of these cases. [For another case where this practice of "amending up" was disapproved of, see *Chatham-Kent (Municipality) v. Lusk* (2008), 2008 CarswellOnt 8318 (Ont. C.J.) where the charge was withdrawn.]

Where the accused was stopped for speeding in a National Park, the charge should have been under the *Canada National Parks Regulations* instead of the *Traffic Safety Act* (Sask.). It would be unfair to allow such an amendment at the conclusion of the evidence, given the nature of the charge and the proceedings which have been undertaken to this stage: *R. v. Walker*, 2008 CarswellSask 185, 2008 SKPC 31, 62 M.V.R. (5th) 138, 315 Sask. R. 114, [2008] S.J. No. 187 (Sask. Prov. Ct.).

5.3.4 PARTICULARS

- The court may order that a particular, further describing any matter relevant to the proceeding, be furnished to the defendant.
- This may be done before or during a trial.
- The court must be satisfied that it is necessary for a fair trial: section 35: See Appendix A.

5.4 JOINDER AND SEVERANCE

5.4.1 THE POA

- Section 38 outlines the power for joint or separate trials of defendants or charges. See Appendix A.

- Section 38 of the POA states that the court may:

  - *Before* trial direct that separate counts, informations or certificates be tried *together* or that persons who are charged separately be tried *together*, where it is satisfied that the ends of justice so require.

  - *Before or during* the trial direct that separate counts, informations or certificates be tried *separately* or that persons who are charged jointly or being tried together be tried *separately*, where it is satisfied that the ends of justice so require.

5.4.2 TRYING MATTERS TOGETHER

- Reasons that the defence may wish to try matters *together* may include the situations listed below:

  - Two defendants are charged separately for the same incident. If the matters are joined together, each defendant is a non-compellable witness by the prosecution under section 46(5) and *Charter* section 11(c). Otherwise, the prosecutor might compel each defendant to testify against the other.

  - The defence may seek to join charges where they can be tried together without prejudice, and the defence wishes to coordinate its witnesses to testify on both matters.

In *Ontario (Ministry of Labour) v. Intracorp Developments (Lombard) Inc.* (2002), 2002 CarswellOnt 1134, [2002] O.J. No. 1209 (Ont. S.C.J.), the justice of the peace exceeded his jurisdiction under section 90(2) in awarding costs to the defendants where the Crown failed to charge both defendants on one information, and brought a motion pursuant to section 38(1) to try the defendants together. Although one of the defendants opposed the motion which was ultimately granted, such omission did not amount to a defect or irregularity as required under section 90: See Appendix A.

- There is statutory authority under section 38 to order that charges within provincial legislation be tried together. The factual underpinnings, the potential for inconsistent verdicts, the potentially common defences, and the issue of judicial resources weigh in favour of this decision. With regard to a joint trial of criminal and provincial hunting charges in the same proceeding, there is no statutory authority that permits this; neither is there statutory prohibition against the same. The administration of justice would be best served by the hunting charges being tried in the same court as the criminal charges, given the factual and legal nexus between the sets of charges. However, there was no consent by the parties on the procedure that could be implemented to ensure that the proper administration of justice actually occurred. The potential for inconsistency would be alleviated by the trial proceedings on the criminal charges and the hunting charges being heard by the same trial judge, but in two separate proceedings. See *R. v. Krisza*, 2007 ONCJ 471, 2007 CarswellOnt 6729, [2007] O.J. No. 4018 (Ont. C.J.).

The two defendants were charged with the same offence: passenger fails to wear complete seatbelt assembly, contrary to the *Highway Traffic Act*. The agent for the defendants brought a motion so that the matters should be heard jointly, which was granted. Both counts arose from the same set of circumstances, and it was an expeditious way to proceed: *R. v. Nikiforos* (June 4, 2008), Tahiri J.P., [2008] O.J. No. 3180 (Ont. C.J.).

A joint trial was ordered for eight defendants who were charged with hunting offences. The factors weighing in favour of a joint trial were the factual circumstances surrounding the allegations, the potential for inconsistent verdicts, the potentially common defences, and the issue of judicial resources: *R. v. Deardorff*, 2008 CarswellOnt 6494, 2008 ONCJ 550, [2008] O.J. No. 4389 (Ont. C.J.).

5.4.3 TRYING MATTERS SEPARATELY

- Reasons that the defence may wish to try matters *separately* may include the situations listed below:
  - The defendant may wish to testify regarding one count but not expose him- or herself to cross-examination on another.
  - Where there are a number of defendants, one defendant might be prejudiced by an admission against another which is hearsay and inadmissible against the first.
  - Where the evidence is complex and there is a danger that the judge will inadvertently lump together distinct issues to the prejudice of the defence, consider trying the matters separately.

5.5 *RES JUDICATA*

- *Before pleading*, the defendant may argue that the charge being faced is in fact and in law the same offence for which he has already been tried.
- This common law rule against "double jeopardy" is now enshrined in section 11(h) of the *Charter* which states the following:

> Any person charged with an offence has the right, if finally acquitted of the offence, not to be tried for it again and, if finally found guilty and punished for the offence, not to be tried or punished for it again.

5.6 OTHER PROCEDURAL DEFENCES*

5.6.1 ABUSE OF PROCESS

- The court may stay (i.e. "stop") a prosecution which amounts to an abuse of process.

---

* For a detailed discussion of the procedural defences which are noted in the following sections, see *Libman on Regulatory Offences in Canada* (Earlscourt, 2002), Chapter 8.

- The power is derived from the common law, which is preserved by section 80 of the POA, as well as the principles of fundamental justice in section 7 of the *Charter*.

- The power to stay a prosecution is only exercised in the "clearest of cases" to prevent "oppressive or vexatious proceedings": see *R. v. Jewitt*, 21 C.C.C. (3d) 7, [1985] 2 S.C.R. 128, [1985] 6 W.W.R. 127, 47 C.R. (3d) 193 (S.C.C.); and *R. v. Young* (1984), 46 O.R. (2d) 520, 40 C.R. (3d) 289, 13 C.C.C. (3d) 1 (Ont. C.A.) at 31.

- The alleged abuse must be by the prosecution, or other executive branch of the government: *R. v. Miles of Music Ltd.* (1989), 48 C.C.C. (3d) 96, 31 O.A.C. 380, 23 C.I.P.R. 16, 24 C.P.R. (3d) 301, 69 C.R. (3d) 361, 74 O.R. (2d) 518 (Ont. C.A.), but see the dissent of Blair J.A. and the reasons of Tarnopolsky J.A.

- Examples of abuse include:

  - Successive prosecutions for the same offence amounting to an oppression of the defendant: *R. v. Keyowski*, [1988] 1 S.C.R. 657, [1988] 4 W.W.R. 97, 40 C.C.C. (3d) 481, (sub nom. *Keyowski v. R.*) 62 C.R. (3d) 349 (S.C.C.).

  - Delay in the laying of charges with the deliberate intention of impairing the defendant's ability to make full answer and defence: *Young*, *supra* at 31-32.

  - Unfair breach of an agreement not to prosecute to the prejudice of the defendant: *R. v. D. (E.)* (1990), 57 C.C.C. (3d) 151, 73 O.R. (2d) 758, 78 C.R. (3d) 112 (Ont. C.A.) at 163-168.

  - Entrapment — when:

    - The authorities provide someone with an opportunity to commit an offence without acting on a reasonable suspicion that he or she is already engaged in criminal activity or in the course of a *bona fide* inquiry; or

- Although having such a reasonable suspicion or acting in the course of a *bona fide* inquiry, going beyond providing an opportunity and inducing the commission of an offence: *R. v. Mack* (1988), 44 C.C.C. (3d) 513, [1988] 2 S.C.R. 903, [1989] 1 W.W.R. 577, 67 C.R. (3d) 1 (S.C.C.).

- A prosecution brought *solely* to collect a civil debt: *R. v. Leroux* (1928), 62 O.L.R. 336, 50 C.C.C. 52 (Ont. C.A.); *R. v. Lee* (1956), 114 C.C.C. 371 (Alta. S.C.); appeal to S.C.C. quashed; but proceedings are not stayed merely because the victim has asked the accused to repay a debt: *R. v. Laird* (1983), 4 C.C.C. (3d) 92 (Ont. H.C.).

5.6.2 OFFICIALLY INDUCED ERROR

- Section 81 of the POA states that: "Ignorance of the law is no excuse for committing the offence".

However, the Ontario Court of Appeal in *R. v. Cancoil Thermal Corp.* (1986), 27 C.C.C. (3d) 295, 11 C.C.E.L. 219, 52 C.R. (3d) 188 (Ont. C.A.) at 303 held that:

> The defence of officially induced error is available as a defence to an alleged violation of a regulatory statute where an accused has reasonably relied upon the erroneous legal opinion or advice of an official who is responsible for the administration or enforcement of the particular law.
>
> In order for the accused to successfully raise this defence, he must show that he relied on the erroneous legal opinion of the official and that his reliance was reasonable. The reasonableness will depend upon several factors including the efforts he made to ascertain the proper law, the complexity or obscurity of the law, the position of the official who gave the advice, and the clarity, definitiveness and reasonableness of the advice given.

- The error must be one of law and not of fact.

- The defendant must take reasonable steps to specifically direct the official's attention to the situation in which the official's opinion is being relied upon.

- The defendant must provide full disclosure to the official of the surrounding circumstances: *R. v. Cancoil Thermal*

Corp. (1988), 1 C.O.H.S.C. 169 (Ont. Prov. Offences Ct.), also digested at 4 W.C.B. (2d) 385.

- The defendant has the burden of proving an officially induced error, on a preponderance of evidence.

- The defence of officially induced error is not available where the defendant was unable to ascertain the existence of a regulation and where there was no erroneous advice given: *Halton Region Conservation Authority v. Cristiano* (1992), 10 C.E.L.R. (N.S.) 154 (Ont. Prov. Div.).

- The defence is in the nature of an excuse which entitles a stay of proceedings rather than an acquittal if six elements are shown: (1) an error of law or of mixed law and fact was made; (2) the person who committed the act considered the legal consequences of his or her actions; (3) the advice obtained came from an appropriate official; (4) the advice was reasonable; (5) the advice was erroneous; and (6) the person relied on the advice in committing the act. See: *Lévis (Ville) c. Tétreault*, 2006 CarswellQue 2911, 2006 CarswellQue 2912, [2006] S.C.J. No. 12, 36 C.R. (6th) 215, 2006 SCC 12, 31 M.V.R. (5th) 1, (sub nom. *Lévis (City) v. Tétreault*) 346 N.R. 331, 207 C.C.C. (3d) 1, [2006] 1 S.C.R. 420, (sub nom. *Lévis (City) v. Trétreault*) 266 D.L.R. (4th) 165 (S.C.C.).

The defence of officially induced error does not apply where there is no reliance on anything said by anyone other than advice from the defendant's own solicitor: *R. v. Catena* (February 1, 2008), No. 02-4122, [2008] O.J. No.1806 (Ont. C.J.).

A mistake of law as to whether the *Income Tax Act* applies to an accused person, where the mistake is based on a belief unsupported by the Act, does not negate the fault requirement of tax evasion: *R. v. Klundert* (2008), 2008 CarswellOnt 6718, 2008 ONCA 767, 62 C.R. (6th) 90, [2009] 2 C.T.C. 108, 93 O.R. (3d) 81, 238 C.C.C. (3d) 6 (Ont. C.A.), at paras. 16-22, 28 [ONCA].

5.6.3 INADEQUATE DISCLOSURE

- The prosecutor has an obligation to provide timely disclosure to the defence, as described in Chapter 3.

- In the clearest of cases, where the defence has been prejudiced and there are no alternative remedies, the court may stay the proceedings if there is inadequate disclosure.
- The usual remedy consists of one or more of the following:
  - An order compelling the prosecutor to produce the material sought.
  - An adjournment to allow the defendant time to prepare the defence.
  - Where necessary, the recalling of witnesses for further examination.
  - Costs.

In *Ontario v. 974649 Ontario Inc.*, 2001 CarswellOnt 4251, 47 C.R. (5th) 316 (sub. nom. *R. v. 974649 Ontario Inc.*) [2001] 3 S.C.R. 575, 56 O.R. (3d) 359 (headnote only), 2001 CarswellOnt 4252, (sub nom. *R. v. 974649 Ontario Inc.*) [2001] S.C.J. No. 79, (sub nom. *R. v. 974649 Ontario Inc.*) 2001 SCC 81, (sub nom. *R. v. 974649 Ontario Inc.*) 206 D.L.R. (4th) 444, (sub nom. *R. v. 974649 Ontario Inc.*) 159 C.C.C. (3d) 321, (sub nom. *R. v. 974649 Ontario Inc.*) 88 C.R.R. (2d) 189, (sub nom. *R. v. 974649 Ontario Inc.*) 279 N.R. 345, (sub nom. *R. v. 974649 Ontario Inc.*) 154 O.A.C. 345 (S.C.C.), the Supreme Court of Canada concluded that the justice of the peace acting as a trial justice under the *Provincial Offences Act* possessed the power to order legal costs against the Crown as a remedy for *Charter* breaches arising from untimely disclosure. The costs were awarded on the defendants' disclosure motion which was brought as a result of the Crown's failure to disclose a copy of the Prosecution Approval Form relating to charges laid under the *Occupational Health and Safety Act.* If defendants were deprived of this remedy, a provincial offences court may be confined to two extreme options for relief — a stay of proceedings or a mere adjournment — neither of which may be appropriate and just in the circumstances.

- The awarding of costs against the prosecution in a provincial offences prosecution is considered to be an "exceptional tool" which is reserved for cases which involve a "marked and unacceptable departure from reasonable prosecution standards". See *R. v. Felderhof* (2002), [2002] O.J. No. 4103, 2002 CarswellOnt 5623 (Ont. S.C.J.), additional reasons at (2003), [2003] O.J. No. 393, 2003 CarswellOnt 488 (Ont. S.C.J.), affirmed (2003), 180 C.C.C.

(3d) 498, 2003 CarswellOnt 4943, [2003] O.J. No. 4819, 68 O.R. (3d) 481, 10 Admin. L.R. (4th) 229, 235 D.L.R. (4th) 131, 180 O.A.C. 288, 17 C.R. (6th) 20 (Ont. C.A.).

- The justice may declare a mistrial rather than ordering a stay of proceedings where an adjournment or further examination of witnesses is *not* an adequate remedy: *R. v. Fineline Circuits Ltd.* (1991), 10 C.R. (4th) 241 (Ont. Prov. Ct.).

- A stay of proceedings should not normally be ordered as the stay is a drastic remedy, and is reserved for those cases where it is not possible to remedy through reasonable means the prejudice to the defendant's right to make full answer and defence. See *R. v. Arcand* (2004), [2004] O.J. No. 5017, 2004 CarswellOnt 5160, 10 C.E.L.R. (3d) 161, 125 C.R.R. (2d) 144, 193 O.A.C. 16, 192 C.C.C. (3d) 57, 73 O.R. (3d) 758 (Ont. C.A.).

While it would have been preferable for the Crown to have been more forthcoming with disclosure, the defendant was in possession of all he needed prior to trial and was not prejudiced by the Crown's conduct: *R. v. Arcand*, 2008 CarswellOnt 4971, 2008 ONCA 595, 240 O.A.C. 286, 238 C.C.C. (3d) 204, 92 O.R. (3d) 444, 38 C.E.L.R. (3d) 1, [2008] O.J. No. 3294 (Ont. C.A.), leave to appeal refused (2008), [2008] S.C.C.A. No. 449, 2008 CarswellOnt 7740, 2008 CarswellOnt 7741 (S.C.C.).

While an officer's notes cannot be expected to record every minute detail, they must contain a complete and accurate record of the significant events in the investigation so as to enable the Crown to fulfill its obligation to make full disclosure: *R. v. Karunakaran*, 2008 CarswellOnt 5210, 2008 ONCJ 397 (Ont. C.J.), at para. 25 [ONCJ].

The defendant was not deprived of her right to make full answer and defence where she was provided with disclosure of the officer's notes, but which did not include information about the officer's qualifications and training to operate the radar gun: *Durham (Regional Municipality) v. Driscoll-Rogers*, 2008 CarswellOnt 6768, 2008 ONCJ 581, [2008] O.J. No. 4572 (Ont. C.J.).

5.6.4 *DE MINIMIS*

- "*De minimis non curat lex.*" is latin for "the law does not concern itself with trifles". In rare circumstances, charges have been dismissed.

- The rationale for the rule is found in *The "Reward"* (1818), 165 E.R. 1482 at 1484, 2 Dods. 265 (Eng. Adm. Ct.):

> The Court is not bound to a strictness at once harsh and pedantic in the application of statutes. The law permits the qualification implied in the ancient maxim *de minimis non curat lex* — Where there are irregularities of very slight consequence, it does not intend that the infliction of penalties should be inflexibly severe. If the deviation were a mere trifle, which, if continued in practice, would weigh little or nothing on the public interest, it might properly be overlooked.

- It is rarely successful. (It was unsuccessful in *The "Reward".*)

Courts generally defer to the power of the legislature to prescribe conduct which might otherwise appear trifling, and the power of prosecution, as agent for the Ministry of the Attorney General, to exercise its discretion in using its prosecutorial resources as it deems fit; see section 3.1 in Chapter 3. However, consider the cases discussed below.

In *R. v. Webster* (1981), 10 M.V.R. 310, 15 M.P.L.R. 60 (Ont. Dist. Ct.), the accused was acquitted of parking illegally contrary to a municipal by-law. He parked where parking was prohibited to facilitate snow removal, but there was no snow on the ground. He was acquitted because it was "an absurdity to convict".

In *R. v. Paleshaty* (1949), 96 C.C.C. 147, 9 C.R. 97, [1950] 1 W.W.R. 108 (Man. C.A.), the doctrine was applied to acquit an individual charged with possession of then-illegal alcohol where the accused was found with two bottles containing about ten drops each.

In *R. v. McIntryre Mines Ltd.* (1978), 5 Alta. L.R. (2d) 201 (Alta. Prov. Ct.), the accused was charged with diverting waters, contrary to provincial water resources legislation. The court held that no diversion had been proved. Even if some had been proved, it was so minimal as to be inconsequential.

In *R. v. Pang* (1987), 5 W.C.B. (2d) 94 (B.C. Co. Ct.), the principle was applied in the context of a misunderstanding between an individual entering Canada and a Canadian customs official. The visitor was believed to have made a misleading or false declaration and was charged. The charge was dismissed because the misunderstanding was minor and short-lived.

Note, however, that in a recent decision the court considered that the *de minimis* defence does not apply in the cases of public welfare offences or strict liability offences, although this statement was *obiter*: *R. v. Williams Operating Corp.* (2008), [2008] O.J. No. 3736, 2008 CarswellOnt 5646, 39 C.E.L.R. (3d) 66 (Ont. S.C.J.).

5.6.5 UNREASONABLE DELAY

- Any person charged with an offence has the right to be tried within a reasonable time: *Charter*, section 11(b).
  - The right extends to corporate accused: *R. v. C.I.P. Inc.*, 12 C.R. (4th) 237, [1992] 1 S.C.R. 843, 7 C.O.H.S.C. 1, 71 C.C.C. (3d) 129 (S.C.C.).
  - The right applies equally to regulatory as to criminal offences: *C.I.P., supra.*
- The relevant time for assessing unreasonableness is between the date of charging the defendant and the date of trial.
- The factors in assessing unreasonableness are: see *R. v. Morin*, 71 C.C.C. (3d) 1, 12 C.R. (4th) 1, [1992] 1 S.C.R. 771 (S.C.C.):
  - The length of delay.
  - The waiver of time periods *(whether the defendant clearly and unequivocally accepted some of the delay with knowledge of his or her Charter rights).*
  - The reasons for the delay, including:
    - Inherent time requirements of the case (a complex trial may take longer to schedule);
    - Actions of the defendant;
    - Actions of the prosecutor;
    - Limitations on institutional resources; and
    - Prejudice to the defendant. *There is a presumption of some prejudice to individuals because of the stress of facing charges, but no presumption for corporations*

— corporations must establish prejudice for this factor to be considered: see C.I.P., supra).

In *R. v. J.I. Case Co.* (May 6, 1991), Doc. No. A1858/91 (Ont. Gen. Div.), a 20-month delay before trial constituted a section 11(b) violation where four months would have been reasonable, there was no explanation for the delay by the Crown, no period of delay was caused by the accused, and there was no waiver.

In *R. v. Boise Cascade Canada Ltd.* (1991), 14 W.C.B. (2d) 259 (Ont. Gen. Div.), a delay of 13 months between the laying of charges under the *Occupational Health and Safety Act* against the defendant corporations and the commencement of the trial was considered reasonable.

In *R. v. Hussain* (2005), [2005] O.J. No. 158, 2005 CarswellOnt 1215 (Ont. C.J.), an 11½ month delay between the laying of the charges under the *Highway Traffic Act* and the *Compulsory Automobile Insurance Act* and the trial date was sufficiently long to investigate the factors set down in *R. v. Morin*, but where some two months related to a reasonable intake period, the remaining delay was within the guideline of 8 to 10 months set down in *R. v. Morin*.

In *R. v. Farokhshadfar* (April 6, 2001), Libman J., [2001] O.J. No. 6015 (Ont. C.J.), it was held that the very short times which govern *Provincial Offences Act* matters make it clear that "speedy justice" is the hallmark of proceedings under the Act. A period of delay of almost 10 months in sending out the Notice of Trial, when the defendant is required to give his/her intention to elect a trial mode within 15 days, was considered excessive. See further *R. v. Mastroianni* (2000), [2000] O.J. No. 3227, 2000 CarswellOnt 6171 (Ont. C.J.) where the accused's s. 11(b) *Charter* rights were found to have been violated on account of his speeding trial taking place nearly 14 months from the offence date. The same period of 14 months delay was considered excessive in *R. v. Omarzadah* (March 3, 2004), Doc. M30824, [2004] O.J. No. 2212 (Ont. C.A.).

- Absent unusual circumstances, a motion to stay proceedings due to unreasonable delay under section 11(b) of the *Charter of Rights* is ordinarily argued before trial. See *Ontario (Ministry of Labour) v. Pioneer Construction Inc.* (2006), 79 O.R. (3d) 641, 209 O.A.C. 379, 54 C.L.R. (3d) 41, 142 C.R.R. (2d) 81, 2006 CarswellOnt 2900, [2006] O.J. No. 1874 (Ont. C.A.).

- Where a defendant declines an offer for an earlier trial date, the resulting delay is attributable to the defendant rather than to the Crown or to institutional delay. Where the defendant does nothing to move the case forward in a timely way, prejudice is accorded little or no weight: *R. v. M. (N.N.)* (2006), [2006] O.J. No. 1802, 2006 CarswellOnt 2721, 209 C.C.C. (3d) 436, 209 O.A.C. 331, 141 C.R.R. (2d) 95 (Ont. C.A.).

In *R. v. Skolney*, 2006 ONCJ 549, 2006 CarswellOnt 8906, [2006] O.J. No. 5506 (Ont. C.J.), it was held that the trial justice erred in law in dismissing the *Charter of Rights* application on the basis that "section 11(b) is strictly for criminal proceedings". The *Charter* applies to charges under the *Provincial Offences Act.*

- Generally speaking, it is considered preferable to deal with section 11(b) issues in advance of trial. A delay of 12.3 months exceeds the recommended guideline for maximum delay in the provincial courts established in *R.* v. *Morin.* The trial judge properly looked at the nature of the specific charges in context, and having regard to the issue of competence inferred prejudice from the combined effects of the passage of time and the fact that three important witnesses were more likely to be found incompetent because they were no longer working with the equipment or following workplace procedures. The trial judge did not err in finding prejudice, which is but one of a number of factors to be taken into account when assessing unreasonable delay. See *R. v. Norwall Group Inc.* (2007), 2007 CarswellOnt 3878, [2007] O.J. No. 2397 (Ont. S.C.J.).

A stay of proceedings was set aside on appeal in *R. v. Norwall Group Inc.*, 2008 CarswellOnt 1742, 2008 ONCA 235, [2008] O.J. No. 1222 (Ont. C.A.), reversing (2007), 2007 CarswellOnt 3878, [2007] O.J. No. 2397, 161 C.R.R. (2d) 39 (Ont. S.C.J.) where the court considered that there was no evidence of actual, irremediable prejudice to the defendant's ability to make full answer and defence. Neither the nature of the allegations in the charges, nor the fact that the employees no longer worked for the employer, standing alone or together, justified any inference of actual prejudice to the ability to make full answer and defence. The stay of proceedings for unreasonable delay was set aside and the matter remitted to the trial court.

In *R. v. Piskun* (2008), 2008 CarswellOnt 4790, [2008] O.J. No. 3705 (Ont. C.J.), a delay of 13 months in an uncomplicated, straightforward speeding prosecution under the *Highway Traffic Act* was held to be excessive. The court noted that it is the duty of the prosecution to bring an accused person to trial; the state and the prosecution apparatus are required to minimize the prejudice inherent in delays, in the disposition of criminal litigation, as well as litigation under the *Provincial Offences Act.*

On the other hand, in *Mississauga (City) v. Berbatiotis*, [2007] O.J. No. 4683, 2007 CarswellOnt 7746, 2007 ONCJ 561 (Ont. C.J.), the court ruled that an overall period of 13 and one-half months from the date of the offence of speeding to the time of trial did not violate s. 11(b). Almost 11 months of this period was due to institutional delay. There was an absence of stigma and any real prejudice.

In *R. v. Hale*, 2005 CarswellOnt 10303, 2005 ONCJ 553, [2005] O.J. No. 6368 (Ont. C.J.), the court observed that one of the ways the management of trial workload is accomplished in the provincial offences court is by the holding of judicial pre-trials. The twin goals of the pre-trial process are to resolve matters capable of resolution, or to narrow the issues if no such resolution is possible so that the time required for trial is shortened by agreed statements of fact obviating the need for some witnesses to testify. To suggest that the pre-trial process be abolished at the Ontario Court of Justice level because it is not specifically provided for by legislation is to invite chaos at the province's busiest level of court. In a case where there was a delay of 15 months from the laying of the information for careless driving until the start of the scheduled trial, and 5.5 months of this delay was due to setting up and conducting the judicial pre-trial and finding a date that was available for trial from the perspective of an appropriate justice of the peace, the defendant's s. 11(b) rights were violated.

In *R. v. Smith* (2008), 2008 CarswellOnt 4286, 2008 CarswellOnt 4287, 175 C.R.R. (2d) 13, [2008] O.J. No. 2841 (Ont. S.C.J.), it was held that the justice of the peace erred in holding that 8 months was an unreasonable period of time to arrange a trial date for careless driving that resulted in a death. The justice of the peace must consider the public interest in having a full trial on the issues when serious charges are laid and an individual has been killed; the failure of the justice to expressly consider this factor amounted to reversible error. There would be a substantial miscarriage of justice as the public interest in having a full trial would not be met if the error was not corrected.

Apart from the requirements of notice under s. 109 of the *Courts of Justice Act* and the rules of court, the defendant must do more than that to assert his rights before the trial judge. Stating that one wishes to bring at some point a s. 11(b) application is not the same as actually bringing the application. While the defendant does not have to assert the right at every court appearance, at some appropriate stage in the proceedings, that is during the trial process, he must muster the evidence, transcripts of the attendance, evidence of prejudice if any, and present argument to the trier of fact: *R. v. Delvecchio*, 2008 ONCJ 511, 2008 CarswellOnt 6281, [2008] O.J. No. 4229 (Ont. C.J.).

5.6.6 PROOF OF BY-LAWS OR SUBORDINATE LEGISLATION

- The basic rule is that judicial notice cannot be taken of municipal by-laws.

- The common law required judicial notice to be taken of public or general statutes but not of private enactments or subordinate legislation such as regulations.

- A copy of a by-law certified by the proper officer of the municipal corporation to be a true copy of the by-law and under the seal of the municipal corporation is admissible in evidence under the *Evidence Act*.

- Speed limit signs are *prima facie* proof of compliance with the regulations under the *Highway Traffic Act: R. v. Clark* (1974), 3 O.R. (2d) 716, 18 C.C.C. (2d) 52 (Ont. C.A.).

5.6.7 BILINGUAL SIGNAGE

- The council of a municipality, which is in a designated area under the *French Language Services Act*, may pass a by-law providing that the administration of the municipality shall be conducted in both English and French, and that all or specified municipal services to the public shall be made available in both languages. See *French Language Services Act*, R.S.O. 1990, c. F.23, s. 14(1).

- Where a municipality is designated a bilingual area under the *French Language Services Act*, the issue arises whether the signage under the *Highway Traffic Act* must be bilingual in order to be valid. See *R. v. Myers* (2004), [2004] O.J. No. 4763, 2004 CarswellOnt 5638 (Ont. C.J.), reversed (2005), 2005 CarswellOnt 10019 (Ont. C.J.).

6

MENS REA OFFENCES

6.1 BURDEN OF PROOF

As described in Chapter 4, and as laid down by the Supreme Court in *R. v. Sault Ste. Marie (City)*, [1978] 2 S.C.R. 1299, 7 C.E.L.R. 53, 3 C.R. (3d) 30, 40 C.C.C. (2d) 353, 1978 CarswellOnt 24, 1978 CarswellOnt 594, 85 D.L.R. (3d) 161, 21 N.R. 295 (S.C.C.):

- The prosecution must prove beyond a reasonable doubt that the defendant committed the illegal act(s).
- The prosecution must also prove beyond a reasonable doubt that the defendant had a particular state of mind.
- The state of mind depends on the offence. For example, it might be intent, knowledge, or recklessness.
- The prosecution can prove the defendant's state of mind in two ways:
  - Admissions by the defendant as to his or her state of mind, or
  - Inferences of the defendant's state of mind based on the common sense principle that people normally intend the natural consequences of their actions.

6.2 THE STATE OF MIND

- "Intention" may be an intention to commit particular acts, or an intention to bring about certain results.

- "Knowledge" may refer to knowledge of fairly limited circumstances or actions, or knowledge of the effect of those actions.

- "Recklessness" means an awareness that there is a risk of certain behaviour and then acting in an unacceptable disregard to that risk.

6.3 PARTIES TO THE OFFENCE

- See heading 7.4 in Chapter 7.

6.4 DEFENCES TO THE ELEMENTS OF THE OFFENCE

6.4.1 DEFENCES TO THE ACT ELEMENT

- Is there any reasonable doubt, on the prosecutor's evidence, that your client voluntarily committed the act(s)?

6.4.2 DEFENCES TO THE MENTAL ELEMENT

- Will the justice likely conclude, beyond a reasonable doubt, that your client had the particular state of mind, based on:

  - Your client's admissions, or

  - Inferences that your client intended the natural consequences of his or her act(s)?

- If the prosecutor has strong proof of the act and mental elements, what evidence can you call for the defence? Will it raise a reasonable doubt?

6.5 OTHER DEFENCES

Section 80 of the POA states:

> Every rule and principle of the common law that renders any circumstance a justification or excuse for an act or a defence to a charge continues in force and applies in respect of offences, except in so far as they are altered by or inconsistent with this or any other Act.

6.5.1 MISTAKE OF FACT

- If the defendant honestly believed in certain facts which, if true, would have rendered his or her actions legal, then the defendant did not intend to commit the offence. In other words, the defendant has rebutted the presumption of intending the natural consequences of his or her actions.

- A court can properly find wilful blindness where the defendant ". . . suspected the fact, realized its probability, but refrained from obtaining the final confirmation because he or she wanted to be able to deny knowledge": *R. v. Malfara* (2006), 2006 CarswellOnt 3164, 211 O.A.C. 200 (Ont. C.A.), endorsement, following *R. v. Jorgensen*, 1995 CarswellOnt 1185, 1995 CarswellOnt 985, [1995] S.C.J. No. 95, [1995] S.C.J. No. 92, EYB 1995-67684, [1995] 4 S.C.R. 55, 43 C.R. (4th) 137, 102 C.C.C. (3d) 97, 129 D.L.R. (4th) 510, 189 N.R. 1, 87 O.A.C. 1, 32 C.R.R. (2d) 189, (sub nom. *R. v. Hawkins*) 25 O.R. (3d) 824 (S.C.C.), at 135 [C.C.C.].

- Generally, a mistake of fact must be honest but not necessarily reasonable.

- As a matter of common sense, a justice may have difficulty believing your client made an honest mistake when a reasonable person in the same situation would not have been mistaken.

- If the defendant honestly believed in mistaken facts because he or she shut his or her mind to the truth, the defendant is "wilfully blind" to the truth and this may be sufficient proof of *mens rea*: *R. v. Sansregret*, (sub nom. *Sansregret v. R.*) [1985] 1 S.C.R. 570, (sub nom. *Sansregret v. R.*) [1985] 3 W.W.R. 701, (sub nom. *Sansregret v. R.*) 45 C.R. (3d) 193, (sub nom. *Sansregret v. R.*) 18 C.C.C. (3d) 223 (S.C.C.).

- "Ignorance of the law by a person who commits an offence is not an excuse for committing the offence": section 81. *But see the defence: "Officially Induced Error" in section 5.6.2 in Chapter 5.*

6.5.2 INTOXICATION

If your client was so befogged by liquor or other toxic substances that he or she was incapable of forming the required state of mind, then he or she may have a defence.

- Determine exactly what state of mind is required for the offence. *In criminal matters, courts have distinguished between specific and general intent crimes, and have minimized the defence of drunkeness for general intent crimes: R. v. Bernard,* 67 C.R. (3d) 113, 45 C.C.C. (3d) 1, [1988] 2 S.C.R. 833 (S.C.C.). *For general intent crimes, the accused must establish, on a balance of probabilities with expert evidence, that he or she was intoxicated to such an extent as to be in a state akin to insanity or automatism: R. v. Daviault,* 33 C.R. (4th) 165, 93 C.C.C. (3d) 21, [1994] 3 S.C.R. 63 (S.C.C.).

- Distinguish between a client who, because of an intoxicant, did not know what he or she was doing at the time from a client who, because of a hangover, knew but cannot now *remember* what he or she did at the time.

6.5.3 ADDITIONAL DEFENCES

- In addition to the procedural defences in Chapter 5, consider the following defences covered in Chapter 8:
  - Involuntariness;

- Causation; and

- Necessity.

6.6 CORPORATE RESPONSIBILITY

The Supreme Court of Canada in *R. v. Sault Ste. Marie (City)*, [1978] 2 S.C.R. 1299, 7 C.E.L.R. 53, 3 C.R. (3d) 30, 40 C.C.C. (2d) 353, 1978 CarswellOnt 24, 1978 CarswellOnt 594, 85 D.L.R. (3d) 161, 21 N.R. 295 (S.C.C.), at 371 [C.C.C.] held:

> The element of control, particularly by those in charge of business activities which may endanger the public, is vital to promote the observance of regulation designed to avoid that danger. This control may be exercised by supervision or inspection, by improvement of . . . business methods or by exhorting those whom may be expected . . . to [be] influence[d] or control[led].

- See section 7.3, "Corporate Responsibility" in Chapter 7.

- The requirements which apply to finding a corporation liable for a regulatory offence which is *mens rea* in nature are the same for a finding of liability for the corporation for a *mens rea* criminal offence: *R. v. Knibb*, [1997] 8 W.W.R. 115, 51 Alta. L.R. (3d) 294, 1997 CarswellAlta 466, [1997] A.J. No. 513, 198 A.R. 161 (Alta. Prov. Ct.), affirmed [1998] A.J. No. 628, 1998 CarswellAlta 489 (Alta. Q.B.).

7

STRICT LIABILITY OFFENCES

7.1 BURDEN OF PROOF

As described in Chapter 4, and as laid down by the Supreme Court in *R. v. Sault Ste. Marie (City)*, [1978] 2 S.C.R. 1299, 7 C.E.L.R. 53, 3 C.R. (3d) 30, 40 C.C.C. (2d) 353, 1978 CarswellOnt 24, 1978 CarswellOnt 594, 85 D.L.R. (3d) 161, 21 N.R. 295 (S.C.C.):

- The prosecution must prove beyond a reasonable doubt that the defendant committed the illegal act(s).
- The defendant must then prove, on a balance of probabilities, that:
  - He or she took reasonable care not to commit the illegal act(s), or
  - He or she made a reasonable mistake of fact which, if true, would have rendered the act(s) lawful.
- A mistake of fact must be reasonable. Normally, the defendant must establish that he or she took all reasonable steps and made all reasonable inquiries to determine the correct information.
- In strict liability cases, the defendant must establish that the mistake of fact was not only an honest one, but that there were reasonable grounds for it.

7.2 CONSIDERATIONS FOR REASONABLE CARE

See the excellent treatise by John Swaigen, entitled *Regulatory Offences in Canada* (Carswell, 1992), Chapters 5, 6 and 7. See also *Libman on Regulatory Offences in Canada* (Earlscourt, 2002) at Chapter 7.3.

7.2.1 ALTERNATIVES

- The defendant must establish, on a balance of probabilities, that there was no reasonable alternative to committing the offence.

- One alternative is to do nothing. If an activity cannot be carried on legally, then it should not be carried on at all. (Economic necessity is not a defence.)

- Some regulations provide that the rules can be deviated from if equivalent or higher standards are followed. For example, Regulation 851, R.R.O. 1990, section 2 under the *Occupational Health and Safety Act* states:

> In applying this Regulation, the composition, design, size and arrangement of any material, object, device or thing may vary from the composition, design, size or arrangement prescribed in this Regulation where the factors of strength, health and safety are equal to or greater than the factors of strength, health and safety in the composition, design, size or arrangement prescribed.

7.2.2 LIKELIHOOD AND GRAVITY OF HARM

- The greater the potential for serious injury, the greater the care required.

- In many businesses, experts make on-going assessments of the probability of minor and serious injuries in order to take special precautions where appropriate.

Due diligence in a traffic offence is a modified objective test — one should appreciate the risk of other drivers speeding, but not necessarily grossly speeding: *R. v. Neal*, [2008] O.J. No. 720, 2008 CarswellOnt 1100, 2008 ONCJ 42, 67 M.V.R. (5th) 277 (Ont. C.J.).

The defendant does not have the onus of demonstrating the precise mechanism by which a prohibited act occurred. Rather, the defence of due diligence is available if the accused can demonstrate that it has exercised due diligence to avoid the specific type of occurrence giving rise to the charges against it: *R. v. Kukuljan*, 2008 CarswellBC 2559, (sub nom. *R. v. Emil K. Fishing Corp.*) 441 W.A.C. 275, (sub nom. *R. v. Emil K. Fishing Corp.*) 262 B.C.A.C. 275, 2008 BCCA 490, [2008] B.C.J. No. 2326 (B.C. C.A.).

7.2.3 DEGREE OF SKILL EXPECTED

As stated in *R. v. Placer Developments Ltd.* (1983), 13 C.E.L.R. 42 (Y.T. Terr.Ct.) at 52:

> Anyone choosing to become involved in activities posing a danger to the public, or to the environment, assumes an obligation to take whatever measures may be necessary to prevent harm. . . Unless equipped with the appropriate professional [trade or technical] skills, no one ought to undertake any activity involving a danger to the public. The degree of professional diligence required depends on commonly accepted practices of that specific activity and upon the specific circumstances.

- Staff must be professionally trained, and in some cases, supervised.

7.2.4 INSPECTIONS AND COMPLIANCE PROGRAMS

- Random inspections and testings are the best means to ensure compliance with regulations and policies.

7.2.5 EQUIPMENT AND TECHNOLOGY

- Reasonable care requires adequate technology and regular maintenance. *For example, an operator of a truck, who tries with all possible effort to slam on the brakes for a red light, may still be liable for failing to stop if his brakes were not properly maintained.*

7.2.6 COSTS OF PREVENTION

- If an activity cannot be carried on legally, then it should not be carried on at all. It is the elected legislature which determines the costs and benefits to society of certain activities.

- However, if the defendant reasonably assesses the possibility of mistake as very unlikely, and reasonably assesses the cost of prevention extremely high, then the standard of care set out in the legislation may have been met: see *R. v. Commander Business Furniture Inc.* (1992), 9

C.E.L.R. (N.S.) 185 at 213-217 (Ont. Prov. Ct.), affirmed (February 18, 1994), Doc. 179/93 (Ont. Gen. Div.).

For example, operating a vehicle with excess weight is a strict liability offence. A trucking company may take all reasonable precautions to ensure that its vehicles comply with the weight requirements. However, in very unusual circumstances, its vehicles exceed those requirements (perhaps a grain cargo gains weight in unusually moist environments). If the additional cost to detect for the unusual possibility is prohibitive, perhaps the standard of reasonable care has been met.

7.2.7 WARNINGS

- Once it is known that an existing system fails to prevent an offence, the reasonable person implements a new system.

As Swaigen writes in *Regulatory Offences in Canada* at 122-123:

> The extent to which such earlier incidents will preclude a defence of reasonable care will depend how similar they were to the events before the court, and the extent to which they caused harm on the previous occasion. The effectiveness of warnings to negate a defence of reasonable care will also depend on how clear they were, how forcefully they were communicated, to whom they were communicated, and whether they were directed at the factors that caused the incident before the court.

7.2.8 START-UP PROBLEMS

- Reasonable care requires investigation prior to starting up a business. *For example, before beginning an activity with environmental issues, an environmental audit should be done.*

7.2.9 EVIDENCE OF DUE DILIGENCE

The "accident as *prima facie* breach" theory of breach was adopted on appeal. As per Spence P.C.J. in *R. v. Lonkar Well Testing Ltd.* (2008), 2008 CarswellAlta 521, 93 Alta. L.R. (4th) 181, [2008] A.J. No. 831 (Alta. Prov. Ct.), "once a breach has been established, *prima facie*, by virtue of an accident in the workplace despite a statutory regime designed to prevent such occurrences, then it is up to the employer to prove that it complied with the regulations and did all that it reasonably could to prevent the accident from happening": *R. v. Rose's Well Services Ltd.*, 2009 CarswellAlta 8, 2009 ABQB 1, [2009] A.J. No. 7 (Alta. Q.B).

In a strict liability offence, reasonableness should not be confused with the issue of recklessness or wilful blindness as it impacts upon a *mens rea* offence, which the Crown must disprove beyond a reasonable doubt. The issue of reasonableness and due diligence has to be proved by the defendant on a balance of probabilities: *R. v. Pham*, 2009 CarswellAlta 236, 2009 ABQB 113, [2009] A.J. No. 173 (Alta. Q.B.).

Documentary support for the accused's mistaken belief is not required to establish a reasonable excuse for failing to comply with an order to register under *Christopher's Law (Sex Offender Registry), 2000*, S.O. 2000, c. 1: *R. v. Sandejas*, 2009 CarswellOnt 1364, 2009 ONCJ 100 (Ont. C.J.), at para. 26 [ONCJ].

7.3 CORPORATE RESPONSIBILITY

The Supreme Court in *R. v. Sault Ste. Marie (City)*, [1978] 2 S.C.R. 1299, 7 C.E.L.R. 53, 3 C.R. (3d) 30, 40 C.C.C. (2d) 353, 1978 CarswellOnt 24, 1978 CarswellOnt 594, 85 D.L.R. (3d) 161, 21 N.R. 295 (S.C.C.), at C.C.C. 371 held:

> The element of control, particularly by those in charge of business activities which may endanger the public, is vital to promote the observance of regulations designed to avoid that danger. This control may be exercised by supervision or inspection, by improvement of . . . business methods or by exhorting those whom may be expected . . . to [be] influence[d] or control[led].

- The test for control is a factual one. It is based on an assessment of the defendant's position — if the defendant can control the activity, then it should take reasonable care.

- A lender, landlord, or business partner may also be in a position to control illegal activity — if he or she can, he or she should take reasonable care.

- Where a corporation purchased a security guard business, retaining the former general manager, and relied on that manager to employ licensed guards, the defence of due diligence was established in relying on experienced personnel to handle the licensing process. See *R. v. Hi-Tec Security & Investigations Ltd.* (2004), [2004] O.J. No. 779, 2004 CarswellOnt 6080 (Ont. C.J.).

- If a "directing mind" of a corporation commits an offence, then the offence is "identified" with the corporation.

The "directing mind" was originally a civil law concept, and simply means those who govern or control the activities of the corporation. Who directs the corporation is a question of fact. It may be that different persons have different areas for which they direct the corporation. For example, a marketing manager may "direct" the marketing program, and an engineer on the board of directors may "direct" the design of equipment.

7.4 PARTIES TO AN OFFENCE

- There are a number of ways a defendant can be liable for illegal acts.
  - Where the defendant actually commits the offence: section 77(1)(a).
  - Where the defendant formed a common intention with another person to carry out an unlawful purpose, and where the defendant knew (or ought to have known) that a probable consequence of the unlawful purpose was the commission of the offence: section 77(2).
  - Where the defendant aids or abets another to commit the offence. To "aid" means to do or omit to do anything to facilitate or assist an offence. To "abet" means to instigate or encourage an offence: section 77(1)(b, c). Specific intent is required to find an accused liable as an aider or abettor to an offence of breaching a publication ban. (*R. v. Helsdon*, [2007] O.J. No. 243, 275 D.L.R. (4th) 209, 2007 CarswellOnt 336, 216 C.C.C. (3d) 1, 2007 ONCA 54, 45 C.R. (6th) 37, 84 O.R. (3d) 544, 220 O.A.C. 302 (Ont. C.A.)).
  - Where the defendant counsels or procures another to be a party to an offence, even if the offence was committed in a way different from that which was counselled or procured: section 78(1). Also, the defendant is a party to every offence where he or she knew or ought to have known the offence was likely to be committed as a result of his or her counselling or procuring: section 78(2).

- In addition, some provincial Acts have special provisions making a director or officer liable. See, for example, section 116 of the *Ontario Water Resources Act*, R.S.O. 1990, c. O.40:

116. (1) Every director or officer of a corporation that engages in an activity that may result in the discharge of any material into or in any waters or any shore or bank thereof or into or in any place that may impair the quality of the water of any waters contrary to this Act or the regulations has a duty to take all reasonable care to prevent the corporation from causing or permitting such unlawful discharge.

(2) Every person who has a duty under subsection (1) and who fails to carry out that duty is guilty of an offence.

(3) A director or officer of a corporation is liable to conviction under this section whether or not the corporation has been prosecuted or convicted.

- Where the defendant is an employee, who worked in a manner that endangered others, he may be culpable under the *Occupational Health and Safety Act* for failure to take reasonable care, although he lacked control of the workplace. See *R. v. Campbell* (2004), [2004] O.J. No. 129, 2004 CarswellOnt 116 (Ont. C.J.).

The defence of self-induced intoxication is available to an accused who is charged with aiding and abetting an offence: *R. v. Wobbes*, 2008 CarswellOnt 4528, 235 C.C.C. (3d) 561, 60 C.R. (6th) 31, 2008 ONCA 567, 242 O.A.C. 7 (Ont. C.A.), at para. 30 [ONCA].

7.5 EVIDENTIARY ISSUES

7.5.1 TIMING OF EVIDENCE

- The prosecution cannot "split" its case. In its case-in- chief, the prosecutor must adduce all evidence rebutting any defence reasonably anticipated — including the defence of reasonable care.

- The defence's cross-examination of the prosecution witnesses will usually indicate whether reasonable care is in issue.

- Only where new and significantly important issues are raised for the first time in the case for the defence, will the prosecutor be permitted to call rebuttal evidence: see *R. v. Montefort* (1987), 79 N.S.R. (2d) 91, 196 A.P.R. 91 (N.S. C.A.); and *R. v. Lefevre* (1987), 77 N.S.R. (2d) 85, 191 A.P.R. 85 (N.S. C.A.).

7.5.2 SIMILAR ACTS *BEFORE* THE INCIDENT

- Generally, bad character or similar fact evidence is inadmissible in criminal and regulatory proceedings to show a disposition to commit the offence.

- However, where the defence is reasonable care, similar facts may be admitted to show that the defendant was warned in the past and failed to exercise reasonable care. The purpose of the evidence is not to show a disposition to commit the offence, but to rebut the suggestion of reasonable care, and so the evidence is admissible.

7.5.3 ACTS *AFTER* BEING CHARGED

- There are two policy reasons not to admit the evidence, as explained in Swaigen in *Regulatory Offences in Canada* at 191-192:

  - Extra care taken after being charged may imply that the defendant should have taken the same care before the incident. Arguably, the prosecutor should be able prove its case *before* charging the defendant.

  - If extra care after being charged is used against defendants, then there is a disincentive to taking extra care — which is contrary to public policy.

7.6 OTHER DEFENCES

- In addition to the procedural defences in Chapter 5, some of the defences detailed under Chapter 8 for absolute liability offences may apply — especially “causation”.

8

ABSOLUTE LIABILITY OFFENCES

8.1 BURDEN OF PROOF

- The prosecution must prove beyond a reasonable doubt that the defendant committed the illegal act(s).

- The defendant is liable whether or not he or she was at fault.

8.2 *CHARTER* ISSUES

- As explained in Chapter 4, any absolute liability with the possibility of imprisonment is contrary to section 7 of the *Charter*, and unless saved as a reasonable limit under section 1, is of no force or effect by section 52(1) of the *Charter*.

8.3 PARTIES TO THE OFFENCE

- See heading 7.4 in Chapter 7.

8.4 PROCEDURAL DEFENCES

- For available defences, see Chapter 5.

8.5 COMMON LAW DEFENCES — GENERALLY

- Section 80 of the POA ensures that every rule and principle of common law continues to be in force as they apply to any justification, excuse or defence to a charge: see *Appendix A*.

8.6 INVOLUNTARINESS DEFENCE

- To some extent, the illegal act(s) must be voluntary and within the control of the defendant.

For example, a driver and passenger are on the highway and, against the driver's will, the passenger slams on the driver's foot, forcing it down on the gas peddle and causing the car to speed. The driver did not commit the act of speeding because he or she did not voluntarily control his or her foot.

In another example, the defendant is drugged by someone, through no fault of the defendant and without his or her knowledge. If he or she becomes incapable of controlling what he or she does, whatever illegal acts occur are not *his or her* acts — they are the involuntary movements of a body beyond his or her control.

See: I. Patient, "Some Remarks about the Element of Voluntariness in Offences of Absolute Liability", [1968] Crim. L.R. 23; see also "The Voluntariness Requirement and the The Doctine of Automatism" Watt J., National Criminal Law Program, Montreal, 1993; see also *R. v. Rabey*, 54 C.C.C. (2d) 1, [1980] 2 S.C.R. 513, 15 C.R. (3d) 225 (Eng.), 20 C.R. (3d) 1 (Fr.) (S.C.C.) per Dickson J. dissenting, cited in *R. v. Parks*, 75 C.C.C. (3d) 287, 303, [1992] 2 S.C.R. 871, 15 C.R. (4th) 289 (S.C.C.) per LaForest J. and voluntariness as it relates to intoxication in *R. v. Daviault*, 33 C.R. (4th) 165, 93 C.C.C. (3d) 21, [1994] 3 S.C.R. 63 (S.C.C.).

8.7 CAUSATION DEFENCE

- The Crown must prove beyond a reasonable doubt that the defendant caused the illegal act(s).
- Where the Crown fails to prove the *actus reus* or the "physical action" element of the offence, the defendant is entitled to be found not guilty.
- Causation is the relationship between the defendant and the illegal act(s) which resulted.
- It is not necessary to prove that the defendant was the sole cause of the illegal act(s).
- It is sufficient that the defendant contributed to the illegal act(s), and that the defendant's contribution was outside the "de minimis" range: see *R. v. Smithers* (1977), 34

C.C.C. (2d) 427, [1978] 1 S.C.R. 506, 40 C.R.N.S. 79 (S.C.C.); *R. v. Cribbin* (1994), 89 C.C.C. (3d) 67, 17 O.R. (3d) 548, 28 C.R. (4th) 137 (Ont. C.A.).

A legally blameworthy cause must be "at least a significant" cause and "more than one that is trifling or minor": *R. v. Trakas*, 2008 CarswellOnt 2889, 241 O.A.C. 52, 233 C.C.C. (3d) 172, 2008 ONCA 410, 61 M.V.R. (5th) 159 (Ont. C.A.), at paras. 42-54 [ONCA].

8.8 NECESSITY DEFENCE

"In urgent situations of clear and imminent peril, when compliance with the law is demonstrably impossible" the defendant has the legal excuse of necessity: *Perka v. R.*, 14 C.C.C. (3d) 385, [1984] 2 S.C.R. 232, [1984] 6 W.W.R. 289, 42 C.R. (3d) 113 (S.C.C.) at 400 citing *R. v. Morgentaler (No. 5)* (1975), 20 C.C.C. (2d) 449, [1976] 1 S.C.R. 616, 30 C.R.N.S. 209 (S.C.C.) at 497.

- To use the defence of necessity, the elements listed below must be present.
  - There must be an imminent risk such that the defendant must act to avoid an immediate peril.
  - There must be no reasonable legal alternative to the course of action taken by the defendant.
  - The harm inflicted by the defendant must be less than the harm avoided.
  - The emergency must not be reasonably foreseeable.
- Once the defence provides some evidence of an emergency, then the Crown must prove beyond a reasonable doubt that the necessity excuse does not apply: see *Perka*, *supra*, at 404-405.
- The first and second requirements – imminent peril and no reasonable legal alternative – are evaluated on the "modified objective standard" – an objective standard that takes into account the situation and characteristics of the particular defendant. The third requirement, proportionality, must

be measured on an objective standard – i.e. community standards. See: *R. v. Latimer*, 2001 CarswellSask 4, 2001 CarswellSask 5, REJB 2001-21909, [2001] S.C.J. No. 1, [2001] 1 S.C.R. 3, [2001] 6 W.W.R. 409, 2001 SCC 1, 80 C.R.R. (2d) 189, 264 N.R. 99, 39 C.R. (5th) 1, 193 D.L.R. (4th) 577, 150 C.C.C. (3d) 129, 203 Sask. R. 1, 240 W.A.C. 1 (S.C.C.).

- Examples of necessity might include:
  - A motorist who exceeds the speed limit, or who drives with a suspended license, or who drives while impaired in order to take an injured person to the hospital: *Perka, supra*, at 393.
  - The accused was driving dangerously (a criminal offence) by speeding at 73 miles per hour, but had to in order to avoid being hit by a tail-gating car: see *R. v. Fry* (1977), 36 C.C.C. (2d) 396 (Sask. Prov. Ct.).
  - In the case of a police officer who failed to stop at a stop sign, while the defence of necessity was not available on the facts of the case, the court observed that the defence would be available in an appropriate fact situation: *R. v. Walker* (1979), 48 C.C.C. (2d) 126, 5 M.V.R. 114 (Ont. Co. Ct.).
  - Shooting a bear contrary to the National Parks Game regulations (a strict liability offence), in order to save a child: see *R. v. Slovack* (1979), [1980] 1 W.W.R. 368 (Alta. Prov. Ct.).

For a recent example of where the defence of duress succeeded, see *R. v. Chu*, 2008 CarswellOnt 3557, 2008 ONCJ 312, [2008] O.J. No. 2733 (Ont. C.J.), a case involving the strict liability offence of selling tobacco to a minor, contrary to the *Smoke Free Ontario Act*, where the court found that the defendant sold the cigarettes to the purchaser and feared for his personal safety.

The necessity defence also succeeded in a case where the defendant was charged with the *Highway Traffic Act* offence of failing to report an accident forthwith, in circumstances where he had been walking in sub-zero weather for several hours in inadequate footwear, and was in the process of warming himself to avoid frost bite prior to reporting the accident to the police: *R. v. Kruchkowsky*, 2008 ONCJ 704, 2008 CarswellOnt 8406, [2008] O.J. No. 5460 (Ont. C.J.).

In another recent case, the court observed that the necessity defence was not formally advanced, although the defence of necessity was suggested by portions of the defendant's testimony. The evidentiary foundation for the defence was insufficient to enable the court to properly determine whether the requirements of the necessity defence had been satisfied: *R. v. Kelleher* (2008), 2008 CarswellOnt 8609, 2009 ONCJ 5, [2009] O.J. No. 670 (Ont. C.J.).

9

SPECIAL PROCEEDINGS

9.1 YOUNG PERSONS

Under the POA:

- A "young person" is between 12 and 16: section 93.
- No person under 12 (at the time of the offence) shall be convicted: section 94.
- The young person must appear during the whole trial, with limited exceptions: sections 95, 98.
- Parents are to be notified as soon as practicable: section 96.
- Generally, the young person's identity is not to be published: section 99.
- An absolute discharge is available: section 101.
- The maximum fine is $1,000: section 101.
- Where proceedings are by a certificate under Part I, the maximum fine is $300: section 97.
- A young person shall not be imprisoned, except for a breach of probation (sections 101, 75) and shall not be imprisoned for non-payment of a fine (section 102).

9.2 BAIL HEARINGS

9.2.1 THE LAW

(a) The Officer at the Police Station

- Regarding adult defendants, the arresting police officer, and later the officer-in-charge at the police station, shall release the defendant as soon as practicable, unless there are reasonable and probable grounds to detain in order to:
  - Establish the identity of the defendant;
  - Secure or preserve evidence related to the offence;
  - Prevent the continuation of the offence or another offence; or
  - The defendant is ordinarily resident outside Ontario, and will not respond to a summons, or to a recognizance without sureties, and/or to a security deposit: sections 149 to 151.
- Regarding young persons, the police must have reasonable and probable grounds to detain in order to:
  - Establish the young person's identity; or
  - Prevent the continuation or repetition of an offence that constitutes a serious danger to the young person or the person or property of another: section 107(2, 3).
- There are rules for notifying the young person's parent(s): section 107(4).
- If an adult or young person is not released, the officer-in-charge shall, as soon as practicable and within 24 hours, bring him or her before a justice.
- With limited exceptions, young persons must be detained separately from adults: section 107(6).

(b) The Justice at the Bail Hearing

- For both young persons and adults, the justice shall release the defendant on an undertaking, unless the prosecutor "shows cause" why a more onerous release or detention is required.

- The justice shall only consider whether the defendant will appear in court. *There is no authority to consider the "public interest" or "the protection or safety of the public" (unlike the "secondary grounds" of a bail hearing under the Criminal Code). And, unlike the police, the justice cannot temporarily detain the defendant to secure or preserve evidence or to prevent the commission of an offence.*

- The justice may order any of the following releases, but the prosecutor must first "show cause" why a less restrictive release is not sufficient. In order of the degree of restriction on the defendant:

  - A recognizance, with appropriate conditions;

  - Where the offence is punishable by imprisonment for 12 months or more, a recognizance with conditions and with sureties, or a cash deposit if consented to by the prosecutor;

  - If the defendant does not ordinarily reside in Ontario, a recognizance with or without sureties and conditions, plus a cash deposit;

  - Detention until trial. (If the defendant is detained, the trial shall be expedited by section 151.)

- The justice's decision and reasons shall be recorded (to allow for an appeal), and the justice may consider any credible or trustworthy information, including hearsay.

- The defendant shall not be examined or cross-examined about the offence charged. (*This may be subject to Charter challenge should the defendant wish to testify about the offence.*)

9.2.2 ACTING FOR THE DEFENDANT AT A BAIL HEARING

- Consider the excellent Practice Guide by D. Garth Burrows, Q.C., *Bail Hearings* (Carswell, 1993).

- All information should have been gathered as described in Chapter 3, including information from the officer-in-charge.

- Speak to the prosecutor before the hearing to get as much disclosure as possible.

  - Is the prosecutor aware of any outstanding charges or a prior record of offences?

- Why does the prosecutor want to detain your client?

  - Is there a record for failing to appear for court? Can that record be explained?

  - Does your client have an alcohol or drug problem? Is your client taking treatment? What evidence can you gather to show improvement?

- Obtain sureties.

  - You must convince the justice that your surety will guarantee the defendant's court appearance.

  - Obtain the following information from the surety:

    1. Name? Relation to accused? Age? Phone number?
    2. Address? Will the defendant live with the surety?
    3. How long has the surety known the defendant?
    4. How frequently has the surety seen the defendant?
    5. Does the surety know the details of the present

charges and prior record of the defendant? If not, you must advise the surety.

6. Ask about the character of the surety — criminal record? Is the surety a responsible person?
7. Does the surety understand his or her duties — a promise to the court to insure that the defendant will appear, and a promise to notify the authorities if the defendant will not appear? (sections 155, 156)
8. How will he or she insure the defendant's appearance?
9. Has he or she ever acted as a surety for the defendant before? If so, did the defendant comply?
10. Does the surety require conditions to the defendant's release?
11. How much money can the surety sign for? What proof can be provided to the justice that the surety can pay that amount if required? Ask about proof of income, property, etc.

9.3 *CHARTER* APPLICATIONS

- By section 109 of the *Courts of Justice Act*, notice of a constitutional question shall be served on the Attorney General of Canada and the Attorney General of Ontario in the following circumstances:

  - The constitutional validity or constitutional applicability of an Act of the Parliament of Canada or the Legislature, of a regulation or by-law made under such an Act or of a rule of common law is in question.

  - A remedy is claimed under subsection 24 (1) of the *Canadian Charter of Rights and Freedoms* in relation to an act or omission of the Government of Canada or the Government of Ontario.

- The notice shall be served as soon as the circumstances requiring it become known and, in any event, at least fifteen days before the day on which the question is to be argued, unless the court orders otherwise.

- If a party fails to give notice in accordance with this section, the Act, regulation, by-law or rule of common law shall not be adjudged to be invalid or inapplicable, or the remedy shall not be granted, as the case may be.

- A court does have some discretion to overlook deficiencies in process when it is in the interests of justice. The requirement of following these rules is an essential safeguard for the protection of the rights of the public, particularly defendants so that matters may be heard in a fair and impartial manner. See *R. v. Elder-Nilson*, 2006 ONCJ 409, [2006] O.J. No. 4359, 2006 CarswellOnt 6721 (Ont. C.J.).

The parties must make sure all the relevant documents are properly before the court, including affidavits which are signed. In one recent case, the trial judge was found to have erred in dismissing the defendant's constitutional challenge on the basis that the defendant's affidavit was not properly executed and signed: *R. v. Bodik* (2008), 2008 CarswellOnt 1948 (Ont. C.J.).

Apart from the requirements of notice under s. 109 of the *Courts of Justice Act* and the rules of court, the defendant must do more than that to assert his rights before the trial judge. Stating that one wishes to bring at some point a. s. 11(b) application is not the same as actually bringing the application. While the defendant does not have to assert the right at every court appearance, at some appropriate stage in the proceedings, that is during the trial process, he must muster the evidence, transcripts of the attendance, evidence of prejudice if any, and present argument to the trier of fact: *R. v. Delvecchio*, 2008 ONCJ 511, 2008 CarswellOnt 6281, [2008] O.J. No. 4229 (Ont. C.J.).

9.4 OTHER APPLICATIONS

- An application provided for by the POA or the rules under the POA shall be commenced by notice of application. R.R.O. 1990, Regulation 200, amended to O. Reg. 567/00.

- A motion provided for by the Act or these rules shall be commenced by notice of motion.

- There shall be at least three days between the giving of notice of application or notice of motion and the day for hearing the application or motion.

- An applicant or moving party shall file notice of application or notice of motion at least two days before the day for hearing the application or motion.

- Evidence on an application or motion may be given

  - by affidavit;

  - with the permission of the court, orally; or

  - in the form of a transcript of the examination of a witness.

- Upon the hearing of an application or motion and whether or not other evidence is given on the application or motion, the justice may receive and base his or her decision upon information the justice considers credible or trustworthy in the circumstances.

- An application or motion may be heard without notice

  - on consent; or

  - where, having regard to the subject-matter or the circumstances of the application or motion, it would not be unjust to hear the application or motion without notice.

10

TRIALS

10.1 PROCEDURE

10.1.1 APPEARANCE FOR TRIAL

- The defendant's appearance for trial is dependent on the procedural "streams" for provincial offences: Part I (Minor Offences), Part II (Parking Infractions), Part III (Serious Offences).

- Where the defendant was served with a notice of trial, but the court house was closed on the trial date due to a power failure, the court retained jurisdiction to proceed with the offence by mailing out a fresh notice of trial. See *York (Regional Municipality) v. Scarcello* (2004), (sub nom. *R. v. Scarcello*) [2004] O.J. No. 1002, 2004 CarswellOnt 6077 (Ont. S.C.J.).

- However, the clerk of the court does not have jurisdiction to adjourn proceedings on account of the absence of the justice of the peace. See *R. v. 1283499 Ontario Inc.* (2003), 65 O.R. (3d) 763, 173 O.A.C. 365, 176 C.C.C. (3d) 522, 2003 CarswellOnt 2497 (Ont. C.A.); *R. v. Colarossi* (2003), [2003] O.J. No. 2629, 2003 CarswellOnt 2496, 65 O.R. (3d) 767 (Ont. C.A.).

In *R. v. Watson* (2007), 2007 CarswellOnt 6283, [2007] O.J. No. 3858 (Ont. C.J.) it was held that the provincial offences court does not lose jurisdiction where a trial is adjourned by a court administrator who is not a judicial officer or a justice of the peace. The court may regain its jurisdiction over the person by mailing out a fresh Notice of Trial, which is certified in the required manner.

(a) Part I: Certificate of Offence

- If a summons is served, the defendant must appear for trial.

- If an offence notice is served, the defendant may plead:

  - Guilty in writing with full payment of the fine: section 8(1);
  - Guilty "with representations" as to penalty, to be made before a justice: section 7(1);
  - Not guilty and appear for trial: section 5(1); or
  - Dispute the charges in writing, if the defendant lives outside a designated jurisdiction where the charges were laid: section 6(1).

- If none of the above is plead within 15 days, or if the defendant fails to appear for trial, he or she is deemed not to dispute the charges and, provided the certificate of offence is complete and regular on its face, the defendant can be convicted in his or her absence: sections 9, 9.1.

- A young person must be summoned for trial: section 95.

  - A notice must be delivered to the parent(s): section 96.

  - The young person must be personally present throughout the trial: section 98.

(b) Part II: Certificate of Parking Infraction

- The defendant has two options:

  - Pay the fine out-of-court: section 16; or
  - Appear for trial by indicating so on the parking infraction notice: section 17.

- If the defendant fails to respond within 15 days, the court may send a notice of impending conviction. If he or she again fails to respond within 15 days, or fails to appear for trial, provided the certificate of parking infraction is complete and regular on its face, the defendant can be convicted in his or her absence: sections 18, 18.1, 18.2, 18.4.

(c) Part III: Information

- The defendant must appear for trial.

10.1.2 MANNER OF DEFENDANT APPEARING FOR TRIAL

- A young person must attend personally throughout the trial: section 98.
- An adult defendant may either attend personally or have a lawyer or agent attend: section 50(1).
- A corporation *must* have a lawyer or agent attend: section 50(2).
- Any defendant may *act* (i.e. be represented) by a lawyer or agent, whether or not the defendant attends: section 82.
- Any agent who is not a lawyer may be barred from representing a defendant if the court finds that the agent is not competent or does not understand and comply with the ethical duties to the court: section 50(3).

In *R. v. Morden* (2000), 2000 CarswellOnt 1037 (Ont. C.J.), it was determined that, although the defendant could choose to be represented by an agent who was not a lawyer, the appellate court has the jurisdiction to allow an appeal if a miscarriage of justice has occurred due to the agent's conduct. Where the agent failed to inquire of the defendant as to whether he wished to testify on his own behalf, the agent's conduct was improper, and a new trial was ordered.

10.1.3 FAILURE OF DEFENDANT TO APPEAR FOR TRIAL

- When the defendant fails to appear for trial and the prosecution proves that procedures for notification were followed (section 54(1)), the court may choose from three alternative procedures:

- Proceed to hear and determine the case in the absence of the defendant;
- Adjourn the hearing and issue a summons to appear or a warrant in the prescribed form for the arrest of the defendant; or
- Choose again from the above if the defendant does not appear in response to the summons or warrant on the date to which the hearing is adjourned: section 54(2).

- Section 54 does not apply to young persons. By section 98(3), a young person must appear throughout the trial.
- Section 54 also does not apply to Part I and Part II offences, where the defendant gave a notice of intention to appear for trial and then failed to appear. In that case, he or she is deemed not to dispute the charges and convicted in his or her absence under sections 9.1 or 18.4.

(a) Compelling the Defendant to Appear for Trial

- The court may order the defendant to attend personally.
- The court may issue a summons in the prescribed form, if it deems it necessary to do so: section 51.

(b) Penalty for Failing to Appear

- Where one is lawfully required to attend the hearing and does not, he or she is guilty of an offence and upon conviction liable to:
  - A fine of not more than $2,000; or
  - Imprisonment for a term of not more than 30 days; or

- Both: section 42(1).

- If the trial proceeds *ex parte*, then the defendant cannot be prosecuted for failing to appear: section 54(2).

- This section does not apply to young persons: section 98(3).

(c) Excluding the Defendant From the Trial

- The court may remove the defendant if he or she interrupts the proceeding to the extent that his or her attendance is not feasible.

- During the trial of an issue as to whether the defendant is, because of mental disorder, unable to conduct his or her defence, the court is satisfied that failure to exclude the defendant might adversely effect his or her mental health: section 52.

10.1.4 FAILURE OF THE PROSECUTOR TO APPEAR FOR TRIAL

- Where the defendant appears for a hearing and the prosecutor does not, the court may:

  - Dismiss the charge; or

  - Adjourn the hearing to another time: section 53(1).

- There is a similar rule if the prosecutor fails to appear at the resumption of an adjourned hearing: section 53(2).

- Certain costs can be awarded to the defendant: section 60.

- However, these costs are not legal costs of the party, but are costs for witness' fees and expenses. Where the proceeding is under Part I or II of the Act, such costs are not to exceed $100. See section 60(2).

- The defendant can request a certified copy of the order of dismissal to bar any subsequent proceedings by the prosecution.

10.1.5 ENSURING THE APPEARANCE OF WITNESSES

(a) By Summons

- Before trial, you (or someone from your office) should appear before a justice to show why your witnesses should be summoned for trial.

- If you expect your witnesses to appear without a summons, consider summoning them anyway. They can use the summons as proof to their employer for being absent from work.

- Also, should they become ill or for some reason not appear at trial, you will more likely succeed in a request for an adjournment if your witnesses were summoned, because the presiding justice cannot fault you for not being prepared to proceed.

- The test that the justice will apply before granting a summons to a witness is found in section 39:

  - The justice must be satisfied that the proposed witness can give *material* evidence in the proceeding.

- The summons shall be served by a provincial offences officer as set out in section 26.

- The witness shall attend to give evidence at the proceeding, and re-attend if the proceeding is adjourned: section 39(4).

- If required by the summons, the witness shall bring any writing or other relevant thing in his or her possession or control: section 39(3).

(b) Arrest of a Witness: Section 40

- The judge may issue a warrant for the arrest of the witness where a judge is satisfied upon sworn evidence that:
  - The witness can give material evidence that is necessary; and
    - The witness will not attend if summoned;
    - The witness is evading service of the summons; or
    - The witness was served but failed to attend court: section 40.

(c) A Witness who is in Jail: Section 41

- Prepare an order in the prescribed form, with a supporting affidavit indicating that he or she is a *material* witness, and indicate the jail and estimated release date for the witness.
- Serve a copy of the judge's order on the superintendant of the jail at least one week before trial, so that the jail can make the necessary transportation arrangements.

10.1.6 ADJOURNMENTS: SECTION 49

- The court may adjourn a trial or hearing.
- Where the defendant is in custody, the adjournment may not be longer than eight days without the consent of the defendant.
- The trial or hearing may be resumed before the expiration of the period with the consent of the defendant and prosecutor.
- Where the trial was commenced under Part I or II, the court shall not adjourn to allow the provincial offences officer

who completed the certificate to attend to give evidence unless the court is satisfied that the interests of justice require it.

- Where the Crown requested an adjournment of the trial, and the defendants had agreed to the adjournment, the justice of the peace has discretion to grant the adjournment in the absence of the defendants. It was a violation of section 7 of the *Charter* to refuse the adjournment, and convict the defendants. See *R. v. Bednis*, [2004] O.J. No. 3992, 2004 CarswellOnt 3958, 2004 ONCJ 215 (Ont. C.J.).

- Where the party becomes aware of the need for an adjournment before the trial date, e.g., a material witness or the defendant is ill, it is advisable to give notice of the adjournment request to the other side. In the case of an adjournment request by the defendant, the prosecutors' office should be contacted.

- A court need not cater to the convenience of the parties at all costs. However, it is imperative that justice and fairness be addressed when considering a request for an adjournment, a process which requires a weighing or balancing of competing interests. The Crown, in representing the public interest, is as entitled as any litigant to these same considerations of justice and fairness. See *R. v. Baxter*, 2006 ONCJ 313, [2006] O.J. No. 3512, 2006 CarswellOnt 5294 (Ont. C.J.).

The justice of the peace erred in refusing to grant an adjournment on the basis that an associate of the defendant's agent, who appeared on the trial date with instructions to seek an adjournment for disclosure, lacked standing on behalf of the defendant: *R. v. Mangat* (January 31, 2006), G. Trotter J., [2006] O.J. No. 1781 (Ont. C.J.).

- The decision of the justice to exercise his discretion to allow an adjournment at the request of the Crown without affidavit evidence in support did not result in a loss of jurisdiction. If the accused had other complaints that the Crown conduct was abusive, it should be advanced at first instance before the trial court rather than on *a certiorari* application. It would be undesirable to fragment the proceedings with an interlocutory judicial review: *R. v. Wilson* (March 22, 2006), Doc. 6609/06, [2006] O.J. No. 5653 (Ont. S.C.J.).

While the Crown disclosed the officer's collision reconstruction report prior to the trial, it failed to disclose the amended report. The defence had not completed its cross-examination of the officer, and the Crown's case was not concluded. The appropriate remedy was not a stay of proceedings, but an order for production of the revised report, and an adjournment to allow the defence to review the revised report with leave to recall Crown witnesses. This remedy removed any prejudice to the defence due to non-disclosure: *R. v. Soo*, 2008 ABPC 221, 2008 CarswellAlta 1077, [2008] A.J. No. 881 (Alta. Prov. Ct.).

In *R. v. Winlow*, 2008 CarswellOnt 3031, 2008 ONCJ 240, [2008] O.J. No. 2085 (Ont. C.J.), leave to appeal granted (April 18, 2008), Doc. M36186 (Ont. C.A. [In Chambers]), it was held that the justice of the peace was entitled to exercise her discretion and refuse the amendment sought by the prosecution in a case involving amending the certificate of offence pursuant to s. 34(2) of the *Provincial Offences Act* to increase the speed alleged against the defendant after it had been reduced by the officer at the time of charge, but to vary it according to the officer's evidence at trial. Where the defendant, minutes or moments before the trial, suddenly finds out that he is facing a defence to a speed that has been doubled in terms of the amount over, it does not affect the defence on the merits he is putting forward, but it does affect the risk he is undergoing. An adjournment for the defendant to seek legal advice would require a further delay, and does not promote the expeditious dealing of these cases. [For another case where this practice of "amending up" was disapproved of, see *Chatham-Kent (Municipality) v. Lusk* (2008), 2008 CarswellOnt 8318 (Ont. C.J.) where the charge was withdrawn.]

An accused has no right to adjourn to get counsel when he has fired counsel to protract the process: *R. v. Maitland Capital Ltd.*, 2008 CarswellOnt 6510, 2008 ONCJ 523, [2008] O.J. No. 4360 (Ont. C.J.).

10.1.7 MENTAL CAPACITY OF THE DEFENDANT TO CONDUCT A TRIAL: SECTION 44

- Where the court has reason to believe that the defendant suffers from a mental disorder, the issue of the defendant's ability to conduct a defence may be tried.

- If the defendant is unable to conduct a defence, the proceedings are suspended.

- The *Mental Health Act*, R.S.O. 1990, c. M.7 defines "mental disorder" as "any disease or disability of the mind".

- The test is similar to that under the *Criminal Code*, R.S.C. 1985, c. C-46, for the capacity to defend a criminal charge: see *R. v. Taylor* (1992), 77 C.C.C. (3d) 551, 17 C.R. (4th) 371, 11 O.R. (3d) 323 (Ont. C.A.).

- Under the *Criminal Code*,

  - The party raising the issue must prove that the accused is unfit to stand trial on a balance of probabilities.

  - The accused is fit to stand trial, provided the accused understands the nature or object of the proceedings, understands the possible consequences, and can communicate with counsel.

  - The accused must be capable of recounting the necessary facts to his lawyer, but he or she need not be capable of acting in his or her own best interests.

- In addition to the powers to order psychiatric assessments under the POA, under the *Mental Health Act*, *supra*, there are various powers to order assessments and the detention of dangerous persons.

10.1.8 ENTERING THE PLEA

- After preliminary motions are decided (see Chapter 5), the defendant is informed of the substance of the charges and must plead guilty or not guilty: section 45(1).

- If the defendant pleads guilty, the court *may* accept the plea and convict: section 45(2).

  - Where the defendant is unrepresented and may not understand the process, the court can wait for the defendant to admit the essential facts alleged by the prosecutor before convicting the defendant.

- If the defendant pleads not guilty to the offence but guilty to any other offence, whether or not it is an included offence, the court may, with consent of the prosecutor, accept the plea and amend the information or substitute the offence to which the defendant pleads guilty, accordingly: section 45(4).

- If the defendant refuses to plead or does not answer directly, the court will enter a plea of not guilty: section 45(3).

- Prior to the defendant pleading guilty, the justice of the peace may conduct a "plea inquiry" so as to ensure that the guilty plea is being freely and voluntarily made. The defendant will be advised, even in cases where he or she is represented by an agent or another, that it is important the defendant understands that by pleading guilty he or she will be giving up the right to have a trial in the provincial offences court and making the prosecution prove its case in court. The defendant will also be told that the matter of penalty or sentence is exclusively up to the justice of the peace and that while the parties have the right to make submissions as to sentence, only the justice can determine what sentence to impose. See *R. v. Shields* (2002), [2002] O.J. No. 4876, 2002 CarswellOnt 4304 (Ont. C.J.). In cases where a guilty plea is being entered by an agent on behalf of the defendant in the defendant's absence, it is important for the agent to indicate to the court that the defendant has instructed the agent to enter the plea on his or her behalf, and that the defendant is aware of the consequences of the guilty plea but has chosen to be represented by an agent to enter the guilty plea. See *Barrie (City) v. Doherty* (2003), [2003] O.J. No. 1105, 2003 CarswellOnt 1235 (Ont. C.J.).

- To be valid, a guilty plea must be voluntary and unequivocal, and the defendant has to understand the nature of the charges. See *Ontario (Ministry of Consumer & Busi-*

ness Services) v. Whiteside (2004), 2004 ONCJ 204, 2004 CarswellOnt 3916, [2004] O.J. No. 3972, 25 C.R. (6th) 373 (Ont. C.J.).

The legal principles governing the withdrawal of a guilty plea were canvassed by Trafford J. in *R. v. Jerome* (2008), 2008 CarswellOnt 528, [2008] O.J. No. 407 (Ont. S.C.J.), a case where the defendant unsuccessfully challenged the validity of her guilty plea to careless driving. The court noted that the appellant has the legal burden of establishing that her plea was invalid, and that the withdrawal of a plea of guilty should be permitted in exceptional circumstances. There is no absolute right to withdraw a plea of guilty. The defendant's plea of guilty to careless driving in the case at bar was informed, voluntary, and unequivocal. Her reasons for entering the plea, namely, to end the stress associated with the accident and the related charges, were considered sufficient and appropriate by her. Those reasons did not vitiate the plea in the circumstances of the case. The plea was an informed admission of guilt, which was made with the knowledge of her right to require the Crown to prove its case. In addition, she admitted the facts alleged by the Crown in support of the plea without any qualification.

The trial justice has a duty to ensure that the defendant's plea of guilty is voluntary, informed and unequivocal. To be informed, the defendant must know the charge and the consequences which the court can impose. However, there is no requirement that the court must inform defendants of all possible consequences of a plea, including administrative and civil consequences: *R. v. Torabi* (September 21, 2007), No. 999-00-86410023-90, [2007] O.J. No. 5402 (Ont. C.J.).

In *R. v. Sholtens*, 2008 CarswellOnt 3605, 2008 ONCJ 282, [2008] O.J. No. 2444 (Ont. C.J.), the appeal court held that where a justice of the peace on his own motion adjourns a sentencing hearing to another date for the purposes of providing reasons as to why he cannot accept the guilty plea, and gives reasons for judgment without providing the prosecutor or unrepresented defendant a real opportunity of making submissions, the proceedings take on the appearance of a public lecture rather than an adversarial process before an impartial decision maker. A reasonable person, reasonably informed, would conclude that that the justice's decision had been arrived at before all the evidence and submissions had been heard. The justice of the peace was bound to follow the law on point and enter a conviction, through the application of the doctrine of *stare decisis*; there was a decision of a judge of the Ontario Court of Justice sitting as an appeal court, indicating that it was appropriate to register a finding of guilt in the circumstances of the case. *Stare decisis* is the glue that binds the court system in Ontario together, and gives purposes to the different levels of court and functions so as to prevent injustice. For a similar case, see *R. v. Bellefeuille*, 2008 CarswellOnt 6641, 2008 ONCJ 575, [2008] O.J. No. 4494 (Ont. C.J.) where the justice of the peace rejected the defendant's guilty plea and erroneously dismissed the charges, rather than set a trial date which was the proper course where a guilty plea is rejected.

In *R. v. Kronshteyn* (2008), 2008 CarswellOnt 4600 (Ont. C.J.), the court set aside a conviction and ordered a new trial where evidence was placed before the court by the trial agent that he misunderstood the defendant's instructions due to a language barrier, and erroneously entered guilty to a lesser charge.

In *R. v. Fuentes*, 2008 ONCJ 598, 2008 CarswellOnt 7068, [2008] O.J. No. 4677 (Ont. C.J.), it was held that it is the client's right to meet with the person who represents him so there will be no misunderstanding as to what occurs in court. It is mandatory that whomever the licensed paralegal hires meets with the client where a paralegal informs the client that another paralegal will represent the client in court. It is not sufficient for the paralegal to merely tell the other agent what the client wants or said. Where the second paralegal pleaded the client guilty without ever speaking to the client, and a licence suspension was imposed, the conviction could not stand.

10.1.9 TRIALS WHERE THE DEFENDANT *DOES* APPEAR: SECTION 46

- The defendant has the following procedural rights:
  - The defendant is entitled to make full answer and defence.
  - The prosecutor or defendant, as the case may be, may examine or cross-examine witnesses.
  - The court may receive and act upon any facts agreed upon by the defendant and prosecutor without proof or evidence.
  - Despite section 8 of the *Evidence Act*, R.S.O. 1990, c. E.23 (EA), the defendant is not a compellable witness for the prosecution: section 46.

10.1.10 TRIALS WHERE THE DEFENDANT DOES *NOT* APPEAR: SECTION 54

- A not guilty plea is entered and the prosecutor must prove its case.

- An *ex parte* trial is still a trial, with all its attendant burdens of proof, formalities and evidentiary requirements.
  - The prosecutor must act fairly and adduce *all* relevant evidence, both indicative of guilt and innocence.
  - The defendant only forfeits the right to be present, to hear and test by cross-examination the evidence of the prosecution witnesses, and to make full answer and defence.
  - The defendant can only be convicted upon legally admissible evidence which establishes proof beyond a reasonable doubt the essential elements of the prosecution's case. See, for example, *R. v. Bandito Video Ltd.* (1986), 52 C.R. (3d) 293 (Ont. Prov. Ct.).
  - An *ex parte* trial, where the defendant does not appear, does not contravene the Charter as the defendant is not deprived of his or her right to be present at trial as he or she need only appear at the time and place fixed for trial: *R. v. Felipa* (1986), 55 O.R. (2d) 362, 27 C.C.C. (3d) 26, 40 M.V.R. 316 (C.A.).

An absent defendant does not give up her right to be convicted only on the basis of legally admissible evidence which establishes beyond a reasonable doubt all essential ingredients of the offences charged. Notwithstanding a lack of any evidence from the defendant, the court is to consider the only other evidence, that is, of the Crown witnesses, to determine whether or not there have been any *Charter* violations and whether any evidence obtained by any such violations should be excluded pursuant to the *Charter*: *R. v. Dumont*, 2008 CarswellOnt 2186, 2008 ONCJ 173, [2008] O.J. No. 1487 (Ont. C.J.).

Where the trial justice raises the issue of voluntariness at the defendants' *ex parte* trial and dismisses the charge on the basis that the identity of the defendants had not been established, the principles of fundamental justice required that the prosecutor be given an opportunity to make submissions in response to the court's concerns about voluntariness. The inconsistency in the spelling of the name of one of the defendants was a point that should have been presented to the prosecution with an opportunity for submissions to be made: *R. v. Jarecsni* (2008), 2008 CarswellOnt 6779, [2008] O.J. No. 4565 (Ont. C.J.).

The defendant did not appear for the resumption of his hearing and was aware that the matter would proceed without further notice to him. He and his co-defendant were both officers and directors of the company and they allegedly acted together. Separating their matters in any way would be inefficient and simply a waste of court time. It was appropriate for the trial to proceed on an *ex parte* basis: *R. v. Maitland Capital Ltd.*, 2008 CarswellOnt 6508, 2008 ONCJ 521, [2008] O.J. No. 4358 (Ont. C.J.).

10.1.11 INCLUDED OFFENCES: SECTION 55

- An included offence is an additional offence to the main charge.
- If the included offence is proved, the defendant may be convicted although the whole offence charged is not proved.

In *R. v. Reiber*, 2007 ONCJ 343, 2007 CarswellOnt 4767, [2007] O.J. No. 2921, 53 M.V.R. (5th) 158 (Ont. C.J.), the court considered section 55 which sets out the concept of an included offence. It is necessary that all of the essential elements of the included offence be part of the original offence. To be an included offence, the accused would necessarily have to commit the included offence in the commission of the offence charged. In the case at bar, the offence of failing to stop for a red light can be committed without committing the offence of failing to stop for an amber light. The essential elements of the amber light offence are not included in the charge of the red light offence.

A lower speed indicated in the certificate of offence is a lesser and included offence of the higher speed. Where the evidence at trial disclosed that a defendant charged with speeding 76 kilometres per hour in a 50 kilometre zone was driving 86 kilometres per hour, the justice of the peace erred by failing to conclude that the speed set out in the certificate of offence was in fact an included offence on the evidence led at trial: *R. v. Mejia* (2008), 2008 CarswellOnt 4439, [2008] O.J. No. 2893 (Ont. C.J.).

10.1.12 EXCLUDING THE PUBLIC OR WITNESSES: SECTION 52(2)

- The court may exclude the public or any member of the public from the hearing where the court believes it is necessary to:
  - Maintain order in the courtroom;
  - Protect the reputation of a minor; or

  - Remove an influence that might affect the testimony of a witness.

- However, an order excluding the public, or a member of the public, from the courtroom is an exceptional order as courtrooms are generally open to the public.

- Request an "order excluding witnesses" pursuant to subsection (c) after your client pleads and before the first witness is called, if you wish to bring out inconsistencies in the prosecution witnesses. If granted, all witnesses shall wait outside the courtroom until summoned to give evidence.

- You might seek an order to protect the defence witnesses. Without such an order, the justice could infer that, because your witnesses heard each other testify, their testimony ought to be given less weight.

10.1.13 PUBLICATION BANS

- In order to protect the reputation of a minor, the court may make an order prohibiting the publication or broadcast of:

  - The identity of the minor; or

  - The evidence or any part of the evidence taken at the hearing.

- The identity of a young person in connection with an offence cannot be published, with some exceptions: section 99.

- Consider the relationship between these sections and the *Charter* section 2(b) right of "freedom of the press and other media of communication".

10.2 EVIDENCE

- The Ontario *Evidence Act*, R.S.O. 1990, c. E.23 applies ("EA").

- Evidence is a complex area of law beyond the scope of this Guide. However, for ease of reference, the following are briefly highlighted: notice rules, documents, number of experts, hearsay, and credibility evidence.

10.2.1 NOTICES REQUIRED UNDER THE EA

- Below follow some examples of Notices required under EA:

  - Seven days notice for business records: EA, section 35(3).

  - Ten days notice for a medical report: EA, section 52(2).

  - Ten days notice for registered land documents: EA, section 53(3).

  - Ten days notice for original of telegram, letter, shipping bill, bill of lading, delivery order, receipt, account or other written instrument used in business or other transactions: EA, section 55(1).

10.2.2 DOCUMENTS

- The following are some examples of documentary rules under the EA:

  - Certified official records: POA, section 47(2).

  - Certified copies of official or public documents in Ontario or certified copies of a document, by-law, rule, regulation or proceeding, or of an entry in a register or other book of a corporation created by charter or statute in Ontario: EA, section 29.

- Certified copies of public books or documents: EA, section 32.

- Copies of governmental books and records made in the usual and ordinary course of business: EA, section 31.

- Business records made in the usual and ordinary course of business: EA, section 35.

- Copies of bank records made in the usual and ordinary course of business: EA, section 33.

- Rules regarding access to bank records: EA, section 33(4).

- Copies of bills of exchange, promissory notes, receipts, instruments: EA, section 34.

- Rules regarding admissibility of electronic records: EA, section 34.1.

10.2.3 NUMBER OF EXPERTS

- No more than three expert witnesses can be called by either party without leave: EA, section 12.

10.2.4 HEARSAY

- Any written, oral or gestured statement by someone who is not testifying at trial to prove the truth of the statement is "hearsay" and generally inadmissible.

- The following are exceptions to the hearsay rule:

  - An out-of-court admission by the defendant. It is hearsay, but admissible.

- The rationale for admitting admissions by a party without concern for the hearsay rule rests on the theory of the adversary system, and not a necessity/reliability analysis: *R. v. Osmar*, 2007 ONCA 50, [2007] O.J. No. 244, 2007 CarswellOnt 339, 220 O.A.C. 186, 150 C.R.R. (2d) 301, 84 O.R. (3d) 321, 217 C.C.C. (3d) 174, 44 C.R. (6th) 276 (Ont. C.A.) at para. 53 [ONCA], leave to appeal refused (2007), 2007 CarswellOnt 4187, 2007 CarswellOnt 4188, 156 C.R.R. (2d) 373 (note) (S.C.C.).

  - If the Crown tenders the statement of a defendant, it cannot pick and choose those parts of the statement that it would like the court to hear; it must take "the good with the bad," and both the "good" and the "bad" are admitted for their truth, for and against the defendant. Moreover, a party wishing to adduce a statement must put in as much of the statement as is necessary to permit a fair understanding of the individual utterances: *R. v. Mallory*, 2007 ONCA 46, 2007 CarswellOnt 348, [2007] O.J. No. 236, 220 O.A.C. 239, 217 C.C.C. (3d) 266 (Ont. C.A.), at para. 203.

  - The documentary business records listed above. They are hearsay, but sufficiently reliable to be admissible.

  - There are other exceptions. You should carefully research the law in order to deliver persuasive objections to hearsay at trial.

- A hearsay statement may be admitted if it is necessary and reliable. "Necessity" may require that the proponent of the evidence made all reasonable efforts to secure the evidence of the declarant in a manner that also preserves the rights of the other party. "Reliability" may require it to be shown that there is no real concern as to whether the statement is true because of the circumstances in which the statement was made, or where concerns can be met through testing the truth and accuracy of the statements by methods that serve as appropriate substitutes for contemporaneous cross-examination: *R. v. Khelawon*, 2006 CarswellOnt 7825, 2006 CarswellOnt 7826, [2006] S.C.J. No. 57, 355 N.R. 267, 274 D.L.R. (4th) 385, 42 C.R. (6th)

1, 2006 SCC 57, 215 C.C.C. (3d) 161, 220 O.A.C. 338, [2006] 2 S.C.R. 787 (S.C.C.).

10.2.5 CREDIBILITY EVIDENCE

- The credibility of a witness is affected by a number of factors, *including*:
  - Mental or physical disabilities affecting perception, or the capacity to tell the truth;
  - Bias or partiality towards the case;
  - Inconsistent statements relevant to the case: EA, sections 20, 21;
  - Criminal record; and
  - Discreditable acts or associations.
- All five factors, if the relevance outweighs the prejudice, can be put to a prosecution witness in cross-examination.
- If the witness denies the suggestion in cross-examination, the first four factors can be proved by calling evidence. The final factor is collateral to the central issue of the guilt of the defendant and so the questioner is stuck with the witness' answer. (See: Sopinka, Lederman and Bryant, *The Law of Evidence in Canada*, Second Edition (Butterworths, 1999), at 963-969.)
- If the witness denies a criminal record, you can prove it under section 22 of the EA and section 57(4) of the POA.
- The prosecutor cannot call evidence or suggest that the defendant is the kind of person to commit the offence, unless the defendant first puts into issue his or her good character.
- The court will consider the issue of credibility by asking itself the following three questions:

- First, if you believe the evidence of the accused, you must acquit.

- Second, if you do not believe the testimony of the accused but you are left in reasonable doubt by it, you must acquit.

- Third, even if you are not left in doubt by the evidence of the accused, you must ask yourself whether, on the basis of the evidence you do accept, you are convinced beyond a reasonable doubt by that evidence of the guilt of the accused.

See *R. v. W. (D.)*, [1991] 1 S.C.R. 742, 63 C.C.C. (3d) 397, EYB 1991-67602, 1991 CarswellOnt 80, 1991 CarswellOnt 1015, [1991] S.C.J. No. 26, 3 C.R. (4th) 302, 122 N.R. 277, 46 O.A.C. 352 (S.C.C.).

The trial judge is not obliged to adopt any particular structure in fashioning his/her reasons or a specific order in reviewing the evidence adduced at trial. Neither is the judge required to articulate the *R. v. W.D.* principles at each stage of his/her analysis of the evidence. The jurisprudence of the Supreme Court of Canada confirms that the steps identified in *W.D.* need not be religiously followed or articulated. What is required is that the trier of fact remains focused on the paramount question, namely, whether on the whole of the evidence, the trier of fact is left with a reasonable doubt about the guilt of the accused: *R. v. S. (M.)*, 2008 CarswellOnt 5225, [2008] O.J. No. 3465, 240 O.A.C. 229, 2008 ONCA 616, 237 C.C.C. (3d) 85 (Ont. C.A.).

The failure of a trial judge to sufficiently articulate how credibility concerns were resolved in the reasons for judgment may constitute a reversible error: *R. v. Dinardo*, EYB 2008-133045, 2008 CarswellQue 3451, 2008 CarswellQue 3452, [2008] S.C.J. No. 24, 374 N.R. 198, 57 C.R. (6th) 48, 293 D.L.R. (4th) 375, 231 C.C.C. (3d) 177, 2008 SCC 24, [2008] 1 S.C.R. 788 (S.C.C.).

A trial judge is not required to refer to every piece of evidence led at trial: *R. v. Haller*, 2008 CarswellOnt 3778, 2008 ONCA 517, 61 M.V.R. (5th) 189 (Ont. C.A.), at para. 2 [ONCA].

The appellate court is not given the power to intervene simply because it thinks the trial court did a poor job of expressing itself. Reasons are sufficient if they are responsive to the case's live issues and the parties' key arguments: *R. v. Walker*, 2008 CarswellSask 347, 2008 CarswellSask 348, [2008] S.C.J. No. 34, [2008] 6 W.W.R. 1, 2008 SCC 34, 375 N.R. 228, 57 C.R. (6th) 212, [2008] 2 S.C.R. 245, 310 Sask. R. 305, 423 W.A.C. 305, 294 D.L.R. (4th) 106, 231 C.C.C. (3d) 289 (S.C.C.), at para. 20 [SCC].

The purpose of adhering to the procedure set out in the *W.D.* case is to foreclose an inadvertent shifting of the burden of proof where the complainant and the accused have both testified, and the trial turns on their credibility as witnesses: *R. v. Y. (C.L.)*, [2008] S.C.J. No. 2, 2008 CarswellMan 19, 2008 CarswellMan 20, [2008] 2 W.W.R. 1, 225 Man. R. (2d) 146, 419 W.A.C. 146, [2008] 1 S.C.R. 5, 227 C.C.C. (3d) 129, 53 C.R. (6th) 207, 2008 SCC 2, 370 N.R. 284, 289 D.L.R. (4th) 1 (S.C.C.).

10.2.6 CHALLENGING AN OFFICER'S EVIDENCE: PART I AND II OFFENCES

- For Part I offences proceeded by way of a notice of offence and for Part II parking infraction offences, if the defendant intends to challenge an officer's testimony, it must be indicated in the notice sent to the court.

- If so indicated, then the clerk of the court will notify the officer to attend trial.

  - For Part I offences, see section 5.2 and on a reopening, section 11(3-4).

  - For Part II offences, see sections 18.1.2, 19(3).

- This rule does not apply to Part III trials and Part I offences where the defendant is summoned.

10.2.7 COMPELLABILITY OF THE DEFENDANT

- Section 46(5) of the POA and section 11(c) of the *Charter* protect the defendant from being compelled to testify.

10.2.8 PROVING AN EXCEPTION: SECTION 47(3)

> The burden of proving that an authorization, exception, exemption or qualification prescribed by law operates in favour of the defendant is on the defendant, and the prosecutor is not required, except by way of rebuttal, to prove that the authorization, exception or qualification does not operate in favour of the defendant, whether or not it is set out in the information.

- This section places a persuasive burden on the defendant to prove, on a balance of probabilities, that an authorization, exception, exemption or qualification absolves him or her of guilt.

- Arguably, in some circumstances, the defendant must prove his or her innocence, which is contrary to the *Charter* section 11(d) right "to be presumed innocent until proven guilty".

- Supreme Court of Canada and Court of Appeal for Ontario decisions have distinguished between essential and collateral elements of an offence.

  - Some authorities have held that *all* elements of an offence, both essential and collateral, must be proven by the prosecution: see *R. v. Holmes*, 41 C.C.C. (3d) 497, 64 C.R. (3d) 97, [1988] 1 S.C.R. 914, 65 O.R. (2d) 639 (S.C.C.) per Dickson J. for the minority; *R. v. Whyte*, 6 M.V.R. (2d) 138, [1988] 2 S.C.R. 3, [1988] 5 W.W.R. 26, 29 B.C.L.R. (2d) 273, 64 C.R. (3d) 123, 42 C.C.C. (3d) 97 (S.C.C.); *R. v. Schwartz* (1988), 45 C.C.C. (3d) 97, [1989] 1 W.W.R. 289, [1988] 2 S.C.R. 443, 66 C.R. (3d) 251 (S.C.C.) per the minority.

- The better authority, it seems, is that only the essential elements of the offence must be proven by the prosecution, and that it *is* constitutional to require the defendant to prove an exemption on the balance of probabilities: see *Holmes*, *supra*, per McIntyre J. for the majority; *Schwartz*, *supra*, per the majority; *R. v. Lee's Poultry Ltd.* (1985), 17 C.C.C. (3d) 539, 43 C.R. (3d) 289 (Ont. C.A.); *Proulx v. Krukowski* (1993), 109 D.L.R. (4th) 606 (C.A.); *Halton Regional Municipality v. Stainton* (1991), 2 O.R. (3d) 170 (Prov. Div.), affirmed (1992), 7 O.R. (3d) 203 (note) (Ont. Prov. Div.).

In a case where the defendants were charged with harvesting timber without a forest resource licence in an area where the defendants held mining claims, the trial court reversed the onus by stating that the Crown had failed to prove that both the defendants did not have an exemption under the *Mining Act* when that onus was on the defendants. The onus was on the defendants to establish an exemption pursuant to s. 47(3) of the *Provincial Offences Act*: *R. v. Wetelainen*, 2008 ONCJ 553, 2008 CarswellOnt 6495, [2008] O.J. No. 4392 (Ont. C.J.).

10.2.9 COMMISSION EVIDENCE: SECTION 43

- Upon motion by the defendant or prosecutor, a judge may order a commissioner to take evidence from a witness who:
  - Is outside of Ontario; or
  - Is unlikely to be able to attend trial because of an illness, physical disability, or other good cause.

10.2.10 UNREASONABLE SEARCH AND SEIZURE AND INSPECTIONS

- A justice may issue search warrants on reasonable grounds: section 158. *Section 159 refers to the detention of things seized, and section 160 deals with the seizure of privileged documents.*

- Other provincial Acts provide for "inspections" *without* any evidence of wrong-doing.

- Courts have held that some regulated activities have lower expectations of privacy. *For example, a corporation might reasonably expect a government auditor to periodically review its business records for compliance with the regulations without any suspicion of wrong-doing.* See *Comité paritaire de l'industrie de la chemise c. Sélection Milton,* 4 C.C.E.L. (2d) 214, (sub nom. *R. v. Potash*) 91 C.C.C. (3d) 315, (sub nom. *Comité paritaire de l'industrie de la chemise c. Potash*) [1994] 2 R.C.S. 406 (S.C.C.); *Canada Inc. c. Québec (Procureur général),* (sub nom. *Québec (Sous-ministre du Revenue) c. 143471 Canada Inc.*) 31 C.R. (4th) 120, 90 C.C.C. (3d) 1, [1994] 2 S.C.R. 339 (S.C.C.); *Johnson v. Ontario (Minister of Revenue)* (1990), 25 M.V.R. (2d) 78, 75 O.R. (2d) 558, 1 C.R.R. (2d) 293 (Ont. C.A.); *R. v. Wholesale Travel Group Inc.,* 67 C.C.C. (3d) 193, 8

C.R. (4th) 145, [1991] 3 S.C.R. 154, 4 O.R. (3d) 799 (note) (S.C.C.).

- If, however, the predominant purpose of a regulatory inquiry is the determination of penal liability, the state is engaged in an adversarial relationship, and the subject of the inquiry must be provided with his or her *Charter* rights: *R. v. Jarvis* (2002), 169 C.C.C. (3d) 1, REJB 2002-35624, 2002 CarswellAlta 1440, 2002 CarswellAlta 1441, [2002] S.C.J. No. 76, [2002] 3 S.C.R. 757, 2002 SCC 73, 2002 D.T.C. 7547, [2003] 1 C.T.C. 135, 6 C.R. (6th) 23, 219 D.L.R. (4th) 233, 295 N.R. 201, [2003] 3 W.W.R. 197, 8 Alta. L.R. (4th) 1, 317 A.R. 1, 284 W.A.C. 1, 101 C.R.R. (2d) 35 (S.C.C.).

Section 8 of the *Charter* guarantees that: "Everyone has the right to be secure against *unreasonable* search or seizure [emphasis added]". Section 24(2) of the *Charter* requires the exclusion of evidence obtained in breach of section 8, if it is established (by the defence on a balance of probabilities) that, having regard to all the circumstances, the admission of the evidence would bring the administration of justice into disrepute.

- The law of search and seizure is complex and should be carefully researched before trial.

- Carefully review the powers of inspection and any legal duties on your client to co-operate with the authorities.

Where the inspector under the *Truck Transportation Act* did not have the authority to direct the defendant's truck to follow him as he had no reasonable grounds to believe that an offence had been committed, the evidence of excessive weight was excluded, and the defendant was acquitted. See *R. v. B. Gottardo Construction Ltd.*, [2004] O.J. No. 2139, 2004 CarswellOnt 2092, 7 M.V.R. (5th) 186, 2004 ONCJ 56 (Ont. C.J.).

- Commercial vehicles operating in a highly controlled industry have a reduced expectation of privacy compared to a private vehicle; therefore, the expectation of privacy in the cargo hold of a commercial vehicle, partially exposed to plain view, is marginal: *R. v. Busat*, 2006 CarswellSask 28, [2006] S.J. No. 42, 33 M.V.R. (5th) 51, 274 Sask. R. 1, 2006 SKQB 36 (Sask. Q.B.), CRWN/2006-038.

- Where a motorist refuses to produce his driver's licence, a police officer is only entitled to arrest without a warrant under section 217 of the *Highway Traffic Act* if the motorist has refused to give other reasonable identification. The officer must make a specific request for identification other than a driver's licence: *R. v. Plummer* (2006), [2006] O.J. No. 4530, 2006 CarswellOnt 7056, 38 M.V.R. (5th) 187, 214 C.C.C. (3d) 84, 217 O.A.C. 201, 45 C.R. (6th) 3, 83 O.R. (3d) 528 (Ont. C.A.).

- A stop based on preventative policing as opposed to another purpose, such as checking for sobriety or documentation pursuant to the *Highway Traffic Act*, violates section 9 of the *Charter*: *R. v. Houben* (2006), 2006 CarswellSask 746, [2007] 2 W.W.R. 195, 39 M.V.R. (5th) 84, 2006 SKCA 129, 214 C.C.C. (3d) 519, [2006] S.J. No. 715, 382 W.A.C. 118, 149 C.R.R. (2d) 244, 44 C.R. (6th) 338, 289 Sask. R. 118 (Sask. C.A.).

The amended search warrant provisions under s. 158.1 of the *Provincial Offences Act* have been proclaimed into force and came into effect on 30 June 2008. These new provisions allow for warrants to be issued by fax by designated justices of the peace, and for a report to be made rather than bringing the actual items seized before a justice.

Tax investigation of criminal activity does not raise *Charter* rights, if the predominant purpose of the investigation is regulatory compliance: *R. v. Tiffin*, [2008] O.J. No. 1525, 2008 CarswellOnt 2424, 57 C.R. (6th) 123, 170 C.R.R. (2d) 151, 235 O.A.C. 52, [2008] 5 C.T.C. 77, 90 O.R. (3d) 575, 232 C.C.C. (3d) 303, 2008 ONCA 306 (Ont. C.A.).

There is a limited expectation of privacy for business records in a regulatory investigation: *Taplin v. Alberta (Securities Commission)*, 2008 CarswellAlta 337, [2008] A.J. No. 286, 442 A.R. 248, 2008 ABQB 173 (Alta. Q.B.).

Evidence was excluded where the police properly stopped a vehicle pursuant to the *Highway Traffic Act*, R.S.O. 1990, c. H.8, but then asked the accused passenger for his identification and ran his name through CPIC. The nature of the detention changed when the police asked the accused for his identification, as they had begun an investigation unrelated to the traffic stop. The accused was being detained by the police and felt compelled to provide his identification. Due to the information available on CPIC, asking for the accused's identification was equivalent to asking him a series of questions regarding his criminal past, his bail status, and any bail conditions by which he was bound: *R. v. Gray*, 2009 CarswellOnt 165, 2009 ONCJ 5 (Ont. C.J.), at paras. 38, 44-47 [ONCJ].

10.2.11 RIGHT TO COUNSEL

Charter section 10(b) states: "Everyone has the right *on arrest or detention* to retain and instruct counsel without delay and to be informed of that right." [emphasis added]

- A defendant who is arrested or detained must be informed, without delay, of the following:
  - The reasons for the arrest or detention;
  - That he or she is entitled to speak to a lawyer without delay;
  - Information about legal aid and any available duty counsel hotline;
  - If there is any indication that the defendant does not understand his or her right to counsel, it should be explained again more clearly;
  - The defendant should not be asked any questions dealing with the offence in the meantime, unless there are urgent or dangerous circumstances, or unless he or she understands and clearly says that he or she does not wish to speak to a lawyer; and
  - If the defendant wishes to speak to a lawyer, he or she should be given a reasonable opportunity to do so in private.
- The law regarding right to counsel is complex and should be carefully researched before trial.
- The fundamental purpose of section 10(b) is to ensure that detainees are sufficiently informed of their jeopardy and their right to counsel and given a reasonable opportunity to exercise that right. However, the police are not required to provide the defendant's counsel detailed information when first detained, if counsel can obtain that information by other means, including by asking the defendant himself:

R. v. Fitzsimmons (2006), 2006 CarswellOnt 8086, 39 M.V.R. (5th) 111, [2006] O.J. No. 5079, 84 O.R. (3d) 266, 219 O.A.C. 200, 216 C.C.C. (3d) 141 (Ont. C.A.), leave to appeal refused (2007), [2007] S.C.C.A. No. 81, 2007 CarswellOnt 2863, 2007 CarswellOnt 2864 (S.C.C.).

- See: *R. v. Bartle*, 92 C.C.C. (3d) 289, 33 C.R. (4th) 1, [1994] 3 S.C.R. 173, 6 M.V.R. (3d) 1, 19 O.R. (3d) 802 (note) (S.C.C.); *R. v. Cobham*, 33 C.R. (4th) 73, 6 M.V.R. (3d) 89, [1994] 3 S.C.R. 360, 92 C.C.C. (3d) 333 (S.C.C.); *R. v. Prosper*, 33 C.R. (4th) 85, 6 M.V.R. (3d) 181, [1994] 3 S.C.R. 236, 92 C.C.C. (3d) 353 (S.C.C.); *R. v. Borden*, 33 C.R. (4th) 147, [1994] 3 S.C.R. 145, 92 C.C.C. (3d) 404 (S.C.C.); and *R. v. Pozniak*, 92 C.C.C. (3d) 472, 33 C.R. (4th) 49, [1994] 3 S.C.R. 310, 6 M.V.R. (3d) 113, 19 O.R. (3d) 802 (note) (S.C.C.).

- Use of tax audit for criminal investigation purposes results in *Charter* violations. (*R. v. Borg* (2007), [2007] O.J. No. 3866, 2007 CarswellOnt 8480, 2007 ONCJ 451, 2008 G.T.C. 1055 (Eng.), 2007 D.T.C. 5671 (Eng.), [2007] G.S.T.C. 154 (Ont. C.J.)).

- A momentary investigatory detention does not trigger section 10(b) of the *Charter*. To require the police to give section 10(b) warnings whenever they momentarily detain a person for routine questioning would be to confuse constitutional vigilance with paranoia: *R. v. Suberu* (2006), 2006 CarswellOnt 3005, 142 C.R.R. (2d) 75 (Ont. S.C.J.), at para. 10, per McIsaac J., sitting as an appeal court, affirmed, 2007 CarswellOnt 430, [2007] O.J. No. 317, 220 O.A.C. 322, 218 C.C.C. (3d) 27, 45 C.R. (6th) 47, 2007 ONCA 60, 151 C.R.R. (2d) 135, 85 O.R. (3d) 127 (Ont. C.A.), leave to appeal allowed (2007), 2007 CarswellOnt 5617, 2007 CarswellOnt 5618, 156 C.R.R. (2d) 375 (note) (S.C.C.). Section 8 held violated where a police officer without lawful justification demands name identification from a passenger detained in a vehicle, and exclusion of evidence under section 24(2) considered in detail. (*R. v. Harris*, [2007] O.J. No. 3185, 87 O.R. (3d) 214, 49 C.R. (6th) 220,

51 M.V.R. (5th) 172, 2007 CarswellOnt 5279, 2007 ONCA 574, 225 C.C.C. (3d) 193, 228 O.A.C. 241 (Ont. C.A.)).

- There is no general right to counsel in proceedings before courts and tribunals. There is however, a possibility that a right to counsel may be recognized in specific and varied situations. *Christie v. British Columbia (Attorney General)*, 2007 SCC 21, 155 C.R.R. (2d) 366, [2007] 1 S.C.R. 873, [2007] 8 W.W.R. 64, 280 D.L.R. (4th) 528, 2007 CarswellBC 1118, 2007 CarswellBC 1117, 2007 G.T.C. 1488 (Eng.), 361 N.R. 322, 66 B.C.L.R. (4th) 1, 2007 G.T.C. 1493 (Fr.), 398 W.A.C. 1, 240 B.C.A.C. 1, 2007 D.T.C. 5229 (Fr.), 2007 D.T.C. 5525 (Eng.) (S.C.C.) at para. 27 [SCC].

- The fact that the accused has spoken to counsel after his or her section 10(b) *Charter* rights were violated does not necessarily immunize any subsequently obtained statements from a section 24(2) analysis. Whether these later statements were obtained in violation of the *Charter* under section 24(2) depends on the "temporal, contextual, and causal connection" between the statements and the original *Charter* breach. *R. v. Lewis*, 2007 ONCA 349, 155 C.R.R. (2d) 94, 219 C.C.C. (3d) 427, 224 O.A.C. 298, 2007 CarswellOnt 2871, 86 O.R. (3d) 46, 48 C.R. (6th) 67 (Ont. C.A.) at para. 31.

Solicitor-client privilege is to be determined by the courts and not administrative boards, generally: *Blood Tribe Department of Health v. Canada (Privacy Commissioner)*, [2008] S.C.J. No. 45, 2008 CarswellNat 2244, 2008 CarswellNat 2245, (sub nom. *Privacy Commissioner of Canada v. Blood Tribe Department of Health*) 2008 C.L.L.C. 210-030, 74 Admin. L.R. (4th) 38, 376 N.R. 327, 294 D.L.R. (4th) 385, 67 C.P.R. (4th) 1, (sub nom. *Canada (Privacy Commissioner) v. Blood Tribe Department of Health*) [2008] 2 S.C.R. 574, 2008 SCC 44 (S.C.C.).

Where a detainee has expressed an intention to exercise his or her s. 10(b) rights, the police must inform that he or she is entitled to a reasonable opportunity to contact a lawyer and that they are required to refrain from taking any statement or requiring the detainee to participate in any potentially incriminating process in the meantime: *R. v. Bell*, 2008 CarswellOnt 1866, 2008 ONCJ 151 (Ont. C.J.), at paras. 37 and 39 [ONCJ].

An accused who is in the company of police officers is not detained for the purposes of the *Charter* simply because the police have reasonable grounds to arrest and have formed the intention to arrest. A broader contextual analysis that accounts for all relevant factors is required to ascertain whether an individual was detained: *R. v. Pomeroy*, 2008 CarswellOnt 3911, [2008] O.J. No. 2550, 2008 ONCA 521, 91 O.R. (3d) 261, 173 C.R.R. (2d) 269 (Ont. C.A.).

10.2.12 VOLUNTARINESS/RIGHT TO SILENCE

- Before the defendant's statement(s) made to a person in authority can be introduced as evidence by the prosecution, it must first be proven *beyond a reasonable doubt* that it was made voluntarily.
  - There can be no threats or promises. A *quid pro quo* offer from the police is an important factor in establishing the existence of a threat or promise, but it is the strength of the inducement, having regard to the particular individual and his or her circumstances, that is to be considered in the overall contextual analysis of voluntariness: *R. v. Spencer*, 2007 SCC 11, [2007] 5 W.W.R. 201, 358 N.R. 278, [2007] S.C.J. No. 11, 44 C.R. (6th) 199, 276 D.L.R. (4th) 565, 2007 CarswellBC 480, 2007 CarswellBC 479, [2007] 1 S.C.R. 500, 392 W.A.C. 1, 237 B.C.A.C. 1, 64 B.C.L.R. (4th) 203, 217 C.C.C. (3d) 353 (S.C.C.), at para. 15 [SCC].
  - It cannot be made in "oppressive circumstances".
  - It cannot be made by a defendant without an "operating mind" (i.e. the defendant must *choose* to make a statement).
- Where the police obtain an involuntary confession from a defendant in an oppressive atmosphere, a subsequent inculpatory statement is tainted where the defendant continues to demonstrate the deleterious effects of the police conduct: *R v. Bateman* (2006), 2006 CarswellOnt 3417, [2006] O.J. No. 2562 (Ont. S.C.J.), at paras. 26-28. Right to silence under section 7 of the *Charter* does not prohibit continued police questioning. (*R. v. Singh* (2007), [2007]

S.C.J. No. 48, 285 D.L.R. (4th) 583, 225 C.C.C. (3d) 103, 2007 SCC 48, 2007 CarswellBC 2589, 2007 CarswellBC 2588, 73 B.C.L.R. (4th) 1, 51 C.R. (6th) 199, [2008] 1 W.W.R. 191 (S.C.C.)).

- In addition, the section 7 *Charter* right to "life, liberty and security of the person and the right not to be deprived thereof except in accordance with the principles of fundamental justice" includes the right to remain silent.

- As mentioned in Chapter 3, some statutes make it an offence not to disclose regulatory information.

  - Arguably, any such compelled statement is involuntary and contrary to the right to silence.

  - Some courts have upheld the power to compel statements but ruled them inadmissible in a later prosecution.

- The issue is complex and should be carefully researched before trial.

- The voluntariness of the statement in this case was not affected by the lack of a caution or warning, but was affected by the failure to completely record the conversation. The officer admitted that he did not have a full recall of the conversation and his notes were merely skeletal. The lack of complete record left doubt about its voluntariness: *R. v. Shilon*, 2004 CarswellOnt 8947, [2004] O.J. No. 6138, CRWN/2006-188 (S.C.J.).

- Cross-examination on the defendant's failure to tell the police his version of events before trial breached his *Charter* and common law right to silence: *R. v. Kwandahor-Mensah*, 2006 CarswellAlta 182, 380 A.R. 321, 363 W.A.C. 321, 2006 ABCA 59, 205 C.C.C. (3d) 321, [2006] A.J. No. 171 (Alta. C.A.).

- Crown permitted to cross-examine accused on "discovery" evidence given in civil proceeding for the purposes of challenging his credibility (and not for the purpose of incrimination) despite the fact that he was required to participate in that process under the *Rules of Civil Procedure*. (*R. v. Nedelcu* (2007), [2007] O.J. No. 1188, 2007 CarswellOnt 1851, 41 C.P.C. (6th) 357, 46 M.V.R. (5th) 129, 154 C.R.R. (2d) 171 (Ont. S.C.J.).

- Statements by an accused person must be proved voluntary if they are tendered as proof of the assertions therein. Where an accused is unrepresented, a trial judge has a limited duty to identify and investigate *Charter* issues if they become apparent. The prosecutor should have identified the basis on which the accused's statement to the officer was led – as part of the narrative to explain the process by which the accused was charged or as an admission. Failing that, it would have been preferable, had the justice of the peace required the prosecution to state the basis for the reference to the statement, given that the accused was unrepresented at trial. No substantial wrong or miscarriage of justice could be said to flow from the unqualified reference to the statement as there was ample independent evidence to identify the defendant as the driver of the motor vehicle involved in the incident: See *R. v. Champion*, 2007 ONCJ 319, 2007 CarswellOnt 4515, [2007] O.J. No. 2782, 53 M.V.R. (5th) 52 (Ont. C.J.).

10.3 TRIAL STRATEGY

10.3.1 DOES THE PROSECUTION HAVE A CASE?

- Review the prosecution's anticipated evidence.
    - Are all the essential elements of the offence provable?
    - Are any inferences required?
    - Are those inferences reasonable?
    - Is any of the evidence inadmissible? If so, how does that affect the prosecution's case?

10.3.2 THEORY OF THE CASE

- The prosecutor will adduce evidence and present a "theory" or "story" of what happened. If the story is compelling, then the defence should present a competing "theory of the defence".

- Any question or evidence which neither detracts from your opponent's theory nor advances your theory should be discarded.

- It is risky to attack the adequacy of a police investigation. It may render relevant evidence which the Crown would otherwise not be permitted to adduce. See: *R. v. Mallory*, 2007 ONCA 46, 2007 CarswellOnt 348, [2007] O.J. No. 236, 220 O.A.C. 239, 217 C.C.C. (3d) 266 (Ont. C.A.).

10.3.3 EFFECTIVE PERSUASION

- Present your evidence and examinations in a simple and logical order, to quickly advance your theory of the case. It will be easier for the Justice to follow and remember your evidence.

- In cross-examination, ask only leading questions so as to control the witness' answers.

- In examination-in-chief, use brief directed questions.

  - Get to the point quickly and convincingly — you will project your own competence and advance the believability of your cause.

- It is too late to be discovering evidence.

  - Do not ask a question unless you expect the answer to help.

- There are excellent texts on advocacy, which are both helpful and entertaining.

- Be prepared to make submissions or legal argument at the end of the case which will assist the justice of the peace to find in your favour, e.g., that the prosecution has not proven its case beyond a reasonable doubt because of the inconsistencies in the witnesses' testimony, or that the defendant's evidence is not credible as it fails to meet the *R. v. W. (D.)* test in assessing credibility (see section 10.2.5 on Credibility Evidence in Chapter 10). Concise submissions which are focused and to the point are of great assistance to the court. If there are any cases or decisions you are going to rely on during your submissions, it is helpful to bring extra copies for the other side and the court.

11

SENTENCING

11.1 RANGE OF SENTENCES

11.1.1 UNDER THE CHARGING ACT

- The maximum penalty in the charging Act takes precedence over the maximum penalty in the POA: section 61.
- Some charging Acts have severe penalties. For example:
  - The maximum under section 122 of the *Securities Act*, R.S.O. 1990, c. S.5, amended 2002, for the misrepresentation of securities information is a fine up to $5,000,000, or imprisonment for five years less a day, or both.
  - The maximum under section 116 of the *Consumer Protection Act*, S.O. 2002, Chapter 30, Schedule A, is a fine up to $50,000 ($250,000 for a corporation), or imprisonment for two years less a day, or both.
  - The maximum under section 66(2) of the *Occupational Health and Safety Act*, R.S.O. 1990, c. O.1, for a corporation failing to comply with the Act or regulations, is a fine up to $500,000.

In *R. v. Macrodyne Technologies Inc.* (2003), [2003] O.J. No. 3582, 2003 CarswellOnt 3438 (Ont. C.J.), the corporate defendant pleaded guilty to a charge relating to the death of a worker operating an overhead crane, where the worker was not a competent person as defined in the Act. The defendant was sentenced to a fine of $130,000 to be paid over a period of three years. Although the actual and potential harm was significant, the defendant pleaded guilty, and had attempted to remedy the issues of training.

11.1.2 UNDER THE POA

- If no maximum punishment is set out in the charging Act, the maximum penalty is a $5,000 fine for offences proceeded under Part III: section 61.

- If the offence is proceeded under Part I (certificate of offence), and *regardless* of the maximum penalty in any charging Act,

  - If the defendant was summoned, the maximum penalty is a $500 fine and no imprisonment: section 12(1); and

  - If the defendant was served with an offence notice, the maximum penalty is a $500 fine and no imprisonment, and there are further limits to any results following a conviction: section 12(2).

- For young persons, regardless of the maximum penalty in any charging Act, except for breach of probation (section 75(d)), the maximum penalty is a $1,000 fine (section 101). For offences proceeded under Part I or Part II, the maximum fine is $300 fine, and an absolute discharge is available: section 97.

11.2 OPTIONS IN SENTENCING

11.2.1 REDUCING MINIMUM FINES AND IMPRISONMENT IN EXCEPTIONAL CIRCUMSTANCES

- Only penalties specifically declared as minimums should be regarded as such: section 59(1).

- The court may impose a fine that is less than the prescribed minimum or suspend the sentence where it finds exceptional circumstances exist such that imposing the minimum would be:

  - Unduly oppressive; or

- Otherwise not in the interests of justice: section 59(2).

In *R. v. McComb*, [2004] O.J. No. 4765, 2004 CarswellOnt 4807, 2004 ONCJ 289 (Ont. C.J.), the sentence was suspended where the defendant was convicted of an offence under the *Compulsory Automobile Insurance Act*, which was an absolute liability offence, and the defendant was not trying to avoid paying or having appropriate coverage for his vehicle. Pursuant to section 59(2), it would be inappropriate and not in the interest of justice to fine him.

- The court may impose a fine of not more than $5,000 in lieu of imprisonment where the minimum penalty prescribed includes imprisonment: section 59(3).

- Under section 59(2), there exists a limited degree of flexibility in exceptional circumstances where the minimum fine could be unduly oppressive or otherwise not in the interest of justice. It may well have been in this case that the justice hearing the matter could have exercised some discretion under section 59(2), but he was not given the benefit of exceptional circumstances because the accused was not present to relay the exceptional circumstances to him. Having failed to do so, he cannot be heard now to complain of the imposition of less than the maximum fines that could have been imposed. See *R. v. Mundy*, 2007 ONCJ 449, 2007 CarswellOnt 6599, [2007] O.J. No. 3954 (Ont. C.J.).

Section 59(2) does not create an unfettered discretion. In the absence of exceptional circumstances, it is not sufficient to reduce the minimum fine out of a degree of compassion for the defendant: *R. v. Zhang* (2007), 2007 CarswellOnt 9713 (Ont. C.J.).

11.2.2 TIME TO PAY A FINE

- A fine becomes due and payable 15 days after its imposition: section 66(1).

- The court will ask the defendant if he or she requires an extension of the 15 days in order to pay the fine: section 66(2).

- Where a fine is imposed in the defendant's absence, the clerk of the court will give the defendant:

  - Notice of the fine;

  - Notice of its due date; and

  - Notice of the defendant's right to make a motion for an extension of the time for payment: section 66(5).

- The defendant may, at any time, request an extension or further extension of time for payment of the fine by:

  - Making a motion in the prescribed form [See Appendix C]; and

  - Filing the motion in the office of the court: section 66(6).

- The motion will be determined by a justice. In respect of the motion, the justice has the same powers as the court has under subsections (3) and (4): section 66(6).

- Where the defendant requests an extension of the time for payment of the fine, the court may:

  - Make inquiries of the defendant, on oath or affirmation, as the court deems necessary. The defendant is not be compelled to answer: section 66(3).

  - May order periodic payments be made unless it finds that the request for the extension of time is not made in good faith or that it would likely be used to evade payment: section 66(4). [See Appendix C]

11.2.3 FINE OPTION PROGRAM

- The Lieutenant Governor in Council has regulation making authority over programs permitting the payment of fines by means of credits for work performed: section 67.

- Under this authority, he or she may:

  - Prescribe classes of work and the conditions under which they are to be performed;

- Prescribe a system of credits; and

- Provide for any matter necessary for the effective administration of the program: section 67.

- Any regulation may limit the program's application to any part or parts of Ontario: section 67.

- According to the annotation to Segal and Libman's *The 2005 Annotated Ontario Provincial Offences Act* (Carswell, 2005) at 233:

> The applicable rules and regulations for the Fine Option Program are set out in R.R.O. 1990, Reg. 948, as amended by O. Reg. 500/91, section 1. There are currently three fine option districts: the Regional Municipality of Hamilton-Wentworth, the Regional Municipality of Niagara; and the whole of the Territorial District of Kenora. However, this Schedule of Fine Option districts has been revoked effective April 1, 1994: O. Reg. 925/93, sections 1, 2. There is not as yet a program established by the province to permit the payment of fines by means of credit for work performed as contemplated by section 67. An undertaking to satisfy fine payment by earning credits for work performed shall be in Form 1: R.R.O. 1990, Reg. 948, as amended by O. Reg. 500/91, section 1. An undertaking to satisfy fine payment by earning credits for work performed shall be in Form 2.

11.2.4 CIVIL ENFORCEMENT OF FINES

- Section 68 prescribes the manner in which a fine can be used as a civil judgment for collection, and if the fine is not paid within 90 days, section 69.1 permits the disclosure of the fine to a consumer reporting agency.

11.2.5 DEFAULT OF FINE

- Failure to pay a fine may lead to cancellation of a provincial permit, licence, registration, or other privilege: section 69.

- A defaulting defendant may be brought before the court by way of the justice's issuance of a warrant for the arrest of the defendant or the clerk's issuance of a summons if other methods of collecting the fine have failed: section 69(6), (7).

In *R. v. Mitchell* (2001), 2001 CarswellOnt 3767, 30 M.V.R. (4th) 134 (Ont. S.C.J.), it was held that the defendant could not bring a motion under section 69 for relief from the fines. The Justice of the Peace had no common law or inherent power to take on jurisdiction. If the doctrine of attornment existed at all, it could not be relied on in criminal or provincial prosecutions as a basis for assuming jurisdiction. Section 69 does not contemplate or authorize initiating a motion by the defendant.

11.2.6 COSTS

- Upon conviction, the defendant may have to pay various fees, up to a maximum of $100, which are enforced like a fine: section 60.

- The Provincial Offences Court is restricted in its power to award costs, and does not have jurisdiction to award legal costs. Under section 60, its power is limited to costs in respect of witnesses and costs fixed by regulation (R.R.O. 1990, Reg. 945 as amended).

In *Ontario v. 974649 Ontario Inc.*, 2001 CarswellOnt 4251, 47 C.R. (5th) 316 (sub. nom. R. v. 974649 Ontario Inc.) [2001] 3 S.C.R. 575, 56 O.R. (3d) 359 (headnote only), 2001 CarswellOnt 4252, (sub nom. *R. v. 974649 Ontario Inc.*) [2001] S.C.J. No. 79, (sub nom. *R. v. 974649 Ontario Inc.*) 2001 SCC 81, (sub nom. *R. v. 974649 Ontario Inc.*) 206 D.L.R. (4th) 444, (sub nom. *R. v. 974649 Ontario Inc.*) 159 C.C.C. (3d) 321, (sub nom. *R. v. 974649 Ontario Inc.*) 88 C.R.R. (2d) 189, (sub nom. *R. v. 974649 Ontario Inc.*) 279 N.R. 345, (sub nom. *R. v. 974649 Ontario Inc.*) 154 O.A.C. 345 (S.C.C.), the Supreme Court of Canada concluded that the regulation referred to in section 60(2) is Reg. 945, R.R.O. 1990, which provides for payment of minimum amounts for matters such as fees to cover travel expenses and each day in attendance for witnesses. The word "expenses" used in section 60(2) has the same meaning in section 29(5), and does not include legal fees.

- Section 90 limits the power to award costs to particular procedural breaches.

In *Ontario v. 974649 Ontario Inc.*, 2001 CarswellOnt 4251, 47 C.R. (5th) 316 (sub. nom. *R. v. 974649 Ontario Inc.*) [2001] 3 S.C.R. 575, 56 O.R. (3d) 359 (headnote only), 2001 CarswellOnt 4252, (sub nom. *R. v. 974649 Ontario Inc.*) [2001] S.C.J. No. 79, (sub nom. *R. v. 974649 Ontario Inc.*) 2001 SCC 81, (sub nom. *R. v. 974649 Ontario Inc.*) 206 D.L.R. (4th) 444, (sub nom. *R. v. 974649 Ontario Inc.*) 159 C.C.C. (3d) 321, (sub nom. *R. v. 974649 Ontario Inc.*) 88 C.R.R. (2d) 189, (sub nom. *R. v. 974649 Ontario Inc.*) 279 N.R. 345, (sub nom. *R. v. 974649 Ontario Inc.*) 154 O.A.C. 345 (S.C.C.), costs were awarded on the defendants' disclosure motion which was brought as a result of the Crown's failure to disclose a copy of the

Prosecution Approval Form relating to charges laid under the *Occupational Health and Safety Act*.

In *Ontario (Ministry of Labour) v. Intracorp Developments (Lombard) Inc.* (2002), 2002 CarswellOnt 1134, [2002] O.J. No. 1209 (Ont. S.C.J.), the court held that before legal costs could be awarded under section 90(2), there must be an irregularity or defect in the substance or form of the document compelling the defendant to answer the charges or a variance between the charges set out in the summons and the charge in the information, and the defendant must have been misled by the irregularity, defect or variance. Accordingly, the justice of the peace exceeded his jurisdiction in awarding costs to the defendants where the Crown failed to charge both defendants on one information as such omission did not amount to a defect or irregularity.

11.2.7 SURCHARGE

- Section 60.1 provides for a surcharge if a fine is imposed in respect of a conviction for an offence commenced under Part I or Part III.

- A surcharge is deemed to be a fine for the purpose of enforcing payment: section 60.1(2).

- The surcharge known as the Victim Fine Surcharge consists of a graduated scale of rates, depending on the amount of the fine, and is administered after a fine has been imposed: O. Reg. 161/00.

In *R. v. Henry Heyink Construction Ltd.* (1999), 118 O.A.C. 261, 1999 CarswellOnt 254, [1999] O.J. No. 238 (Ont. C.A.), the Court of Appeal found that it was entirely appropriate for the trial judge in imposing sentence to consider the surcharges and their economic impact in determining the fitness of the sentence. The surcharge is a real life consideration that affects the economic circumstances of the defendant and his or her capacity to pay.

11.2.8 PROBATION

- Where a defendant is convicted of an offence under Part III, the court may suspend sentence and direct the defendant to complete a term of probation with various conditions, having regard to the following factors:

  - o The age, character and background of the defendant;
  - o The nature of the offence; and
  - o The circumstances surrounding its commission: section 72.

- o The probation order contains certain statutory conditions, including that the defendant not commit the same offence or any related or similar offence [See copy of Probation Order in Appendix C].
- o The court may impose a period of probation of up to two years under subsection 72(4).
- o A copy of the probation order must be given to the defendant.
- o A probation order may be imposed after a trial held on an *ex parte* basis: the trial justice has jurisdiction to impose probation in the absence of the defendants: *R. v. Viera*, 2007 ONCJ 496, 2007 CarswellOnt 6959, [2007] O.J. No. 4177 (Ont. C.J.).

A justice of the peace is entitled to impose as a condition of probation that the offender not engage directly or indirectly in the business of environmental consulting, under the authority of s. 72(3)(c) of the *Provincial Offences Act* "to prevent similar unlawful conduct": *R. v. Carter*, 2008 CarswellOnt 5301, 39 C.E.L.R. (3d) 1, 2008 ONCA 630, [2008] O.J. No. 3533 (Ont. C.A.), affirming (2008), 2008 CarswellOnt 4339 (Ont. C.J.), varying (2007), 2007 CarswellOnt 9472 (Ont. C.J.).

In *Ontario (Ministry of Labour) v. Creations by Helen Inc.*, 2007 CarswellOnt 9561, 2007 ONCJ 713, [2007] O.J. No. 5560 (Ont. C.J.), it was held that while s. 72(1)(a) authorizes suspending sentence and imposing probation if the proceedings are commenced by information, where the proceedings were instituted by a certificate of offence, there was no jurisdiction for the justice of the peace to place the defendant on a probation order.

11.2.9 BREACH OF PROBATION

- Breach of probation is punishable under section 75.
- A defendant may breach the statutory conditions of the probation order in one of two ways:
  - Commit the same or similar offence.
  - Commit an offence under a provincial or federal statute that is punishable by imprisonment.
- Once a defendant has breached a condition of the probation order, section 75 provides for two offences relating to breaching a probation order.
  - For the offence of breach of probation, the defendant must be convicted of an offence that constitutes a breach of the probation order, and the time for appeal has elapsed or any appeal filed has been dismissed or abandoned.
  - For the offence of willfully failing to comply with a probation order, the prosecution must prove to the court that the defendant was aware of the probation order and its conditions, and chose to ignore them.
- Upon conviction under section 75, the court may impose a fine of up to $1,000 or imprisonment of not more than 30 days, or both.

11.2.10 IMPRISONMENT

- The only offence for which a youth can be imprisoned is breach of probation, which has a maximum of 30 days (sections 75, 101), and any sentence for the youth shall be served in open custody (section 103).
- Pre-sentence reports for any defendant can be ordered under section 56 and must be ordered for a youth facing a prison term under section 100(2).

- In determining the sentence to be imposed on a person convicted of an offence, the justice may take into account any time spent in custody by the person as a result of the offence: section 58.

- The term of prison shall, unless otherwise directed, commence on the date taken into custody, though the court may order custody to commence up to 30 days after sentencing: section 63.

- Sentences shall be served consecutively, unless otherwise ordered: section 64.

11.3 SUBMISSIONS ON SENTENCE

- The prosecution and defence shall have an opportunity to make submissions as to an appropriate sentence: section 57.

- You, as counsel or agent, should make the submissions and generally your client should remain silent. Anything positive can be said by you, and the risk of your client making matters worse will be greatly reduced.

- However, the justice of the peace may ask the defendant if there is anything he or she wishes to say before sentence is imposed. This is the practice in criminal courts. The defendant may wish to address the court after pleading guilty to make an apology or express remorse for his or her conduct. This can be an effective part of the sentencing process, but the defendant's counsel or agent should discuss this beforehand to ensure that what will be said is appropriate and relevant to the issue of sentencing.

- There have also been some recent cases where the prosecutor has been permitted to tender into evidence a victim impact statement so that the victim's views on sentencing can be communicated to the provincial offences court. See *R. v. Hutchings*, [2004] O.J. No. 3950, 2004 ONCJ 200, 2004 CarswellOnt 3907 (Ont. C.J.); *R. v. Messercola*,

[2005] O.J. No. 126, 2005 ONCJ 6, 2005 CarswellOnt 148, 16 M.V.R. (5th) 82 (Ont. C.J.); *R. v. Robinson*, 2008 CarswellBC 1854, 2008 BCSC 1195, [2008] B.C.J. No. 1691 (B.C. S.C.).

- Consider the following issues in your submissions.
  - General deterrance.
    - How prevalent is the offence in the community?
    - What social interests are at stake?
    - What is the normal range of sentence?
    - What sentence would likely deter others?
  - Specific deterrance.
    - Why did your client commit the offence?
    - Was it done before?
    - What has and can be done to prevent it from happening again?
    - Will the sentence affect his or her dependants, and if so, will it decrease the likelihood of your client repeating the offence?

General deterrence was a key sentencing factor in the case of an aboriginal person who unlawfully hunted moose in partnership with a non-native person contrary to the *Fish and Wildlife Conservation Act*. Each defendant received a fine of at least $5,000, and had their hunting privileges suspended for two years. The illegal hunting had an adverse effect on the local economy, and resulted in an abuse of aboriginal treaty rights. The defendant, who was an aboriginal, committed a breach of trust to his community, and this abuse resulted in tension between the native and non-native communities. See *Ontario (Ministry of Natural Resources) v. Bruyere* (2003), [2003] O.J. No. 5927, 2003 CarswellOnt 6275 (Ont. S.C.J.).

In *R. v. Kang*, 2007 ONCJ 362, 2007 CarswellOnt 5123, [2007] O.J. No. 3085 (Ont. C.J.) Quon J. discussed the use of a pre-sentence report as provided under section 56(1) of the *Provincial Offences Act*. He observed that the purpose of a pre-sentence report is to supply to the court a picture of the offender as a person in society. A probation officer's recommendation for community supervision only means that he is not unsuitable for community supervision: the probation officer, in developing recommendations, does not take into account deterrence and other sentencing objectives that a sentencing court has to consider in finding a fit and suitable sentence for the offender. A pre-sentence report should be confined to portraying the background, family, education, employment record, physical and mental health, associates, social activities, potential, and motivation of the person; its function is not to tell the court what sentence should be imposed.

In an *Occupational Health and Safety Act* case involving two fatalities, the trial judge took account of the impact of the tragic events on the families of the deceased as indicated by his having permitted the widow of one of the deceased workers to read a victim impact statement into the record, even though there is no provision expressly permitting this under the *Provincial Offences Act*: *R. v. Delgant 2000 Ltd.* (2008), 2008 CarswellOnt 1244, [2008] O.J. No. 879 (Ont. S.C.J.).

In *R. v. Sholtens*, 2008 ONCJ 282, 2008 CarswellOnt 3605, [2008] O.J. No. 2444 (Ont. C.J.), the appeal court held that where a justice of the peace on his own motion adjourns a sentencing hearing to another date for the purposes of providing reasons as to why he cannot accept the guilty plea, and gives reasons for judgment without providing the prosecutor or unrepresented defendant a real opportunity of making submissions, the proceedings take on the appearance of a public lecture rather than an adversarial process before an impartial decision maker. A reasonable person, reasonably informed, would conclude that that the justice's decision had been arrived at before all the evidence and submissions had been heard. The justice of the peace was bound to follow the law on point and enter a conviction, through the application of the doctrine of *stare decisis*; there was a decision of a judge of the Ontario Court of Justice sitting as an appeal court, indicating that it was appropriate to register a finding of guilt in the circumstances of the case. *Stare decisis* is the glue that binds the court system in Ontario together, and gives purposes to the different levels of court and functions so as to prevent injustice. For a similar case, see *R. v. Bellefeuille*, 2008 CarswellOnt 6641, 2008 ONCJ 575, [2008] O.J. No. 4494 (Ont. C.J.) where the justice of the peace rejected the defendant's guilty plea and erroneously dismissed the charges, rather than set a trial date which was the proper course where a guilty plea is rejected.

In a sentencing hearing, hearsay evidence that is credible and trustworthy is admissible, unless such evidence is disputed in which event it must be proved by the rules as if in a trial: *R. v. Janes Family Foods Ltd.*, 2008 ONCJ 13, 2008 CarswellOnt 177, 36 C.E.L.R. (3d) 290, [2008] O.J. No. 158 (Ont. C.J.).

The maximum sentence provided for an offence may be appropriate even where the offender is not the worst possible and the offence is not committed in the worst way. If a proper and fit sentence, as determined by the court acting judicially, is at the maximum of the range set by Parliament, then the sentence is fit. The sentencing court must determine the appropriate punishment within the limits established by

Parliament: *R. v. Solowan*, 2008 CarswellBC 2396, 2008 CarswellBC 2397, [2008] S.C.J. No. 55, 2008 SCC 62, 299 D.L.R. (4th) 577, 261 B.C.A.C. 27, 440 W.A.C. 27, 70 M.V.R. (5th) 1, (sub nom. *R. v. S. (K.S.T.)*) 237 C.C.C. (3d) 129, 61 C.R. (6th) 268, 381 N.R. 191, [2008] S.C.J. No. 55 (S.C.C.).

In *R. v. Kronshteyn* (2008), 2008 CarswellOnt 4600 (Ont. C.J.), the court set aside a conviction and ordered a new trial where evidence was placed before the court by the trial agent that he misunderstood the defendant's instructions due to a language barrier, and erroneously entered guilty to a lesser charge.

In *R. v. Fuentes*, 2008 ONCJ 598, 2008 CarswellOnt 7068, [2008] O.J. No. 4677 (Ont. C.J.), it was held that it is the client's right to meet with the person who represents him so there will be no misunderstanding as to what occurs in court. It is mandatory that whomever the licensed paralegal hires meets with the client where a paralegal informs the client that another paralegal will represent the client in court. It is not sufficient for the paralegal to merely tell the other agent what the client wants or said. Where the second paralegal pleaded the client guilty without ever speaking to the client, and a licence suspension was imposed, the conviction could not stand.

12

APPEALS

12.1 RE-OPENING A PART I OR PART II CONVICTION

12.1.1 PART I OFFENCES

- In order for a conviction to be struck out where the defendant was convicted without a hearing
  - The defendant must:
    - Attend at the court office during regular office hours within 15 days of becoming aware of the conviction; and
    - Appear before a justice requesting that the conviction be struck out: section 11(1) [See Record of Re-opening Application in Appendix C].
  - The justice will strike out the conviction if he or she is satisfied by affidavit of the defendant that, through no fault of the defendant [See Affidavit in Support of a Request for Re-opening in Appendix C]:
    - The defendant was unable to appear for a hearing; or
    - A notice or document relating to the offence was not delivered: section 11(1) [See Certificate of Striking Out Conviction in Appendix C].
- The justice will give the defendant and the prosecutor a notice of trial or proceed under section 7 where the justice strikes out the conviction: section 11(2).

- The evidence that is required in support of a re-opening request must be an affidavit of the defendant, and not that of an agent. See *Mississauga (City) v. Saleira* (2002), [2002] O.J. No. 5422, 2002 CarswellOnt 5311 (Ont. S.C.J.).

In a case dealing with the delegation of filing and processing notices of appeals from the province to the municipalities, Wake ACJ held in *Solda v. Brampton (City)*, 2006 ONCJ 246, 35 M.V.R. (5th) 103, 82 O.R. (3d) 312, 2006 CarswellOnt 4197, [2006] O.J. No. 2801 (Ont. C.J.) that a clerk of the court employed by the province, and a clerk of the court employed by the municipality but assigned to perform some appeal duties by virtue of the Memorandum of Understanding between the municipality and the Attorney General, have concurrent jurisdiction to receive notices of appeal.

The 15-day requirement under s. 11(1) began to run when the defendant had actual knowledge of his conviction. In the instant case, the defendant's agent learned of his client's conviction on January 31, 2008 but was unable to contact his client and inform him of it until February 22, 2008. The defendant's re-opening application on March 4, 2008 was therefore within the time limits prescribed by s. 11(1). While the justice of the peace may have rejected the defendant's explanation that he had lost his ticket, and that the agent, who had been contacted before the conviction was entered, could not obtain information regarding the charge until he received the defendant's authorization, there was evidence in the defendant's affidavit, supplemented by what the justice heard from the defendant and the agent, to support the re-opening decision. The reviewing court was not prepared to say that the exercise of discretion was an error of law. There were no exceptional circumstances to justify an awarding of costs: *Thunder Bay (City) v. Kandiah* (2008), 2008 CarswellOnt 2685, [2008] O.J. No. 1863 (Ont. S.C.J.).

A justice of the peace who convicts a defendant under ss. 9 or 9.1 is not precluded from presiding at a subsequent trial if a re-opening has been granted: *Charron v. Ontario (Justice of the Peace)* (2008), 2008 CarswellOnt 3421, (sub nom. *Charron v. Squires*) 91 O.R. (3d) 305, [2008] O.J. No. 2288 (Ont. S.C.J.).

12.1.2 PART II PARKING OFFENCES

- Section 19(1) and (2) is substantially the same rule for reopening parking infraction cases where the defendant was convicted without a hearing.

12.2 APPEAL PROCEDURE

12.2.1 PART I AND PART II APPEALS

For an *adult* defendant:

- The defendant or prosecutor (or Attorney General by way of intervention) may appeal an acquittal, conviction or sentence to the Ontario Court of Justice: section 135(1).

- The appeal shall be heard by a provincial court judge: section 135(1).

For a *youth* defendant:

- The appeal lies to the Ontario Superior Court of Justice, but the procedures and powers of the court shall be the same as for an adult appeal to the Ontario Court of Justice: section 105.

- The notice of appeal shall:

  - Be in the prescribed form; [See Schedule C]

  - Shall state the reasons why the appeal is taken; and

  - Shall be filed with the court within 15 days of the decision: section 135(2).

- The defendant must pay any fine imposed before filing the notice of appeal, unless waived by a judge (section 111), and there is no stay pending appeal, unless a judge so orders (section 112).

- There is no requirement to order transcripts or file a factum.

- The appeal shall be conducted by means of a *review* and the court may "make such inquiries as are necessary to ensure that the issues are fully and effectively defined": section 136. In particular, the court may:

  - Hear and rehear the recorded evidence or any part thereof and may require any party to provide a transcript of the evidence, or any part thereof, or to produce any further exhibit;

  - Receive the evidence of any witness whether or not the witness gave evidence at the trial;

  - Require the justice presiding at the trial to report in writing on any matter specified in the request; or

  - Receive and act upon statements of agreed facts or admissions.

- The appeal court "may affirm, reverse or vary the decision appealed from or where, in the opinion of the court, it is necessary to do so to satisfy the ends of justice, direct a new trial": section 138(1).

- Where a new trial is directed, it will be before a different justice than the one who presided originally, unless the parties consent otherwise: section 138(2).

- In addition, with the consent of the parties, the court may direct that the justice to hear the new trial will be the Provincial Judge hearing the appeal: section 138(2).

- Costs can be awarded: section 138(3).

- With leave, further appeals are to the Court of Appeal for Ontario: section 139.

In *London (City) v. Young*, 2008 CarswellOnt 3091, [2008] O.J. No. 2118, 2008 ONCA 429, 237 O.A.C. 357, 233 C.C.C. (3d) 10, 75 Admin. L.R. (4th) 280, 91 O.R. (3d) 215, 65 M.V.R. (5th) 208 (Ont. C.A.), it was held that no regular avenue of appeal is provided where a proceeding is quashed under s. 9(1) of the *Provincial Offences Act.* If the prosecuting authority or the Attorney General believes a justice has misconstrued what constitutes an error going to the regularity or completeness of the certificate, a prerogative remedy can be sought.

A *Charter* violation was found in a provincial offences appeal case where the trial transcripts took from 15 and one-half months to 27 months to produce. The four appellants had been convicted under Part I Certificate of Offence proceedings. The court ruled that the appellants' fairness of trial rights were compromised due to the delays occasioned in the preparation of the trial transcripts, and resulted in an abuse of process, contrary to s. 7 of the *Charter*. A stay of proceedings was imposed on appeal, and costs were ordered against the prosecutor: *R. v. Ovided*, [2008] O.J. No. 2780, 2008 CarswellOnt 4181, 91 O.R. (3d) 593, 2008 ONCJ 317, 174 C.R.R. (2d) 189 (Ont. C.J.).

The Court of Appeal has jurisdiction to allow an appeal, quash the decision of the provincial judge dismissing the appeal under s. 135 of the *Provincial Offences Act*, as well as the underlying conviction, and to order a new trial. The court's authority for doing this is the result of the combined effect of the definition of "court" in s. 109 and the provisions of s. 138(1). A new trial was necessary to satisfy the ends of justice as the provincial judge treated the hearing for an extension of time as an appeal on the merits, and dismissed the appeal without providing the appellant an opportunity to be heard: *R. v. Baccus*, 2008 CarswellOnt 3726, 2008 ONCA 508, [2008] O.J. No. 2503 (Ont. C.A.).

12.2.2 PART III APPEALS

(a) Procedure and Forum for Appeal

- The defendant or prosecutor or the Attorney General may, by way of intervention, appeal, as to sentence or in order to conduct a defence, from a conviction or dismissal or from a finding as to ability, because of mental disorder, where:
  - The proceeding is commenced by information under Part III; and
    - Where the appeal is from the decision of a justice of the peace, to the Ontario Court of Justice presided over by a provincial judge; or
    - Where the appeal is from the decision of a provincial judge, to the Ontario Superior Court of Justice: section 116(1, 2).
- The appellant will give notice of appeal as is provided for by the rules of court: section 116(3) [See Appendix C].

In a case dealing with the delegation of filing and processing notices of appeals from the province to the municipalities, Wake ACJ held in *Solda v. Brampton (City)*, 2006 ONCJ 246, 35 M.V.R. (5th) 103, 82 O.R. (3d) 312, 2006 CarswellOnt 4197, [2006] O.J. No. 2801 (Ont. C.J.) that a clerk of the court employed by the province, and a clerk of the court employed by the municipality but assigned to perform some appeal duties by virtue of the Memorandum of Understanding between the municipality and the Attorney General, have concurrent jurisdiction to receive notices of appeal.

In a case involving a Crown appeal against a verdict of acquittal where the provincial offences appeal court substituted verdicts of guilt, the Court of Appeal ruled that it was unfair to permit the Crown to raise a new issue on appeal when the defendant had no notice that this was an issue at trial. A Crown appeal is not the time for the prosecution to advance a new theory of liability. As the errors by the appeal judge infected her assessment of the due diligence defence, the Court of Appeal was not convinced that an appeal court would necessarily have reached the same conclusions on liability in the absence of the errors. A re-hearing of the Crown's appeal in the provincial offences appeal court was ordered: *Ontario (Ministry of Labour) v. Modern Niagara Toronto Inc.*, 2008 CarswellOnt 4799, 2008 ONCA 590, 240 O.A.C. 278, 91 O.R. (3d) 774, (sub nom. *R. v. Modern Niagara Toronto Inc.*) 297 D.L.R. (4th) 156, [2008] O.J. No. 3168 (Ont. C.A.).

12.2.3 APPEALING A PROVINCIAL OFFENCE — APPEAL POINTERS

- Either the defendant or prosecutor may bring an appeal to challenge the decision of the trial court — the party launching the appeal is called the appellant; the party responding to the appeal is called the respondent; in rare cases the Crown attorney if not the appellant or respondent may intervene and participate in the appeal, as may other third parties, such as an organization or association affected by the decision under appeal, and where permitted to do so such parties to the appeal are called intervenors.

- There are two streams of appeals under the *Provincial Offences Act*:

  - where the trial proceedings are by certificate of offence under Part I of the Act, or certificate of parking infraction under Part II of the Act, the appeal provisions which govern are the more informal requirements set out under sections 135-139;

- where the trial proceedings are by way of information under Part III of the Act, the appeal provisions which govern are the more formal requirements set out under sections 116-134.

- It is therefore very important to first determine whether the decision being appealed from is in relation to a trial matter under Parts I or II of the *Provincial Offences Act*, or under Part III. Significant differences between the two appeal streams include:

  - Part I and Part II appeals must be filed within 15 days after the decision being appealed from whereas Part III appeals must be filed within 30 days of the decision being appealed from.

  - The forms required to be filed on appeals, such as the Notice of Appeal, are different for the two appeal streams.

  - Part I and Part II appeals are typically heard by a judge of the Ontario Court of Justice whereas Part III appeals are typically heard by a judge of the Ontario Court of Justice if the trial was held before a justice of the peace, but where the trial was held before a judge of the Ontario Court of Justice the appeal court is the Ontario Superior Court of Justice.

  - There are different appeal rules which apply, governing matters such as manner of service of documents: O. Reg. 722/94 for Part I and II appeals, and O. Reg. 723/94 for Part III appeals.

- Further appeals may be brought to the Ontario Court of Appeal, but leave to appeal from a judge of the Court of Appeal is required. There are separate rules which apply to such appeals: O. Reg. 721/94.

- To launch an appeal, the following steps must be followed:
  - Complete a Notice of Appeal in Form 1 under the appropriate appeal rules. Important considerations at this stage include:
    - Is this an appeal against conviction, sentence, or both? The notice of appeal should clearly state this, or the court may decline to allow the appeal to proceed or adjourn it to allow the other side to properly prepare.
    - The basis for the appeal must be stated, e.g., the defendant is appealing the conviction because the justice of the peace entered a conviction which is unreasonable and not supported by the evidence; the prosecutor is appealing the sentence as the fine imposed is not a fit sentence and fails to adequately denounce the defendant's unlawful conduct.
    - It is important for the party bringing the appeal to find out as much information about the trial proceedings as possible, especially where a different party is arguing the appeal than the one who argued the trial — what are grounds for the appeal: did the justice rule evidence admissible or inadmissible that he/she should not have, or did the justice not indicate adequately the basis for finding the defendant guilty, or err in interpreting a legal requirement of the offence or statute? Given the short time periods for bringing the appeal after trial (15 days or 30 days), there will likely not be a copy of the justice's reasons available for review – what was the basis of the conviction or acquittal? Factual information will also be required as to the name of the justice of the peace who heard the trial, date of decision, location of the court and so on.
    - If the appeal is going to involve a question as to the conduct of the parties at trial, e.g., the ground of appeal alleges that the agent did not have authority to plead guilty for the defendant, it is important to contact the party and give him/her an opportunity to provide an

explanation as to what happened to the appeal court, such as by swearing an affidavit and being available for examination before the appeal court.

- Where the appeal is not being brought within the required time frames as set out below, the party seeking to appeal must apply for an extension of time and explain to the appeal court the reasons for the delay, including its intention to appeal in time and the merits of the appeal.

- Serve the Notice of Appeal on the other party within the required time frame (15 days for Part I or II appeals; 30 days for Part III appeals).

- File the Notice of Appeal in the court office where the appeal is to be heard within the required time frame (15 days for Part I or II appeals; 30 days for Part III appeals), including proof of service of the Notice of Appeal where necessary (proof of service may be acknowledged in writing on the Notice of Appeal which is filed in the court, otherwise an affidavit of service will be required).

- Order transcripts of the evidence taken at trial for the appeal, including the reasons for judgment and/or sentence — ordinarily 3 copies are required for the appeal — one for the appellant, one for the respondent and one for the court hearing the appeal. Each respondent is entitled to a transcript of the proceedings. The transcript must be ordered from the court reporter or monitor and there will be a fee charged to the party who is appealing the decision. The fee for the transcript is usually based on the number of pages which are transcribed.

- File a certificate in Form 2 regarding trial transcripts with the clerk of the court indicating that the transcript of the evidence has been ordered for Part III appeals. Although there is no similar transcript requirement for Part I and II appeals, it is often of practical assistance to order a trial transcript so that the parties can review in written form the proceedings in the trial court, and not have to rely on the playing of a tape in the appeal court. A transcript will allow the appeal court to better review the trial proceedings and give the parties more time to argue the appeal instead of having to play the tape. Trial transcripts of Part I or II matters are generally shorter than Part III proceedings, although in some cases, such as where the defendant fails to appear for trial or does not respond to the certificate of offence, there will not be a transcript of these "default" proceedings.

- Serve one copy of the trial transcript on the other side and the court, and keep one copy for the arguing of the appeal.

- File cases and/or written argument in the appeal court where appropriate to do so. Although appeals under Parts I or II are informal in nature, it is helpful to the court and good advocacy to bring to court any decisions or a case book that the party is relying on, e.g., a decision of the court ruling that a defect on the certificate renders the document defective in a case where the certificate in question has a similar defect, or a number of decisions showing that the sentence imposed for a similar offence for similar offenders is greater than the one imposed by the justice in the instant case. Written argument or a factum may be required by the court where the issue is novel or involves a new law or has the potential to impact on other cases.

- Attend the appeal court at the time and date specified for arguing the appeal. Attend the appeal court well in advance of the time set for the hearing, as there will usually be several other appeal cases being argued at that time, or motions for extensions of time to file an appeal, or enter into a fine recognizance on appeal rather than paying the fine. Bail pending appeal may also be granted where a period of imprisonment is imposed. There may also be a number of other lawyers or agents at the appeal court, and a number of prosecutors from different municipalities or agencies.

- Other appeal pointers:

  - Prior to arguing an appeal, attend the appeal court to observe the proceedings and see how matters are argued, e.g., does the appeal judge call on the parties to review the trial transcript or grounds of appeal before launching into argument, or does the appeal judge go right to the argument and question the parties about the grounds for the appeal? Attending the appeal court beforehand will also allow the parties to familiarize themselves with where to go in the court to argue the appeal, observe the judge and other parties.

  - Speak to the other side in advance of the appeal, to introduce yourself and let the other side know that you are ready for the appeal and to present any cases or written materials, as well as to check that the appropriate materials are in the appeal file, such as a copy of the Notice of Appeal and any transcripts. This may also give the appellant an opportunity to ask the respondent what its position is on the appeal — for example, where the appellant is seeking a new trial as he/she did not show up for trial, but wishes to plead guilty to provide an explanation for speeding although at a lesser speed, the prosecutor may consent to the appellant providing an explanation to the appeal court and having the appeal heard and determined at such time, rather than arguing whether a new trial should be granted.

  - The party bringing the appeal generally will have only one opportunity to argue an appeal, as further appeals to the Ontario Court of Appeal and even the Supreme Court of Canada require special grounds of appeal and permission (leave) of the court to do so. The appellant should therefore cast its appeal in its strongest grounds, and remember that the appeal court is to review the proceedings in the court below, and not merely substitute its view of the evidence or the witnesses. As a result, the appellant should be prepared to demonstrate where the trial court made an error by accepting or rejecting the evidence of a witness, or failed to consider a relevant factor, since "a trial is a trial, not a trial run". The appeal court will generally be reluctant to second guess the trial court on findings of fact or credibility, unless they appear not to be supported by the evidence. Where the appellant wishes to argue that the error in the trial court relates to a point of law, such as the interpretation of the essential elements of the offence, it is very helpful to bring decisions of other courts to the appeal court so that other legal authorities are placed before the court for its consideration.

- For the Court of Appeal to grant leave for a further appeal, the legal issue should be of broad public importance. The focus is not on the subject matter of the appeal but on the questions of law to be resolved. For example, the fact that prosecution of securities tipping offences is of public importance is not enough for a leave to be granted. Leave to appeal to the Ontario Court of Appeal will only be granted if the appeal raises questions of law on which the court's guidance is essential in the public interest or for the due administration of justice: *R. v. Rankin*, 2007 ONCA 127, [2007] O.J. No. 719, 2007 CarswellOnt 1045, 221 O.A.C. 184, 216 C.C.C. (3d) 481 (Ont. C.A. [In Chambers]), at para. 30 [ONCA], additional reasons at 2007 CarswellOnt 3698, 2007 ONCA 426, 225 O.A.C. 11, 86 O.R. (3d) 399 (Ont. C.A. [In Chambers]), per Gillese J.A., in chambers.

- If an appellant can show that it was trial counsel and not the appellant who decided that he would not testify at trial, and that the appellant would have testified if he understood that it was his decision, then he will have established a claim of incompetent representation: *R. v. Archer* (2005), 202 C.C.C. (3d) 60, 2005 CarswellOnt 4964, [2005] O.J. No. 4348, 34 C.R. (6th) 271, (sub nom. *R. v. R.W.A.*) 203 O.A.C. 56 (Ont. C.A.), at para. 139 [C.C.C.], followed in *R. v. McKenzie*, 2007 ONCA 470, 2007 CarswellOnt 5294, 228 O.A.C. 182, 51 C.R. (6th) 316 (Ont. C.A.) at paras. 67 & 78 [ONCA].

- Claims of ineffective assistance of counsel at trial based on allegations of inadequate preparation only lead to a miscarriage of justice if it can be shown that the lack of preparation undermined the reliability of the verdict reached at trial: *R. v. Jex*, 2007 ONCA 737, 2007 CarswellOnt 6813, 230 O.A.C. 79 (Ont. C.A.), endorsement.

- See also, Segal and Libman, *The 2007 Annotated Ontario Provincial Offences Act* (Carswell, 2007) at 329, for a checklist based on the rules in R.R.O. 1990, Reg. 196 [re-enacted as O. Reg. 723/94].

In *Hill v. Toronto (City)*, 2007 ONCJ 253, 48 M.V.R. (5th) 55, (sub nom. *Toronto (City) v. Hill*) 221 C.C.C. (3d) 189, 2007 CarswellOnt 3578, [2007] O.J. No. 2232 (Ont. C.J.), it was held that allegations made by a paralegal agent on appeal that a paralegal agent at trial has not acted properly, so as to amount to professional incompetence or to have otherwise contributed to a miscarriage of justice, must be made only after careful consideration. More particularly, such allegations should only be brought forward after the appeal agent has satisfied himself or herself, by means of personal investigations or inquiries, that there is some factual foundation for the allegation, apart from the instructions of the appellant. There must also be afforded to the trial agent a fair opportunity to respond, specifically by providing notice to the trial agent of the allegations being made before the appeal court, and ensuring that a record of this response is placed before the appeal court so that a proper assessment of the allegations may be made by the judge on appeal. Such a procedure or protocol, which places on the paralegal agent on appeal the obligation to investigate and furnish the paralegal trial agent with an opportunity to respond, and thus the appeal court with a proper basis to evaluate such allegations, reflects the need to ensure fairness, openness, and transparency in the provincial offences court, which is so aptly regarded as the "people's court" given the pervasive nature of public welfare/regulatory offences. At the same time, it is in keeping with the new responsibilities of ethical behaviour now mandated by the Law Society of Upper Canada for paralegal practitioners, which includes the required standard of a "competent paralegal", pursuant to the *Paralegal Rules of Conduct*.

A *Charter* violation was found in a provincial offences appeal case where the trial transcripts took from 15 and one-half months to 27 months to produce. The four appellants had been convicted under Part I Certificate of Offence proceedings. The court ruled that the appellants' fairness of trial rights were compromised due to the delays occasioned in the preparation of the trial transcripts, and resulted in an abuse of process, contrary to s. 7 of the *Charter*. A stay of proceedings was imposed on appeal, and costs were ordered against the prosecutor: *R. v. Ovided*, [2008] O.J. No. 2780, 2008 CarswellOnt 4181, 91 O.R. (3d) 593, 2008 ONCJ 317, 174 C.R.R. (2d) 189 (Ont. C.J.).

In *R. v. Kronshteyn* (2008), 2008 CarswellOnt 4600 (Ont. C.J.), the court set aside a conviction and ordered a new trial where evidence was placed before the court by the trial agent that he misunderstood the defendant's instructions due to a language barrier, and erroneously entered guilty to a lesser charge.

To succeed on an incompetence of counsel appeal, there must be a reasonable probability that the verdict would have been different or that the appellant was deprived of a fair trial because of the conduct of counsel: *R. v. Davies*, 2008 CarswellOnt 1673, 2008 ONCA 209, 234 O.A.C. 291 (Ont. C.A.), at para. 37 [ONCA].

In *R. v. Fuentes*, 2008 ONCJ 598, 2008 CarswellOnt 7068, [2008] O.J. No. 4677 (Ont. C.J.), it was held that it is the client's right to meet with the person who represents him so there will be no misunderstanding as to what occurs in court. It is mandatory that whomever the licensed paralegal hires meets with the client where a paralegal informs the client that another paralegal will represent the client in court. It is not sufficient for the paralegal to merely tell the other agent what the client wants or said. Where the second paralegal pleaded the client guilty without ever speaking to the client, and a licence suspension was imposed, the conviction could not stand.

(a) Custody Pending Appeal

- An appealing defendant will remain in custody, if already in custody: section 110.
- A judge may order the defendant's release upon any of the conditions prescribed under subsection 150(2): section 110.

(b) Payment of Fine Pending Appeal

- The defendant must pay in full the fine imposed by the original decision before a notice appeal will be accepted for filing: section 111(1).
- The judge may:
  - Waive the paying of the full fine as presecribed in subsection 111(1) (section 111(2)); and

  - Direct the appellant to enter into a recognizance, to appear on the appeal, in such amount and with or without sureties as the judge deems fits: section 111(2).

(c) Stay Pending Appeal

- The conviction is not stayed by filing of a notice of appeal, unless the judge so orders: section 112.

(d) Attendance and Right to Counsel

- The appellant or respondent may appear and act personally or by counsel: section 118(1).
- The court may impose sentence in the absence of the appellant or respondent: section 118(3).
- Where the appellant or respondent is in custody due to the original decision, he or she is entitled to be present at the hearing of the appeal: section 118(2).

(e) Written Argument

- The appellant or respondent may present his or her case on appeal and argument in writing rather than orally: section 119.
- The court must consider any case or argument when presented in writing: section 119.

(f) Procedural Powers of Appeal Court

- The court may, where it considers it to be in the interest of justice,
  - Order the production of any writing, exhibit or other thing relevant to the appeal (section 117(1)(a));

- Order any witness who would have been a compellable witness at the trial, whether or not he or she was called at the trial, to:

    - Attend and be examined before the court; or

    - Be examined in the manner provided by the rules of court before a judge of the court, or before any officer of the court or justice of the peace or other person appointed by the court for the purpose (section 117(1)(b));

- Admit, as evidence, an examination that is taken under subclause (b)(ii) (section 117(1)(c));

- Receive the evidence, if tendered, of any witness (section 117(1)(d));

- Order that any question arising on the appeal be referred for inquiry and report to a special commissioner appointed by the court, in the manner provided by the rules of court, that:

    - Involves prolonged examination of writings or accounts, or scientific investigation; and

    - Cannot in the opinion of the court conveniently be inquired into before the court (section 117(1)(e));

and

- Act upon the report of a commissioner who is appointed under clause (e) in so far as the court thinks fit to do so (section 117(1)(f)).

- The appellant or the respondent or their counsel are entitled to cross-examine witnesses and, in any inquiry under clause (1)(e), are entitled to be present during the inquiry and to adduce evidence and to be heard: section 117(2).

(g) Decisional Powers on Appeal Against Conviction Or a Finding of Incapacity to Conduct a Defence

- On the hearing of an appeal against conviction or against a finding as to the ability, because of mental disorder, to conduct a defence, the court may order:
  - The appeal allowed where the court is of the opinion that:
    - The finding should be set aside on the ground that it is unreasonable or cannot be supported by the evidence;
    - The judgment of the trial court should be set aside on the ground of a wrong decision on a question of law; or
    - There was a miscarriage of justice, on any ground: section 120(1)(a).
  - The appeal dismissed where:
    - The court is of the opinion that the appellant, while not properly convicted on a count or part of an information, was properly convicted on another count or part of the information;
    - The appeal is not decided in favour of the appellant on any ground mentioned in clause (a); or
    - The court finds that no substantial wrong or miscarriage of justice has occurred, although the court is of the opinion that on any ground mentioned in subclause (a)(ii) the appeal might be decided in favour of the appellant: section 120(1)(b).
- Where the court allows an appeal, it shall:

  - Direct a finding of acquittal to be entered, where the appeal is from a conviction;

  - Order a new trial, where the appeal is from a conviction: section 120(2)(a); or

  - Order a new trial, subject to section 44 (the mental disorder provisions) where the appeal is from a finding as to the ability, because of mental disorder, to conduct a defence: section 120(2)(b).

- Where the court dismisses an appeal, it may substitute the decision that in its opinion should have been made and:

  - Affirm the sentence passed by the trial court; or

  - Impose a sentence that is warranted in law: section 120(3).

(h) Decisional Powers on Appeal Against Acquittal

- Where an appeal is from an acquittal, the court may:

  - Dismiss the appeal; or

  - Allow the appeal, set aside the finding, and:

    - Order a new trial; or

    - Enter a finding of guilt with respect to the offence of which, in its opinion, the accused should have been found guilty, and pass the sentence that is warranted in law: section 121.

(i) Decisional Powers on Appeal Against Sentence

- Where an appeal is against sentence, the court shall consider the fitness of the sentence appealed from and may:

  - Dismiss the appeal; or
  - Vary the sentence within the limits prescribed by law for the offence of which the defendant was convicted: section 122(1). The court may take into account any time spent in custody by the defendant as a result of the offence.
- Where a court varies a sentence, the new sentence has the same force and effect as if it were a sentence passed by the trial court: section 122(2).
- Where one sentence is passed upon a finding of guilt on two or more counts, the sentence is good if any of the counts would have justified the sentence: section 123.

(j) Appeal Based on Defect in Information or Process

- Unless it is shown that objection was taken at the trial and that, in the case of a variance, an adjournment of the trial was refused although the variance had misled the appellant, judgment shall not be given in favour of an appellant based on:
  - Any alleged defect in the substance or form of an information, certificate or process; or
  - Any variance between the information, certificate or process and evidence adduced at trial: section 124(1).
- The court shall make an order curing the defect where an appeal is based on a defect in a conviction or an order: section 124(2).

(k) Additional Powers for Appeal Court

- The court may make any order that justice requires, where it exercises any of the powers conferred by sections 117 to 124: section 125.

Where a plea of guilty is set aside and the Crown has withdrawn other charges in exchange for the guilty plea, the court may rescind the withdrawal by the Crown of the other counts and direct a new trial on all the counts together: *R. v. K. (S.)* (1995), 1995 CarswellOnt 2340, 24 O.R. (3d) 199, 99 C.C.C. (3d) 376, 82 O.A.C. 132, [1995] O.J. No. 1627 (Ont. C.A.); *R. v. Yanover (No. 1)* (1985), 1985 CarswellOnt 1114, 9 O.A.C. 93, 20 C.C.C. (3d) 300 (Ont. C.A.).

Where the defendant argued on appeal that it was improperly named as Deneen Allen & Associates rather than Deneen Allen & Associates Ltd. and that the amendment should not be allowed on appeal, the appeal court granted the amendment on the basis that the amendment could have been made at trial if the misnomer was noticed by the prosecutor, the defendant was aware of the charge, and the amendment would not result in the substitution of one corporate entity for another: *Deneen Allen & Associates v. Barrie (City)*, 2008 CarswellOnt 6043, 2008 ONCJ 488, [2008] O.J. No. 4005 (Ont. C.J.).

It is an error of law for a justice sitting as an appeal court on a provincial offences matter to conclude that he did not have jurisdiction to deal with *Charter* arguments: *R. v. Peric*, 2008 CarswellOnt 7217, 2008 ONCA 827 (Ont. C.A. [In Chambers]), per Weiler J.A. The error of law, however, only requires the Court of Appeal to grant leave to appeal if it would result in a miscarriage of justice and undermine public confidence in the administration of justice.

(l) New Trials

- Where a court orders a new trial, it shall:
  - Be held in the Ontario Court of Justice;
  - Be presided over by a justice other than the justice who tried the defendant in the first instance unless the appeal court directs otherwise: section 126(1).
- Where a court orders a new trial, it may:
  - Make an order for the release of the appellant pending such trial as may be made by a justice under subsection 150(2).
  - The release order may be enforced in the same manner as if it had been made by a justice under that subsection: section 126(2).

(m) Trial *de novo* Before the Appeal Court

- The court may order that the appeal shall be heard by way of a new trial in the appeal court, where, the court, upon the motion of the appellant or respondent, is of the opinion that the interests of justice would be better served by hearing and determining the appeal by holding a new trial in the appeal court, because of the condition of the record of the trial in the trial court or for any other reason: section 127(1).

- For this purpose, this Act applies with necessary modifications in the same manner as to a proceeding in the trial court: section 127(1).

- The appeal court may, for the purpose of hearing and determining an appeal by way of trial *de novo*, permit the evidence of any witness taken before the trial court to be read if that evidence has been authenticated and if:

  - The appellant and respondent consent;

  - The court is satisfied that the attendance of the witness cannot reasonably be obtained; or

  - By reason of the formal nature of the evidence or otherwise the court is satisfied that the opposite party will not be prejudiced: section 127(2).

- Any evidence that is read under the authority of section 127 has the same force and effect as if the witness had given the evidence before the court: section 127(2).

(n) Abandonment or Dismissal of Appeal

- The court may order the appeal dismissed, upon proof that notice of an appeal has been given and that,

  - The appellant has failed to comply with any order made under section 110 or 111 or with the conditions of any recognizance entered into under either of those sections; and

- The appeal has not been proceeded with or has been abandoned: section 128.

(o) Miscellaneous

- Costs can be awarded under section 129.
- With leave, further appeals lie to the Ontario Court of Appeal: section 131.

12.3 REVIEWS TO THE ONTARIO SUPERIOR COURT OF JUSTICE

- Sections 140 through 142 of the POA, sections 1 through 10 of the *Habeas Corpus Act*, R.S.O. 1990 c. H.1, and sections 1 through 11 of the *Judical Review Procedure Act*, R.S.O. 1990, c. J.1, set out the procedures for invoking extraordinary remedies.
- Examples of extraordinary remedies include:
  - *Certiorari*: It is an order to the inferior court to present its record of the proceedings before the Ontario Superior Court of Justice for a review for jurisdictional error(s).

In *Ontario (Ministry of Labour) v. Intracorp Developments (Lombard) Inc.* (2002), 2002 CarswellOnt 1134, [2002] O.J. No. 1209 (Ont. S.C.J.), an application for certiorari was granted where the justice of the peace exceeded his jurisdiction under section 90(2) in awarding costs to the defendants where the Crown brought a motion pursuant to section 38(1) to try the defendants together. Although one of the defendants opposed the motion which was ultimately granted, such omission did not amount to a defect or irregularity as required under section 90.

  - Prohibition: It is an order to the inferior court not to exercise or attempt to exercise a power for which it has no jurisdiction. *For example, where the inferior court pro-*

ceeds under an unconstitutional statute or where the justice is biased.

In *Enbridge Gas Distribution Inc. v. Ontario* (2005), [2005] O.J. No. 688, 2005 CarswellOnt 691 (Ont. S.C.J.), affirmed (2005), 2005 CarswellOnt 7811 (Ont. C.A.), an application for prohibition was refused where the defendant was charged under both the *Technical Standard and Safety Act* and the *Occupational Health and Safety Act* for a fatal gas explosion. The defendant submitted that the two sets of charges duplicated each other, and arose out of the same delict. Prohibition was available to deal with a jurisdictional error, and where there was an objection with the underlying statute, rather than the content of the information.

  - *Mandamus*: It is an order to the inferior court to do that which it is required by law; *for example, where the inferior court declines to exercise its jurisdiction. It is used more by the prosecution.*

  - *Habeas Corpus*: It is an order reviewing the detention or imprisonment of a person.

- Extaordinary remedies are not to be brought unless all appeal routes are exhausted: section 141(3).

- At common law, certiorari and prohibition are discretionary remedies and the superior court should generally decline to grant the remedy where there is an adequate appellate remedy. See *R. v. Arcand* (2004), [2004] O.J. No. 5017, 2004 CarswellOnt 5160, 10 C.E.L.R. (3d) 161, 125 C.R.R. (2d) 144, 193 O.A.C. 16, 192 C.C.C. (3d) 57, 73 O.R. (3d) 758 (Ont. C.A.).

- Intervention by the superior court in the middle of a trial defeats not only the integrity of the trial process, but also the efficacy of the appeal process. See *R. v. Felderhof* (2002), [2002] O.J. No. 4103, 2002 CarswellOnt 5623 (Ont. S.C.J.), additional reasons at (2003), [2003] O.J. No. 393, 2003 CarswellOnt 488 (Ont. S.C.J.), affirmed (2003), 180 C.C.C. (3d) 498, 2003 CarswellOnt 4943, [2003] O.J. No. 4819, 68 O.R. (3d) 481, 10 Admin. L.R. (4th) 229, 235 D.L.R. (4th) 131, 180 O.A.C. 288, 17 C.R. (6th) 20 (Ont. C.A.).

- It is clear that it is only in exceptional circumstances that review of a pre-trial ruling, such as a stay application based on section 11(b) of the *Charter*, by way of *certiorari* would be appropriate. Special and exceptional circumstances would involve a palpable infringement of a constitutional right that has taken place or is clearly threatened. See *R. v. 1353837 Ontario Ltd.* (2005), [2005] O.J. No. 166, 2005 CarswellOnt 163 (Ont. S.C.J.).

In *London (City) v. Young*, 2008 CarswellOnt 3091, [2008] O.J. No. 2118, 2008 ONCA 429, 237 O.A.C. 357, 233 C.C.C. (3d) 10, 75 Admin. L.R. (4th) 280, 91 O.R. (3d) 215, 65 M.V.R. (5th) 208 (Ont. C.A.), it was held that no regular avenue of appeal is provided where a proceeding is quashed under s. 9(1) of the *Provincial Offences Act*. If the prosecuting authority or the Attorney General believes a justice has misconstrued what constitutes an error going to the regularity or completeness of the certificate, a prerogative remedy can be sought.

The public has an interest in the consistent and correct application of *Charter* principles when a justice of the peace acts as trial judge. Where a justice of the peace is a trial judge and there is no other right of appeal under s. 116, *certiorari* should be available to correct errors of law which result in a substantial wrong or miscarriage of justice as set out under s. 141(4). *Certiorari* is not limited to jurisdictional error in these circumstances. The justice of the peace erred in holding that 8 months was an unreasonable period of time to arrange a trial date for careless driving that resulted in a death. The justice of the peace must consider the public interest in having a full trial on the issues when serious charges are laid and an individual has been killed; the failure of the justice to expressly consider this factor amounted to reversible error. There would be a substantial miscarriage of justice as the public interest in having a full trial would not be met if the error was not corrected: *R. v. Smith* (2008), 2008 CarswellOnt 4286, 2008 CarswellOnt 4287, 175 C.R.R. (2d) 13, [2008] O.J. No. 2841 (Ont. S.C.J.).

Extraordinary remedies are discretionary; they do not issue as of right or where no useful purpose would be served by their issuance: *R. v. Alrifai*, 2008 CarswellOnt 4338, [2008] O.J. No. 2870, 64 M.V.R. (5th) 159, (sub nom. *Alrifai v. Ontario*) 235 C.C.C. (3d) 374, 2008 ONCA 564, 242 O.A.C. 88 (Ont. C.A.), affirming (2007), 2007 CarswellOnt 2913, 48 M.V.R. (5th) 144, [2007] O.J. No 1805 (Ont. S.C.J.).

In a recent case involving an administrative process for a "first attendance notice" employed by the City of Brampton, the court ruled that although the justice of the peace quashed the certificate of offence, the entire proceedings were illegal. The certificate of offence was a nullity and the offence notice was illegal as misleading. No substantial wrong or miscarriage of justice therefore resulted by the quashing order: *R. v. Nandalall* (October 14, 2008), Doc. Brampton CV-06-338900 (Ont. S.C.J.).

Where the trial justice erred in quashing the count charging stunt driving in the absence of a defect in the information, the Crown's only recourse was to seek the remedy of *certiorari* and mandamus: *R. v. Saragosa* (2008), 2008 CarswellOnt 7114, [2008] O.J. No. 4848 (Ont. S.C.J.).

In *R. v. Fortese* (September 25, 2008), Ferguson J., [2008] O.J. No. 5159 (Ont. S.C.J.), it was held that a police officer has jurisdiction to lay a charge for an offence committed anywhere in Ontario. There is no provision in the *Provincial Offences Act* that requires a proceeding to be commenced in the county, district or regional municipality where the offence occurred. The place of the offence only becomes relevant if the defendant appears and disputes the charge, in which case the court must consider the possible application of s. 29 governing the venue of the proceeding. However, where the defendant fails to appear for trial, the justice was required to proceed in the defendant's absence and enter a conviction and impose sentence pursuant to s. 9.1. If the court does nothing, when it is required to act, the court commits jurisdictional error.

13

CHECKLISTS

13.1 DEFENDING A PROVINCIAL OFFENCE

- What is the offence charged? How is it worded?
- Is it a *mens rea*, strict liability or absolute liability offence? What must the prosecution prove? (See Chapter 4)
- What evidence is admissible? If some evidence is inadmissible, how does that affect the case? (See section 10.2 "Evidence" and 10.3 "Trial Strategy")
- Are there any *Charter* issues? (See section 5.2 "Constitutional Defences")
- Are there any procedural defences? (See Chapter 5)
- **What is your client's story?**

  The Trial:

  - **It wasn't me.** (prosecution must prove "identity" beyond a reasonable doubt and the defendant can remain silent)
  - **I wasn't there.** (section 3.2.5 "Initial Advice" and the requirement to disclose alibis evidence before trial)
  - **I didn't do it.** (proof of *actus reus*; section 8.6 "Involuntariness Defence", section 8.7 "Causation Defence" and section 7.4 "Parties to an Offence")
  - **I did it, but I didn't mean to.** (proof of intent – section 6.2 as to "state of mind", section 4.1.1 as to "reckless-

ness" and "awareness of the risk", and section 6.5.2 as to the "intoxication" defence)

- **I did it; I was aware of the risk, but I used reasonable care.** (section 6.5.1 "Mistake of Fact" and section 7.2 "Considerations for Reasonable Care")

- **I had to do it.** (section 8.8 "Necessity Defence")

- **I was told by an official that I could do it.** (section 5.6.2 "Officially Induced Error")

- **It was such a trivial incident that the prosecution ought to be stayed.** (section 5.6.4 "de minimus")

Sentencing:

- **Okay, I did it; it wasn't so trivial; I shouldn't have done it, but I've never done it before.** (first time offenders – in some cases, the emphasis is on rehabilitation rather than punishment)

- **I've done it before, but not for a while. (**the "gap principle" in sentencing may apply)

- **I've done it before, consistently and recently, but I've started treatment or corrective measures.** (if the corrective measures will prevent repetition, then specific deterrence may be partially satisfied)

- **I've done it consistently before; I've failed to break the cycle; I'm not taking treatment; but I plead guilty early – I've saved the prosecution the expense of a trial.** (a guilty plea can be a mitigating circumstance on sentencing)

- **I wish to remain silent.**

Appendix A

Provincial Offences Act

R.S.O. 1990, c. P.33, as am. S.O. 1992, c. 20, s. 1(1); 1993, c. 31, s. 1(2), (3), (5), (7), (8), (10), (11), (14), (19), (23), (25); 1994, c. 17, ss. 30, 131; 1994, c. 27, s. 52(6); 1995, c. 6, s. 7; 1998, c. 4, s. 1(1); 2000, c. 26, Sched. A, s. 13(3), (5), items 1, 3-6, (6), items 1, 7, 8; 2002, c. 17, Sched. F, s. 1; 2002, c. 18, Sched. A, s. 15(1)-(3), (5), (6), item 1 [Sched. A, s. 15 not in force at date of publication.]; 2006, c. 19, Sched. B, s. 15(1), (3) [Sched. B, s. 15, conditions not yet satisfied.], Sched. D, s. 18(2); 2006, c. 21, Sched. C, s. 131(1), (2), (6), (9), (11), (16), (18), (19)

Definitions

1. (1) In this Act,

"certificate" means a certificate of offence issued under Part I or a certificate of parking infraction issued under Part II;
"court" means the Ontario Court of Justice;
"judge" means a provincial judge;
"justice" means a provincial judge or a justice of the peace;
"offence" means an offence under an Act of the Legislature or under a regulation or by-law made under the authority of an Act of the Legislature;
"police officer" means a chief of police or other police officer but does not include a special constable or by-law enforcement officer;
"prescribed" means prescribed by the rules of court;
"prosecutor" means the Attorney General or, where the Attorney General does not intervene, means the person who issues a certificate or lays an information and includes an agent acting on behalf of either of them;

2006, c. 21, Sched. C, s. 131(1)

"provincial offences officer" means a police officer or a person designated under subsection (3);
"representative" means, in respect of a proceeding to which this Act applies, a person authorized under the Law Society Act to represent a person in that proceeding;

2006, c. 21, Sched. C, s. 131(2)

"set fine" means the amount of fine set by the Chief Justice of the Ontario Court of Justice for an offence for the purpose of proceedings commenced under Part I or II.

(2) [Repealed 2002, c. 17, Sched. F, s. 1.]

Designation of provincial offences officers

(3) A minister of the Crown may designate in writing any person or class of persons as a provincial offences officer for the purposes of all or any class of offences.

2000, c. 26, Sched. A, s. 13(6), item 1; 2002, c. 17, Sched. F, s. 1; 2002, c. 18, Sched. A, s. 15(6), item 1

Purpose of Act — Interpretation

2. (1) The purpose of this Act is to replace the summary conviction procedure for the prosecution of provincial offences, including the provisions adopted by reference to the *Criminal Code* (Canada), with a procedure that reflects the distinction between provincial offences and criminal offences.

(2) Where, as an aid to the interpretation of provisions of this Act, recourse is had to the judicial interpretation of and practices under corresponding provisions of the *Criminal Code* (Canada), any variation in wording without change in substance shall not, in itself, be construed to intend a change of meaning.

Intention to appear — Notice of trial

5. (1) A defendant who is served with an offence notice may give notice of intention to appear in court for the purpose of entering a plea and having a trial of the matter by so indicating on the offence notice and delivering the notice to the court office specified in it.

(2) Where an offence notice is received under subsection (1), the clerk of the court shall, as soon as is practicable, give notice to the defendant and prosecutor of the time and place of the trial.

1993, c. 31, s. 1(2)

Challenge to officer's evidence — Notifying officer

5.2 (1) A defendant who gives notice of an intention to appear in court for the purpose of entering a plea and having a trial of the matter shall indicate on the notice of intention to appear or offence notice if the defendant intends to challenge the evidence of the provincial offences officer.

(2) If the defendant indicates an intention to challenge the officer's evidence, the clerk of the court shall notify the officer.

S.O. 1993, c. 31, s. 1(3)

Dispute without appearance — Disposition — Hearing — Application of section

6. (1) Where an offence notice is served on a defendant whose address as shown on the certificate of offence is outside the county or district in which the office of the court specified in the notice is situate, and the defendant wishes to dispute the charge but does not wish to attend or be represented at a trial, the defendant may do so by signifying that intention on the offence notice and delivering the offence notice to the office of the court specified in the notice together with a written dispute setting out with reasonable particularity the defendant's dispute and any facts upon which the defendant relies.

(2) Where an offence notice is delivered under subsection (1), a justice shall, in the absence of the defendant, consider the dispute and,

(*a*) where the dispute raises an issue that may constitute a defence, direct a hearing; or

(*b*) where the dispute does not raise an issue that may constitute a defence, convict the defendant and impose the set fine.

(3) Where the justice directs a hearing under subsection (2), the court shall hold the hearing and shall, in the absence of the defendant, consider the evidence

in the light of the issues raised in the dispute, and acquit the defendant or convict the defendant and impose the set fine or such lesser fine as is permitted by law.

(4) This section applies in such part or parts of Ontario as are prescribed by the regulations.

Plea of guilty with representations — Submissions under oath

7. (1) Where an offence notice is served on a defendant who does not wish to dispute the charge but wishes to make submissions as to penalty, including the extension of time for payment, the defendant may attend at the time and place specified in the notice and may appear before a justice sitting in court for the purpose of pleading guilty to the offence and making submissions as to penalty, and the justice may enter a conviction and impose the set fine or such lesser fine as is permitted by law.

(2) The justice may require submissions under subsection (1) to be made under oath, orally or by affidavit.

Payment out of court — Conviction

8. (1) Where an offence notice is served on a defendant who does not wish to dispute the charge, the defendant may sign the plea of guilty on the offence notice and deliver the offence notice and amount of the set fine to the office of the court specified in the notice.

(2) Acceptance by the court office of payment under subsection (1) constitutes a plea of guilty whether or not the plea is signed and endorsement of payment on the certificate of offence constitutes the conviction and imposition of a fine in the amount of the set fine for the offence.

Failure to respond to offence notice — Where conviction without proof of by-law

9. (1) Where at least fifteen days have elapsed after the defendant was served with the offence notice and the offence notice has not been delivered in accordance with section 6 or 8 and a plea of guilty has not been accepted under section 7, the defendant shall be deemed to not wish to dispute the charge and a justice shall examine the certificate of offence and,

(*a*) where the certificate of offence is complete and regular on its face, the justice shall enter a conviction in the defendant's absence and without a hearing and impose the set fine for the offence; or

(*b*) where the certificate of offence is not complete and regular on its face, the justice shall quash the proceeding.

(2) Where a defendant is deemed to not wish to dispute a charge under subsection (1) in respect of an offence under a by-law of a municipality, the justice shall enter a conviction under clause (1)(a) without proof of the by-law that creates the offence if the certificate of offence is complete and regular on its face.

Failure to appear at trial — Examination by justice — Quashing proceeding

9.1 (1) If a defendant who has given notice of an intention to appear fails to appear at the time and place appointed for the hearing, the defendant shall be deemed not to dispute the charge.

(2) If subsection (1) applies, section 54 does not apply, and a justice shall examine the certificate of offence and shall without a hearing enter a conviction in the defendant's absence and impose the set fine for the offence if the certificate is complete and regular on its face.

(3) The justice shall quash the proceeding if he or she is not able to enter a conviction.

1993, c. 31, s. 1(3)

Reopening — If conviction struck out — Trial — Notifying officer — Certificate

11. (1) If a defendant who has been convicted without a hearing attends at the court office during regular office hours within fifteen days of becoming aware of the conviction and appears before a justice requesting that the conviction be struck out, the justice shall strike out the conviction if he or she is satisfied by affidavit of the defendant that, through no fault of the defendant, the defendant was unable to appear for a hearing or a notice or document relating to the offence was not delivered.

(2) If the justice strikes out the conviction, he or she shall give the defendant and the prosecutor a notice of trial or proceed under section 7.

(3) If a notice of trial is given, the defendant shall indicate on the notice of intention to appear or offence notice if the defendant intends to challenge the evidence of the provincial offences officer who completed the certificate of offence.

(4) If the defendant indicates an intention to challenge the officer's evidence, the clerk of the court shall notify the officer.

(5) A justice who strikes out a conviction under subsection (1) shall give the defendant a certificate of the fact in prescribed form.

S.O. 1993, c. 31, s. 1(5)

Payment out of court

16. A defendant who does not wish to dispute the charge may deliver the notice and amount of the set fine to the place shown on the notice.

1992, c. 20, s. 1(1)

Intention to appear — Proceeding commenced — Idem — Notice of trial — Certificate not invalid without by-law number

17. (1) A defendant who is served with a parking infraction notice may give notice of intention to appear in court for the purpose of entering a plea and having a trial of the matter by so indicating on the parking infraction notice and delivering the notice to the place specified in it.

(2) If a defendant gives notice of an intention to appear, a proceeding may be commenced in respect of the charge if it is done within seventy-five days after the day on which the alleged infraction occurred.

(3) The proceeding shall be commenced by filing in the office of the court,

(*a*) the certificate of parking infraction; and

(*b*) if the parking infraction is alleged against the defendant as owner of a vehicle, evidence of the ownership of the vehicle.

(4) As soon as practicable after the proceeding is commenced, the clerk of the court or a person designated by the regulations shall give notice to the defendant and prosecutor of the time and place of the trial.

(5) A certificate of parking infraction issued for an infraction under a by-law of a municipality is not insufficient or irregular by reason only that it does not identify the by-law that creates the offence if the notice of trial given to the defendant identifies the by-law.

1992, c. 20, s. 1(1); 1993, c. 31, s. 1(7), (8)

Failure to respond — Form of notice — Contents of notice

18. (1) The person designated by the regulations may give the defendant a notice of impending conviction if,

(*a*) at least fifteen days and no more than thirty-five days have elapsed since the alleged infraction occurred;

(*b*) the defendant has not paid the fine; and

(*c*) a notice of intention to appear has not been received.

(2)The notice shall be in the form prescribed under section 20.

(3) The notice shall,

(*a*) indicate the set fine for the infraction; and

(*b*) indicate that a conviction will be registered against the defendant unless the defendant pays the set fine or gives notice of an intention to appear in court for the purpose of entering a plea and having a trial of the matter.

1992, c. 20, s. 1(1); 1993, c. 31, s. 1(10), (11)

Challenge to officer's evidence — Notifying officer

18.1.2 (1) A defendant who gives notice of an intention to appear under subsection 17(1), 17.1(3), 18.1(1) or 18.1.1(3) shall indicate on the notice of intention to appear or parking infraction notice if the defendant intends to challenge the evidence of the provincial offences officer who completed the certificate of parking infraction.

(2) If the defendant indicates an intention to challenge the officer's evidence, the clerk of the court or a person designated by the regulations shall notify the officer.

S.O. 1993, c. 31, s. 1(14)

Reopening — If conviction struck out — Trial — Notifying officer

19. (1) If a defendant who has been convicted of a parking infraction without a hearing applies to a justice within fifteen days after becoming aware of the conviction requesting that the conviction be struck out, the justice shall strike out the conviction if he or she is satisfied by affidavit of the defendant or otherwise that, through no fault of the defendant, the defendant was unable to appear for the hearing or the defendant never received any notice or document relating to the parking infraction.

(2) If the justice strikes out the conviction, he or she shall give the defendant and the prosecutor a notice of trial or accept a plea of guilty and impose the set fine.

(3) If a notice of trial is given, the defendant shall indicate on the notice of intention to appear or such form as is prescribed if the defendant intends to challenge the evidence of the provincial offences officer who completed the certificate of parking infraction.

(4) If the defendant indicates an intention to challenge the officer's evidence, the clerk of the court shall notify the officer.

S.O. 1992, c. 20, s. 1; 1993, c. 31, s. 1(19)

Summons before information laid

22. Where a provincial offences officer believes, on reasonable and probable grounds, that an offence has been committed by a person whom the officer finds at or near the place where the offence was committed, he or she may, before an information is laid, serve the person with a summons in the prescribed form.

Counts — Allegation of offence — Reference to statutory provision — Idem — More than one count — Particulars of count — Sufficiency — Idem — Need to negative exception, etc.

25. (1) Each offence charged in an information shall be set out in a separate count.

(2) Each count in an information shall in general apply to a single transaction and shall contain and is sufficient if it contains in substance a statement that the defendant committed an offence therein specified.

(3) Where in a count an offence is identified but the count fails to set out one or more of the essential elements of the offence, a reference to the provision creating or defining the offence shall be deemed to incorporate all the essential elements of the offence.

(4) The statement referred to in subsection (2) may be,
(*a*) in popular language without technical averments or allegations of matters that are not essential to be proved;
(*b*) in the words of the enactment that describes the offence; or
(*c*) in words that are sufficient to give to the defendant notice of the offence with which the defendant is charged.

(5) Any number of counts for any number of offences may be joined in the same information.

(6) A count shall contain sufficient detail of the circumstances of the alleged offence to give to the defendant reasonable information with respect to the act or omission to be proved against the defendant and to identify the transaction referred to.

(7) No count in an information is insufficient by reason of the absence of details where, in the opinion of the court, the count otherwise fulfils the requirements of this section and, without restricting the generality of the foregoing, no count in an information is insufficient by reason only that,
(*a*) it does not name the person affected by the offence or intended or attempted to be affected;
(*b*) it does not name the person who owns or has a special property or interest in property mentioned in the count;
(*c*) it charges an intent in relation to another person without naming or describing the other person;
(*d*) it does not set out any writing that is the subject of the charge;

(*e*) it does not set out the words used where words that are alleged to have been used are the subject of the charge;
(*f*) it does not specify the means by which the alleged offence was committed;
(*g*) it does not name or describe with precision any person, place or thing; or
(*h*) it does not, where the consent of a person, official or authority is required before proceedings may be instituted for an offence, state that the consent has been obtained.

(8) A count is not objectionable for the reason only that,
(*a*) it charges in the alternative several different matters, acts or omissions that are stated in the alternative in an enactment that describes as an offence the matters, acts or omissions charged in the count; or
(*b*) it is double or multifarious.

(9) No exception, exemption, proviso, excuse or qualification prescribed by law is required to be set out or negatived, as the case may be, in an information.

Summons — Service — Service outside Ontario — Service on corporation — Substitutional service — Proof of service

26. (1) A summons issued under section 22 or 24 shall,
(*a*) be directed to the defendant;
(*b*) set out briefly the offence in respect of which the defendant is charged; and
(*c*) require the defendant to attend court at a time and place stated therein and to attend thereafter as required by the court in order to be dealt with according to law.

(2) A summons shall be served by a provincial offences officer by delivering it personally to the person to whom it is directed or if that person cannot conveniently be found, by leaving it for the person at the person's last know or usual place of abode with an inmate thereof who appears to be at least sixteen years of age.

(3) Despite subsection (2), where the person to whom a summons is directed does not reside in Ontario, the summons shall be deemed to have been duly served seven days after it has been sent by registered mail to the person's last known or usual place of abode.

(4) Service of a summons on a corporation may be effected by delivering the summons personally,
(*a*) in the case of a municipal corporation, to the mayor, warden, reeve or other chief officer of the corporation or to the clerk of the corporation; or
(*b*) in the case of any other corporation, to the manager, secretary or other executive officer of the corporation or person apparently in charge of a branch office thereof, or by mailing the summons by registered mail to the corporation at an address held out by the corporation to be its address, in which case the summons shall be deemed to have been duly served seven days after the day of mailing.

(5) A justice, upon motion and upon being satisfied that service cannot be made effectively on a corporation in accordance with subsection (4), may by order authorize another method of service that has a reasonable likelihood of coming to the attention of the corporation.

(6) Service of a summons may be proved by statement under oath or affirmation, written or oral, of the person who made the service.

Dividing counts — Idem

33. (1) A defendant may at any stage of the proceeding make a motion to the court to amend or to divide a count that,

(*a*) charges in the alternative different matters, acts or omissions that are stated in the alternative in the enactment that creates or describes the offence; or

(*b*) is double or multifarious,

on the ground that, as framed, it prejudices the defendant in the defendant's defence.

(2) Upon a motion under subsection (1), where the court is satisfied that the ends of justice so require, it may order that a count be amended or divided into two or more counts, and thereupon a formal commencement may be inserted before each of the counts into which it is divided.

Amendment of information or certificate — Idem — Variances between charge and evidence — Considerations on amendment — Amendment, question of law — Endorsement of order to amend

34. (1) The court may, at any stage of the proceeding, amend the information or certificate as may be necessary if it appears that the information or certificate,

(*a*) fails to state or states defectively anything that is requisite to charge the offence;

(*b*) does not negative an exception that should be negatived; or

(*c*) is in any way defective in substance or in form.

(2) The court may, during the trial, amend the information or certificate as may be necessary if the matters to be alleged in the proposed amendment are disclosed by the evidence taken at the trial.

(3) A variance between the information or certificate and the evidence taken on the trial is not material with respect to,

(*a*) the time when the offence is alleged to have been committed, if it is proved that the information was laid or certificate issued within the prescribed period of limitation; or

(*b*) the place where the subject-matter of the proceeding is alleged to have arisen, except in an issue as to the jurisdiction of the court.

(4) The court shall, in considering whether or not an amendment should be made, consider,

(*a*) the evidence taken on the trial, if any;

(*b*) the circumstances of the case;

(*c*) whether the defendant has been misled or prejudiced in the defendant's defence by a variance, error or omission; and

(*d*) whether, having regard to the merits of the case, the proposed amendment can be made without injustic being done.

(5) The question whether an order to amend an information or certificate should be granted or refused is a question of law.

(6) An order to amend an information or certificate shall be endorsed on the information or certificate as part of the record and the trial shall proceed as if the information or certificate has been originally laid as amended.

Particulars

35. The court may, before or during trial, if it is satisfied that it is necessary for a fair trial, order that a particular, further describing any matter relevant to the proceeding, be furnished to the defendant.

Motion to quash information or certificate — Grounds for quashing

36. (1) An objection to an information or certificate for a defect apparent on its face shall be taken by motion to quash the information or certificate before the defendant has pleaded, and thereafter only by leave of the court.

(2) The court shall not quash an information or certificate unless an amendment or particulars under section 33, 34 or 35 would fail to satisfy the ends of justice.

Joinder of counts or defendants — Separate trials

38. (1) The court may, before trial, where it is satisfied that the ends of justice so require, direct that separate counts, informations or certificates be tried together or that persons who are charged separately be tried together.

(2) The court may, before or during the trial, where it is satisfied that the ends of justice so require, direct that separate counts, informations or certificates be tried separately or that persons who are charged jointly or being tried together be tried separately.

Issuance of summons — Service — Attendance — Remaining in attendance

39. (1) Where a justice is satisfied that a person is able to give material evidence in a proceeding under this Act, the justice may issue a summons requiring the person to attend to give evidence and bring with him or her any writings or things referred to in the summons.

(2) A summons shall be served and the service shall be proved in the same manner as a summons under section 26.

(3) A person who is served with a summons shall attend at the time and place stated in the summons to give evidence and, if required by the summons, shall bring with him or her any writing or other thing that the person has in his or her possession or under his or her control relating to the subject-matter of the proceeding.

(4) A person who is served with a summons shall remain in attendance during the hearing and the hearing as resumed after adjournment from time to time unless the person is excused from attendance by the presiding justice.

Arrest of witness — Idem — Bringing before justice — Release on recognizance — Bringing before judge — Detention — Release on recognizance — Maximum imprisonment — Release when no longer required — Arrest on breach of recognizance — Commission evidence of witness in custody

40. (1) Where a judge is satisfied upon evidence under oath or affirmation, that a person is able to give material evidence that is necessary in a proceeding under this Act and,

(*a*) will not attend if a summon is served; or

(*b*) attempts to serve a summons have been made and have failed because the person is evading service,

the judge may issue a warrant in the prescribed form for the arrest of the person.

(2) Where a person who has been served with a summons to attend to give evidenc in a proceeding does not attend or remain in attendance, the court may, if it is established,

(*a*) that the summons has been served; and

(*b*) that the person is able to give material evidence that is necessary,

issue or cause to be issued a warrant in the prescribed form for the arrest of the person.

(3) The police officer who arrests a person under a warrant isued under subsection (1) or (2) shall immediately take the person before a justice.

(4) Unless the justice is satisfied that it is necessary to detain a person in custody to ensure his or her attendance to give evidence, the justice shall order the person released upon condition that the person enter into a recognizance in such amount and with such sureties, if any, as are reasonably necessary to ensure his or her attendance.

(5) Where a person is not released under subsection (4), the justice of the peace shall cause the person to be brought before a judge within two days of the justice's decision.

(6) Where the judge is satisfied that it is necessary to detain the person in custody to ensure his or her attendance to give evidence, the judge may order that the person be detained in custody to testify at the trial or to have his or her evidence taken by a commissioner under an order made under subsection (11).

(7) Where the judge does not make an order under subsection (6), he or she shall order that the person be released upon condition that the person enter into a recognizance in such amount and with such sureties, if any, as are reasonably necessary to ensure his or her attendance.

(8) A person who is ordered to be detained in custody under subsection (6) or is not released in fact under subsection (7) shall not be detained in custody for a period longer than ten days.

(9) A judge, or the justice presiding at a trial, may at any time order the release of a person in custody under this section where he or she is satisfied that the detention is no longer justified.

(10) Where a person who is bound by a recognizance to attend to give evidence in any proceeding does not attend or remain in attendance, the court may issue a warrant in the prescribed form for the arrest of that person and,

(*a*) where the person is brought directly before the court, subsections (6) and (7) apply; and

(*b*) where the person is not brought directly before the court, subsections (3) to (7) apply.

(11) A judge or the justice presiding at the trial may order that the evidence of a person held in custody under this section be taken by a commissioner under section 43, which applies thereto in the same manner as to a witness who is unable to attend by reason of illness.

Order for person in a prison to attend — Idem — Idem

41. (1) Where a person whose attendance is required in court to stand trial or to give evidence is confined in a prison, and a judge is satisfied, upon evidence under oath or affirmation orally or by affidavit, that the person's attendance is necessary to satisfy the ends of justice, the judge may issue an order in the prescribed form that the person be brought before the court, from day to day, as may be necessary.

(2) An order under subsection (1) shall be addressed to the person who has custody of the prisoner and on receipt thereof that person shall,

(*a*) deliver the prisoner to the police officer or other person who is named in the order to receive the prisoner; or

(*b*) bring the prisoner before the court upon payment of the person's reasonable charges in respect thereof.

(3) An order made under subsection (1) shall direct the manner in which the person shall be kept in custody and returned to the prison from which he or she is brought.

Penalty for failure to attend

42. (1) Every person who, being required by law to attend or remain in attendance at a hearing, fails without lawful excuse to attend or remain in attendance accordingly is guilty of an offence and on conviction is liable to a fine of not more than $2,000, or to imprisonment for a term of not more than thirty days, or to both.

Order for evidence by commission — Admission of commission evidence — Attendance of accused — Application of rules in civil cases

43. (1) Upon the motion of the defendant or prosecutor, a judge or, during trial, the court may by order appoint a commissioner to take the evidence of a witness who is out of Ontario or is not likely to be able to attend the trial by reason of illness or physical disability or for some other good and sufficient cause.

(2) Evidence taken by a commissioner appointed under subsection (1) may be read in evidence in the proceeding if,

(*a*) it is proved by oral evidence or by affidavit that the witness is unable to attend for a reason set out in subsection (1);

(*b*) the transcript of the evidence is signed by the commissioner by or before whom it purports to have been taken; and

(*c*) it is proved to the satisfaction of the court that reasonable notice of the time and place for taking the evidence was given to the other party, and the party had full opportunity to cross-examine the witness.

(3) An order under subsection (1) may make provision to enable the defendant to be present or represented by representative when the evidence is taken, but failure of the defendant to be present or to be represented by representative in accordance with the order does not prevent the reading of the evidence in the proceeding if the evidence has otherwise been taken in accordance with the order and with this section.
2006, c. 21, Sched. C, s. 131(6)

(4) Except as otherwise provided by this section or by the rules of court, the practice and procedure in connection with the appointment of commissioners under

this section, the taking of evidence by commissioners, the certifying and return thereof, and the use of the evidence in the proceeding shall, as far as possible, be the same as those that govern like matters in civil proceedings in the Superior Court of Justice.

S.O. 2000, c. 26, Sched. A, s. 13(5), item 1

Trial of issue as to capacity to conduct defence — Examination — Finding — Application for rehearing as to capacity — Order for Examination — Idem — Limitation on suspension of proceeding

44. (1) Where at any time before a defendant is sentenced a court has reason to believe, based on,

(*a*) the evidence of a legally qualified medical practitioner or, with the consent of the parties, a written report of a legally qualified medical practitioner; or

(*b*) the conduct of the defendant in the courtroom,

that the defendant suffers from mental disorder, the court may,

(*c*) where the justice presiding is a judge, by order suspend the proceeding and direct the trial of the issue as to whether the defendant is, because of mental disorder, unable to conduct his or her defence; or

(*d*) where the justice presiding is a justice of the peace, refer the matter to a judge who may make an order referred to in clause (c).

(2) For the purposes of subsection (1), the court may order the defendant to attend to be examined under subsection (5).

(3) The trial of the issue shall be presided over by a judge and,

(*a*) where the judge finds that the defendant is, because of mental disorder, unable to conduct his or her defence, the judge shall order that the proceeding remain suspended;

(*b*) where the judge finds that the defendant is able to conduct his or her defence, the judge shall order that the suspended proceeding be continued.

(4) At any time within one year after an order is made under subsection (3), either party may, upon seven days notice to the other, make a motion to a judge to rehear the trial of the issue and where upon the rehearing the judge finds that the defendant is able to conduct his or her defence, the judge may order that the suspended proceeding be continued.

(5) For the purpose of subsection (1) or a hearing or rehearing under subsection (3) or (4), the court or judge may order the defendant to attend at such place or before such peron and at or within such time as are specified in the order and submit to an examination for the purpose of determining whether the defendant is, because of mental disorder, unable to conduct his or her defence.

(6) Where the defendant fails or refuses to comply with an order under subsection (5) without reasonable excuse or where the person conducting the examination satisfies a judge that it is necessary to do so, the judge may by warrant direct that the defendant be taken into such custody as is necessary for the purpose of the examination and in any event for not longer than seven days and, where it is necessary to detain the defendant in a place, the place shall be, where practicable, a psychiatric facility.

(7) Where an order is made under subsection (3) and one year has elapsed and no further order is made under subsection (4), no further proceeding shall be taken in respect of the charge or any other charge arising out of the same circumstances.

Taking of plea — Conviction on plea of guilty

45. (1) After being informed of the substance of the information or certificate, the defendant shall be asked whether the defendant pleads guilty or not guilty of the offence charged therein.

(2) Where the defendant pleads guilty, the court may accept the plea and convict the defendant.

Trial on plea of not guilty — Right to defend — Right to examine witnesses — Agreed facts — Defendant not compellable

46. (1) Subject to section 6, where the defendant pleads not guilty, the court shall hold the trial.

(2) The defendant is entitled to make full answer and defence.

(3) The prosecutor or defendant, as the case may be, may examine and cross-examine witnesses.

(4) The court may receive and act upon any facts agreed upon by the defendant and prosecutor without proof of evidence.

(5) Despite section 8 of the *Evidence Act*, the defendant is not a compellable witness for the prosecution.

Burden of proving exception, etc.

47. (3) The burden of proving that an authorization, exception, exemption or qualification prescribed by law operates in favour of the defendant is on the defendant, and the prosecutor is not required, except by way of rebuttal, to prove that the authorization, exception, exemption or qualification does not operate in favour of the defendant, whether or not it is set out in the information.

Adjournments — Early resumption — Adjournment

49. (1) The court may, from time to time, adjourn a trial or hearing but, where the defendant is in custody, an adjournment shall not be for a period longer than eight days without the consent of the defendant.

(2) A trial or hearing that is adjourned for a period may be resumed before the expiration of the period with the consent of the defendant and the prosecutor.

(3) Despite subsection (1), if the trial is being held in respect of a proceeding commenced under Part I or II, the court shall not adjourn the trial for the purpose of having the provincial offences officer who completed the certificate attend to give evidence unless the court is satisfied that the interests of justice require it. S.O. 1993, c. 31, s. 1(23).

Compelling attendance of defendant

51. Although a defendant appears by representative, the court may order the defendant to attend personally, and, where it appears to be necessary to do so, may issue a summons in the prescribed form.

2006, c. 21, Sched. C, s. 131(9)

Excluding public from hearing

52. (2) The court may exclude the public or any member of the public from a hearing where, in the opinion of the court, it is necessary to do so,

(*a*) for the maintenance of order in the courtroom;

(*b*) to protect the reputation of a minor; or

(*c*) to remove an influence that might affect the testimony of a witness.

Failure of prosecutor to appear

53. (1) Where the defendant appears for a hearing and the prosecutor, having had due notice, does not appear, the court may dismiss the charge or may adjourn the hearing to another time upon such terms as it considers proper.

Conviction in the absence of the defendant — Proceeding arising from failure to appear

54. (1) Where a defendant does not appear at the time and place appointed for a hearing and it is proved by the prosecutor, having been given a reasonable opportunity to do so, that a summons was served, a notice of trial was given under Part I or II, an undertaking to appear was given or a recognizance to appear was entered into, as the case may be, or where the defendant does not appear upon the resumption of a hearing that has been adjourned, the court,

(*a*) may proceed to hear and determine the proceeding in the absence of the defendant;

(*b*) may, if it thinks fit, adjourn the hearing and issue a summons to appear or issue a warrant in the prescribed form for the arrest of the defendant; or

(*c*) may, where the defendant does not appear in response to the summons or warrant on the date to which the hearing is adjourned, proceed under clause (*a*) or (*b*).

(2) Where the court proceeds under clause (1)(*a*), no proceeding arising out of the failure of the defendant to appear at the time and place appointed for the hearing or for the resumption of the hearing shall be instituted or if instituted shall be proceeded with, except with the consent of the Attorney General or his or her agent.

Included offences

55. Where the offence as charged includes another offence, the defendant may be convicted of an offence so included that is proved, although the whole offence charged is not proved.

SENTENCING

Pre-sentence report — Service

56. (1) Where a defendant is convicted of an offence in a proceeding commenced by information, the court may direct a probation officer to prepare and file with the court a report in writing relating to the defendant for the purpose of assisting the court in imposing sentence.

(2) Where a report is filed with the court under subsection (1), the clerk of the court shall cause a copy of the report to be provided to the defendant or the defendant's representative and to the prosecutor.

2006, c. 21, Sched. C, s. 131(11)

Proof of previous conviction

57. (4) A certificate setting out with reasonable particularity the finding of guilt or acquittal or conviction and sentence in Canada of a person signed by,

(*a*) the person who made the adjudication; or

(*b*) the clerk of the court where the adjudication was made,

is, upon the court being satisfied that the defendant is the person referred to in the certificate, admissible in evidence and is proof, in the absence of evidence to the contrary, of the facts stated therein without proof of the signature or the official character of the person appearing to have signed the certificate.

Provision for minimum penalty — Relief against minimum fine — Idem, re imprisonment

59. (1) No penalty prescribed for an offence is a minimum penalty unless it is specifically declared to be a minimum.

(2) Although the provision that created the penalty for an offence prescribes a minimum fine, where in the opinion of the court exceptional circumstances exist so that to impose the minimum fine would be unduly oppressive or otherwise not in the interests of justice, the court may impose a fine that is less than the minimum or suspend the sentence.

(3) Where a minimum penalty is prescribed for an offence and the minimum penalty includes imprisonment, the court may, despite the prescribed penalty, impose a fine of not more than $5,000 in lieu of imprisonment.

Fixed costs on conviction — Costs respecting witnesses — Costs collectable as a fine

60. (1) Upon conviction, the defendant is liable to pay to the court an amount by way of costs that is fixed by the regulations.

(2) The court may, in its discretion, order costs towards fees and expenses reasonably incurred by or on behalf of witnesses in amounts not exceeding the maximum fixed by the regulations, to be paid,

(*a*) to the court or prosecutor by the defendant; or

(*b*) to the defendant by the person who laid the information or issued the certificate, as the case may be,

but where the proceeding is commenced by means of a certificate, the total of such costs shall not exceed $100.

(3) Costs payable under this section shall be deemed to be a fine for the purpose of enforcing payment.

Note: Reproduced from Segal and Libman, The 2007 Annotated Ontario Provincial Offences Act, s. 60.

The defendant is liable to pay court costs upon conviction, the amount of which is fixed by regulations: subsection 60(1). These costs are set out in R.R.O. 1990, Reg. 945, as amended by O. Reg. 678/92, section 1; 501/93, section 1; 555/93, section 1; 493/94; 240/98; 461/05:

1.	For service of offence notice or summons	5.00
2.	Upon conviction under section 9 of the Act	5.00
3.	Upon conviction under section 9.1 of the Act	10.00

4. Upon conviction under section 18 of the Act, as it read on August 31, 1993 .... 3.75
5. Upon conviction under subsection 18.2(6) of the Act 16.00
6. Upon conviction under section 18.4 of the Act 12.75
7. Upon conviction under subsection 54(1) of the Act 30.00
8. For service of a parking infraction notice issued other than under a municipal by-law 3.75

Pursuant to subsection 60(2), the court has the discretion to order costs to either the court, prosecutor or defendant in respect of witness' fees and expenses. This provision does not purport to authorize the payment of *legal costs* of the party. Where the proceeding is commenced by a certificate under Parts I or II, the costs shall not exceed $100 in total. These costs are set out in R.R.O. 1995, Reg. 945, section 2, as amended by O. Reg. 678/92, section 1:

> 2. Costs may be awarded under subsection 60(2) of the Act for the items and to a maximum of the amounts following:
>
> 1. Fee for each witness for each day necessarily in attendance when trial scheduled 6.00
>
> 2. Travel expenses for each witness,
>   i. where witness resides in place where trial held 2.50
>   ii. where witness does not reside in place where trial held, a kilometre allowance as set out in Revised Regulation 11 of the Revised Regulations of Ontario, 1990 entitled "Kilometre Allowances".

Kilometre allowances are set out in R.R.O. Reg. 11. The allowance for each kilometre travelled in northern Ontario is 30.5 cents and in southern Ontario 30 cents: section 1. The dividing line between northern Ontario and southern Ontario is contained in section 2.

Surcharge — Collection — Priorities — Part X agreements — Special purpose account — Same — Regulations

60.1(1) If a person is convicted of an offence in a proceeding commenced under Part I or III and a fine is imposed in respect of that offence, a surcharge is payable by that person in the amount determined by regulations made under this Act.

(2) The surcharge shall be deemed to be a fine for the purpose of enforcing payment.

(3) Any payments made by a defendant shall be credited towards payment of the fine until it is fully paid and then towards payment of the surcharge.

(3.1) When an agreement made under Part X applies to a fine, payments made by the defendant shall first be credited towards payment of the surcharge, not as described in subsection (3).

(4) Surcharges paid into the Consolidated Revenue Fund shall be credited to the victims' justice fund account and shall be deemed to be money received by the Crown for a special purpose.

(4.1) Subsection (4) also applies to payments received under clause 165(5)(*a*).

(5) [Repealed 1995, c. 6, s. 7(2).]

(6) [Repealed 1995, c. 6, s. 7(2).]

(7) The Lieutenant Governor in Council may make regulations,
(*a*) prescribing the amount of the surcharges or the method by which they are to be calculated;
(*b*) [Repealed 1995, c. 6, s. 7(2).]
(*c*) exempting any offence or class of offence from the application of subsection (1).

(8) [Repealed 1995, c. 6, s. 7(2).] S.O. 1994, c. 17, s. 30; 1995, c. 6, s. 7(1); 1998, c. 4, s. 1(1)

General penalty

61. Except where otherwise expressly provided by law, every person who is convicted of an offence is liable to a fine of not more than $5,000.

When fine due — Extension of time for payment of a fine — Inquiries — Granting of extension — Notice where convicted in the absence of the defendant — Further motion for extension

66. (1) A fine becomes due and payable fifteen days after its imposition.

(2) Where the court imposes a fine, the court shall ask the defendant if the defendant wishes an extension of the time for payment of the fine.

(3) Where the defendant requests an extension of the time for payment of the fine, the court may make such inquiries, on oath or affirmation or otherwise, of and concerning the defendant as the court considers desirable, but the defendant shall not be compelled to answer.

(4) Unless the court finds that the request for extension of time is not made in good faith or that the extension would likely be used to evade payment, the court shall extend the time for payment by ordering periodic payments or otherwise.

(5) Where a fine is imposed in the absence of the defendant, the clerk of the court shall give the defendant notice of the fine and its due date and of the defendant's right to make a motion for an extension of the time for paymnt under subsection (6).

(6) The defendant may, at any time by motion in the prescribed form filed in the office of the court, request an extension or further extension of time for payment of a fine and the motion shall be determined by a justice and the justice has the same powers in respect of the motion as the court has under subsections (3) and (4).

Regulation for work credits for fines

67. The Lieutenant Governor in Council may make regulations establishing a program to permit the payment of fines by means of credits for work performed, and, for the purpose and without restricting the generality of the foregoing may,
(*a*) prescribe classes of work and the conditions under which they are to be performed;
(*b*) prescribe a system of credits;
(*c*) provide for any matter necessary for the effective administration of the program,
and any regulation may limit its application to any part or parts of Ontario.

Civil enforcement of fines — Limitation — Certificate of discharge — Costs of enforcement — More than one fine

68. (1) When the payment of a fine is in default, the clerk of the court may complete a certificate in the prescribed form as to the imposition of the fine and the amount remaining unpaid and file the certificate in a court of competent jurisdiction and upon filing, the certificate shall be deemed to be an order or judgment of that court for the purposes of enforcement.

(2) A certificate shall not be filed under subsection (1) after two years after the default in respect of which it is issued.

(3) Where a certificate has been filed under subsection (1) and the fine is fully paid, the clerk shall file a certificate of payment upon which the certificate of default is discharged and, where a writ of execution has been filed with the sheriff, the clerk shall file a certificate of payment with the sheriff, upon which the writ is cancelled.

(4) Costs incurred in enforcing the deemed court order or judgment shall be added to the order or judgment and form part of it.

(5) The clerk may complete and file one certificate under this section in respect of two or more fines imposed on the same person.

S.O. 1993, c. 31, s. 1(25); 1994, c. 27, s. 52(6)

Disclosure to consumer reporting agency — Same

69.1(1) When a fine has been in default for at least 90 days, the Ministry of the Attorney General may disclose to a consumer reporting agency the name of the defaulter, the amount of the fine and the date the fine went into default.

(2) When a fine disclosed to a consumer reporting agency has been paid in full, the Ministry of the Attorney General shall inform the agency of this fact as soon as possible after payment.

S.O. 1994, c. 17, s. 131

Breach of probation order

75. Where a defendant who is bound by a probation order is convicted of an offence constituting a breach of condition of the order and,

(*a*) the time within which the defendant may appeal or make a motion for leave to appeal against that conviction has expired and the defendant has not taken an appeal or made a motion for leave to appeal;

(*b*) the defendant has taken an appeal or made a motion for leave to appeal against the conviction and the appeal or motion for leave has been dismissed or abandoned; or

(*c*) the defendant has given written notice to the court that convicted the defendant that the defendant elects not to appeal,

or where the defendant otherwise wilfully fails or refuses to comply with the order, the defendant is guilty of an offence and upon conviction the court may,

(*d*) impose a fine of not more than $1,000 or imprisonment for a term of not more than thirty days, or both, and in lieu of or in addition to the penalty, continue the probation order with such changes or additions and for such extended term, not exceeding an additional year, as the court considers reasonable; or (*e*) where the justice presiding is the justice who made the original order, in lieu of imposing the penalty under clause (*d*), revoke the probation order and impose the sentence the passing of which was suspended upon the making of the probation order.

PART V

GENERAL PROVISIONS

Limitation — Extension

76. (1) A proceeding shall not be commenced after the expiration of any limitation period prescribed by or under any Act for the offence or, where no limitation period is prescribed, after six months after the date on which the offence was, or is alleged to have been, committed.

(2) A limitation period may be extended by a justice with the consent of the defendant.

Common law defences

80. Every rule and principle of the common law that tenders any circumstance a justification or excuse for an act or a defence to a charge continues in force and applies in respect of offences, except in so far as they are altered by or inconsistent with this or any other Act.

Ignorance of the law

81. Ignorance of the law by a person who commits an offence is not an excuse for committing the offence.

Irregularities in form — Adjournment to meet irregularities

90. (1) The validity of any proceeding is not affected by,

(*a*) any irregularity or defect in the substance or form of the summons, warrant, offence notice, parking infraction notice, undertaking to appear or recognizance; or

(*b*) any variance between the charge set out in the summons, warrant, parking infraction notice, offence notice, undertaking to appear or recognizance and the charge set out in the information or certificate.

(2) Where it appears to the court that the defendant has been misled by any irregularity, defect or variance mentioned in subsection (1), the court may adjourn the hearing and may make such order as the court considers appropriate, including an order under section 60 for the payment of costs.

Offence notice not to be used

95. A proceeding commenced against a young person by certificate of offence shall not be initiated by an offence notice under clause 3(2)(a).

Notice to parent — Where no notice given — Saving

96. (1) Where a summons is served upon a young person or a young person is released on a recognizance under this Act, the provincial offences officer, in the case of a summons, or the officer in charge, in the case of a recognizance, shall as soon as practicable give notice to a parent of the young person by delivering a copy of the summons or recognizance to the parent.

(2) Where notice has not been given under subsection (1) and no person to whom notice could have been given appears with the young person, the court may,

(*a*) adjourn the hearing to another time to permit notice to be given; or

(*b*) dispense with notice.

(3) Failure to give notice to a parent under subsection (1) does not in itself invalidate the proceeding against the young person.

Young person to be present at trial — Court may permit absence — Application of ss. 42, 54 — Failure of young person to appear — Compelling young person's attendance

98. (1) Subject to subsection 52(1) and subsection (2) of this section, a young person shall be present in court during the whole of his or her trial.

(2) The court may permit a young person to be absent during the whole or any part of his or her trial, on such conditions as the court considers proper.

(3) Sections 42 and 54 do not apply to a young person who is a defendant.

(4) Where a young person who is a defendant does not appear at the time and place appointed for a hearing and it is proved by the prosecutor, having been given a reasonable opportunity to do so, that a summons was served, an undertaking to appear was given or a recognizance to appear was entered into, as the case may be, or where the young person does not appear upon the resumption of a hearing that has been adjourned, the court may adjourn the hearing and issue a summons to appear or issue a warrant in the prescribed form for the arrest of the young person.

(5) Where a young person does not attend personally in response to a summons issued under section 51 and it is proved by the prosecutor, having been given a reasonable opportunity to do so, that the summons was served, the court may adjourn the hearing and issue a further summons or issue a warrant in the prescribed form for the arrest of the young person.

Pre-sentence report mandatory where imprisonment considered

100. (2) Where a young person who is bound by a probation order is convicted of an offence under section 75 and the court is considering imposing a sentence of imprisonment, the court shall direct a probation officer to prepare and file with the court a report in writing relating to the defendant for the purpose of assisting the court in imposing sentence, and the clerk of the court shall cause a copy of the report to be provided to the defendant or his or her representative and to the prosecutor.

2006, c. 21, Sched. C, s. 131(16)

S. 149 does not apply — Release after arrest by officer — Release by officer in charge — Notice to parent — ss. 150, 151 apply — Place of custody — Idem

107. (1) Section 149 does not apply to a young person who has been arrested.

(2) Where a police officer acting under a warrant or other power of arrest arrests a young person, the police officer shall, as soon as is practicable, release the

young person from custody unconditionally or after serving him or her with a summons unless the officer has reasonable and probable grounds to believe that it is necessary in the public interest for the young person to be detained in order to,

(*a*) establish the young person's identity; or

(*b*) prevent the continuation or repetition of an offence that constitutes a serious danger to the young person or property of another.

(3) Where a young person is not released from custody under subsection (2), the police officer shall deliver the young person to the officer in charge who shall, where in his or her opinion the conditions set out in clause (2)(*a*) or (*b*) do not or no longer exist, release the young person,

(*a*) unconditionally;

(*b*) upon serving the young person with a summons; or

(*c*) upon the young person entering into a recognizance in the prescribed form without sureties conditioned for his or her appearance in court.

(4) Where the officer in charge does not release the young person under subsection (3), the officer in charge shall as soon as possible notify a parent of the young person by advising the parent, orally or in writing, of the young person's arrest, the reason for the arrest and the place of detention.

(5) Sections 150 and 151 apply with necessary modifications to the release of a young person from custody under this section.

(6) No young person who is detained under section 150 shall be detained in any part of a place in which an adult who has been charged with or convicted of an offence is detained unless a justice so authorizes, on being satisfied that,

(*a*) the young person cannot, having regard to the young person's own safety or the safety of others, be detained in a place of temporary detention for young persons; or

(*b*) no place of temporary detention for young persons is available within a reasonable distance.

(7) Wherever practicable, a young person who is detained in custody shall be detained in a place of temporary detention designated under the *Youth Criminal Justice Act* (Canada).

S.O. 2006, c. 19, Sched. D, s. 18(2)

Custody pending appeal

110. A defendant who appeals shall, if in custody, remain in custody, but a judge may order his or her release upon any of the conditions set out in subsection 150(2).

Payment of fine before appeal — Exception with recognizance

111. (1) A notice of appeal by a defendant shall not be accepted for filing if the defendant has not paid in full the fine imposed by the decision appealed from.

(2) A judge may waive compliance with subsection (1) and order that the appellant enter into a recognizance to appear on the appeal, and the recognizance shall be in such amount, with or without sureties, as the judge directs.

APPEALS UNDER PART III

Appeal — Appeal court — Notice of appeal

116. (1) Where a proceeding is commenced by information under Part III, the defendant or the prosecutor or the Attorney General by way of intervention may appeal from a conviction or dismissal or from a finding as to ability, because of mental disorder, to conduct a defence or as to sentence.

(2) An appeal under subsection (1) shall be,
(*a*) where the appeal is from the decision of a justice of the peace, to the Ontario Court of Justice presided over by a provincial judge; or
(*b*) where the appeal is from the decision of a provincial judge, to the Superior Court of Justice.

(3) The appellant shall give notice of appeal in such manner and within such period as is provided by the rules of court.

S.O. 2000, c. 26, Sched. A, s. 13(5), item 3, (6), item 7

Powers of court — Rights of parties

117. (1) The court may, where it considers it to be in the interests of justice,
(*a*) order the production of any writing, exhibit or other thing relevant to the appeal;
(*b*) order any witness who would have been a compellable witness at the trial, whether or not he or she was called at the trial,
(i) to attend and be examined before the court, or
(ii) to be examined in the manner provided by the rules of court before a judge of the court, or before any officer of the court or justice of the peace or other person appointed by the court for the purpose;
(*c*) admit, as evidence, an examination that is taken under subclause (*b*)(ii);
(*d*) receive the evidence, if tendered, of any witness;
(*e*) order that any question arising on the appeal that,
(i) involves prolonged examination of writings or accounts, or scientific investigation, and
(ii) cannot in the opinion of the court conveniently be inquired into before the court,
be referred for inquiry and report, in the manner provided by the rules of court, to a special commissioner appointed by the court; and
(*f*) act upon the report of a commissioner who is appointed under clause (e) in so far as the court thinks fit to do so.

(2) Where the court exercises a power under this section, the parties or their representatives are entitled to examine or cross-examine witnesses and, in an inquiry under clause (1)(e), are entitled to be present during the inquiry and to adduce evidence and to be heard.

2006, c. 21, Sched. C, s. 131(18)

Right to representation — Attendance while in custody — Sentencing in absence

118. (1) An appellant or respondent may appear and act personally or by representative.

2006, c. 21, Sched. C, s. 131(19)

(2) An appellant or respondent who is in custody as a result of the decision appealed from is entitled to be present at the hearing of the appeal.

(3) The power of a court to impose sentence may be exercised although the appellant or respondent is not present.

Written argument

119. An appellant or respondent may present the case on appeal and argument in writing instead of orally, and the court shall consider any case or argument so presented.

Powers on appeal against conviction — Idem — Idem

120. (1) On the hearing of an appeal against a conviction or against a finding as to the ability, because of mental disorder, to conduct a defence, the court by order,

(*a*) may allow the appeal where it is of the opinion that,

(i) the finding should be set aside on the ground that it is unreasonable or cannot be supported by the evidence,

(ii) the judgment of the trial court should be set aside on the ground of a wrong decision on a question of law, or

(iii) on any ground, there was a miscarriage of justice; or

(*b*) may dismiss the appeal where,

(i) the court is of the opinion that the appellant, although the appellant was not properly convicted on a count or part of an information, was properly convicted on another count or part of the information,

(ii) the appeal is not decided in favour of the appellant on any ground mentioned in clause (*a*), or

(iii) although the court is of the opinion that on any ground mentioned in subclause (*a*)(ii) the appeal might be decided in favour of the appellant, it is of the opinion that no substantial wrong or miscarriage of justice has occurred.

(2) Where the court allows an appeal under clause (1)(*a*), it shall,

(*a*) where the appeal is from a conviction,

(i) direct a finding of acquittal to be entered, or

(ii) order a new trial; or

(*b*) where the appeal is from a finding as to the ability, because of mental disorder, to conduct a defence, order a new trial, subject to section 44.

(3) Where the court dismisses an appeal under clause (1)(*b*), it may substitute the decision that in its opinion should have been made and affirm the sentence passed by the trial court or impose a sentence that is warranted in law.

Powers on appeal against acquittal

121. Where an appeal is from an acquittal, the court may by order,

(*a*) dismiss the appeal; or

(*b*) allow the appeal, set aside the finding and,

(i) order a new trial, or

(ii) enter a finding of guilt with respect to the offence of which, in its opinion, the person who has been accused of the offence should have been found guilty, and pass a sentence that is warranted in law.

Appeal against sentence — Variance of sentence

122. (1) Where an appeal is taken against sentence, the court shall consider the fitness of the sentence appealed from and may, upon such evidence, if any, as it thinks fit to require or receive, by order,

(*a*) dismiss the appeal; or

(*b*) vary the sentence within the limits prescribed by law for the offence of which the defendant was convicted,

and, in making any order under clause (*b*), the court may take into account any time spent in custody by the defendant as a result of the offence.

(2) A judgment of a court that varies a sentence has the same force and effect as if it were a sentence passed by the trial court.

One sentence on more than one count

123. Where one sentence is passed upon a finding of guilt on two or more counts, the sentence is good if any of the counts would have justified the sentence.

Appeal based on defect in information or process — Idem

124. (1) Judgment shall not be given in favour of an appellant based on any alleged defect in the substance or form of an information, certificate or process of any variance between the information, certificate or process and the evidence adduced at trial unless it is shown that objection was taken at the trial and that, in the case of a variance, an adjournment of the trial was refused although the variance has misled the appellant.

(2) Where an appeal is based on a defect in a conviction or an order, judgment shall not be given in favour of the appellant, but the court shall make an order curing the defect.

Additional orders

125. Where a court exercises any of the powers conferred by sections 117 to 124, it may make any order, in addition, that justice requires.

New trial — Order for release

126.(1) Where a court orders a new trial, it shall be held in the Ontario Court of Justice presided over by a justice other than the justice who tried the defendant in the first instance unless the appeal court directs that the new trial be held before the justice who tried the defendant in the first instance.

(2) Where a court orders a new trial, it may make such order for the release or detention of the appellant pending such trial as may be made by a justice under subsection 150(2) and the order may be enforced in the same manner as if it had been made by a justice under that subsection.

S.O. 2000, c. 26, Sched. A, s.13(6), item 8

Appeal by way of new trial — Evidence

127. (1) Where, because of the condition of the record of the trial in the trial court or for any other reason, the court, upon the motion of the appellant or respondent, is of the opinion that the interests of justice would be better served by hearing and determining the appeal by holding a new trial in the court, the court may order that the appeal shall be heard by way of a new trial in the court and for this purpose this Act applies with necessary modifications in the same manner as to a proceeding in the trial court.

(2) The court may, for the purpose of hearing and determining an appeal under subsection (1), permit the evidence of any witness taken before the trial court to be read if that evidence has been authenticated and if,

(*a*) the appellant and respondent consent;

(*b*) the court is satisfied that the attendance of the witness cannot reasonably be obtained; or

(*c*) by reason of the formal nature of the evidence or otherwise the court is satisfied that the opposite party will not be prejudiced,

and any evidence that is read under the authority of this subsection has the same force and effect as if the witness had given the evidence before the court.

Dismissal or abandonment

128. The court may, upon proof that notice of an appeal has been given and that,

(*a*) the appellant has failed to comply with any order made under section 110 or 111 or with the conditions of any recognizance entered into under either of those sections; or

(*b*) the appeal has not been proceeded with or has been abandoned,

order that the appeal be dismissed.

REVIEW

Application for relief in nature of mandamus, prohibitions, certiorari — Notice of application — Appeal

140. (1) On application, the Superior Court of Justice may by order grant any relief in respect of matters arising under this Act that the applicant would be entitled to in an application for an order in the nature of mandamus, prohibition or certiorari.

(2) Notice of an application under this section shall be served on,

(*a*) the person whose act or omission gives rise to the application;

(*b*) any person who is a party to a proceeding that gives rise to the application; and

(*c*) the Attorney General.

(3) An appeal lies to the Court of Appeal from an order made under this section.

S.O. 2000, c. 26, Sched. A, s. 13(5), item 4

Notice re certiorari — Filing material — Motion to Continue Proceeding — Where appeal available — Substantial wrong — Order for immunity from civil liability

141. (1) A notice under section 140 in respect of an application for relief in the nature of certiorari shall be given at least seven days and not more than ten days before the date fixed for the hearing of the application and the notice shall be served within thirty days after the occurrence of the act sought to be quashed.

(2) Where a notice referred to in subsection (1) is served on the person making the decision, order or warrant or holding the proceeding giving rise to the application,

such person shall forthwith file with the Superior Court of Justice for use on the application, all material concerning the subject-matter of the application.

(2.1) Where a notice referred to in subsection (1) is served in respect of an application, a person who is entitled to notice of the application under subsection 140(2) may make a motion to the Superior Court of Justice for an order that a trial in the proceeding giving rise to the application may continue despite the application and the Court may make the order if it is satisfied that it is in the interests of justice to do so.

(3) No application shall be made to quash a conviction, order or ruling from which an appeal is provided by this Act, whether subject to leave or otherwise.

(4) On an application for relief in the nature of certiorari, the Superior Court of Justice shall not grant relief unless the court finds that a substantial wrong or miscarriage of justice has occurred, and the court may amend or validate any decision already made, with effect from such time and on such terms as the court considers proper.

(5) Where an application is made to quash a decision, order, warrant or proceeding made or held by a justice on the ground that the justice exceeded his or her jurisdiction, the Superior Court of Justice may, in quashing the decision, order, warrant or proceeding, order that no civil proceeding shall be taken against the justice or against any officer who acted under the decision, order or warrant or in the proceeding or under any warrant issued to enforce it.

S.O. 2000, c. 26, Sched. A, s. 13(3), (5), item 5

Application for habeas corpus — Procedure on application for relief in nature of habeas corpus — Idem — Idem — Costs

142. (1) On application, the Superior Court of Justice may by order grant any relief in respect of a matter arising under this Act that the applicant would be entitled to in an application for an order in the nature of *habeas corpus*.

(2) Notice of an application under subsection (1) for relief in the nature of *habeas corpus* shall be served upon the person having custody of the person in respect of whom the application is made and upon the Attorney General and upon the hearing of the application the presence before the court of the person in respect of whom the application was made may be dispensed with by consent, in which event the court may proceed to dispose of the matter forthwith as the justice of the case requires.

(3) Subject to subsections (1) and (2), the *Habeas Corpus Act* applies to applications under this section, but an application for relief in the nature of certiorari may be brought in aid of an application under this section.

(4) The *Judicial Review Procedure Act* does not apply to matters in respect of which an application may be made under section 140.

(5) A court to which an application or appeal is made under section 140 or this section may make any order with respect to costs that it considers just and reasonable.

S.O. 2000, c. 26, Sched. A, s. 13(5), item 6

BAIL

Release after arrest by officer — Release by officer in charge — Cash bail by non-resident

149. (1) Where a police officer, acting under a warrant or other power of arrest, arrests a person, the police officer shall, as soon as is practicable, release the person from custody after serving him or her with a summons or offence notice unless the officer has reasonable and probable grounds to believe that,

(*a*) it is necessary in the public interest for the person to be detained, having regard to all the circumstances including the need to,

(i) establish the identity of the person,

(ii) secure or preserve evidence of or relating to the offence, or

(iii) prevent the continuance or repetition of the offence or the commission of another offence; or

(*b*) the person arrested is ordinarily resident outside Ontario and will not respond to a summons or offence notice.

(2) Where a defendant is not released from custody under subsection (1), the police officer shall deliver him or her to the officer in charge who shall, where in his or her opinion the conditions set out in clauses (1)(*a*) and (*b*) do not or no longer exist, release the defendant,

(*a*) upon serving the defendant with a summons or offence notice;

(*b*) upon the defendant entering into a recognizance in the prescribed form without sureties conditioned for his or her appearance in court.

(3) Where the defendant is held for the reason only that he or she is not ordinarily resident in Ontario and it is believed that the defendant will not respond to a summons or offence notice, the officer in charge may, in addition to anything required under subection (2), require the defendant to deposit cash or other satisfactory negotiable security in an amount not to exceed,

(*a*) where the proceeding is commenced by certificate under Part I or II, the amount of the set fine for the offence or, if none, $300; or

(*b*) where the proceeding is commenced by information under Part III, $500.

Person in custody to be brought before justice — Order for conditional release — Idem — Order for detention — Reasons — Evidence at hearing — Adjournments

150. (1) Where a defendant is not released from custody under section 149, the officer in charge shall, as soon as is practicable but in any event within twenty-four hours, bring the defendant before a justice and the justice shall, unless a plea of guilty is taken, order that the defendant be released upon giving his or her undertaking to appear unless the prosecutor having been given an opportunity to do so shows cause why the detention of the defendant is justified to ensure his or her appearance in court or why an order under subsection (2) is justified for the same purpose.

(2) Subject to subsection (1), the justice may order the release of the defendant,

(*a*) upon the defendant entering into a recognizance to appear with such conditions as are appropriate to ensure his or her appearance in court;

(*b*) where the offence is one punishable by imprisonment for twelve months or more, conditional upon the defendant entering into a recognizance before a justice with sureties in such amount and with such conditions, if any, as are appropriate to ensure his or her appearance in court or, with the consent of the prosecutor, upon the defendant depositing with the justice such sum of money or other valuable security as the order directs in an amount not exceeding,

(i) where the proceeding is commenced by certificate under Part I or II, the amount of the set fine for the offence or, if none, $300, or

(ii) where the proceeding is commenced by information under Part III, $1,000; or

(*c*) if the defendant is not ordinarily resident in Ontario, upon the defendant entering into a recognizance before a justice, with or without sureties, in such amount and with such conditions, if any, as are appropriate to ensure his or her appearance in court, and depositing with the justice such sum of money or other valuable security as the order directs in an amount not exceeding,

(i) where the proceeding is commenced by certificate under Part I or II, the amount of the set fine for the offence or, if none, $300, or

(ii) where the proceeding is commenced by information under Part III, $1,000.

(3) The justice shall not make an order under clause (2)(*b*) or (*c*) unless the prosecutor shows cause why an order under the immediately proceeding clause should not be made.

(4) Where the prosecutor shows cause why the detention of the defendant in custody is justified to ensure his or her appearance in court, the justice shall order the defendant to be detained in custody until he or she is dealt with according to law.

(5) The justice shall include in the record a statement of the reasons for his or her decision under subsection (1), (2) or (4).

(6) Where a person is brought before a justice under subsection (1), the justice may receive and base his or her decision upon information the justice considers credible or trustworthy in the circumstances of each case except that the defendant shall not be examined or cross-examined in respect of the offence with which he or she is charged.

(7) Where a person is brought before a justice under subsection (1), the matter shall not be adjourned for more than three days without the consent of the defendant.

Proposed Addition—150(8)

Alternative to physical presence

(8) Where a defendant is to be brought before a justice under this section, the defendant's actual physical attendance is required, but the justice may, subject to subsection (9), allow the defendant to appear by means of any suitable telecommunication device, including telephone, that is satisfactory to the justice.

2002, c. 18, Sched. A, s. 15(1) [Not in force at date of publication.]

Proposed Amendment—Conditional Amendment—150(8)

On the later of the coming into force of 2002, c. 18, Sched. A, s. 15(1) [Not in force at date of publication.] and the day the Good Government Act, 2006 receives Royal

Assent [S.O. 2006, c. 19 received Royal Assent June 22, 2006.], subsection 150(8) is replaced by the following:

Alternative to physical presence

(8) Where a defendant is to be brought before a justice under this section, the defendant's actual physical attendance is required, but the justice may, despite any other Act and subject to subsection (9), allow the defendant to appear by means of any suitable telecommunication device, including telephone, that is satisfactory to the justice.

2006, c. 19, Sched. B, s. 15(1) [Conditions not yet satisfied.]

Proposed Addition—150(9)

Consent required

(9) The consent of the prosecutor and the defendant is required for the purpose of an appearance if,

(a) the evidence of a witness is to be taken at the appearance; and

(b) it is not possible for the defendant to appear by closed-circuit television or any other means that allow the justice and the defendant to engage in simultaneous visual and oral communication.

2002, c. 18, Sched. A, s. 15(1) [Not in force at date of publication.]

Expediting trial of person in custody — Further orders

151. (1) Where a defendant is not released from custody under section 149 or 150, he or she shall be brought before the court forthwith and, in any event, within eight days.

(2) The justice presiding upon any appearance of the defendant in court may, upon the motion of the defendant or prosecutor, review any order made under section 150 and make such further or other order under section 150 as to the justice seems appropriate in the circumstances.

SEARCH WARRANTS

Search warrant — Expiration — When to be executed

158. (1) Where a justice is satisfied by information upon oath that there is reasonable ground to believe that there is in any building, receptacle or place,

(*a*) anything upon or in respect of which an offence has been or is suspected to have been committed; or

(*b*) anything that there is reasonable ground to believe will afford evidence as to the commission of an offence,

the justice may at any time issue a warrant in the prescribed form under his or her hand authorizing a police officer or person named therein to search such building, receptacle or place for any such thing, and to seize and carry it before the justice issuing the warrant or another justice to be dealt with by him or her according to law.

Proposed Amendment—158(1)

(1) A justice may at any time issue a warrant under his or her hand if the justice is satisfied by information upon oath that there are reasonable grounds to believe that there is in any place,

(a) anything on or in respect of which an offence has been or is suspected to have been committed; or

(b) anything that there are reasonable grounds to believe will afford evidence as to the commission of an offence.

2002, c. 18, Sched. A, s. 15(2) [Not in force at date of publication.]

Proposed Addition—158(1.1)

Same

(1.1) The search warrant authorizes a police officer or person named in the warrant,

(a) to search the place named in the information for any thing described in clause (1)(a) or (b); and

(b) to seize the thing and deal with it in accordance with section 158.2.

2002, c. 18, Sched. A, s. 15(2) [Not in force at date of publication.]

(2) Every search warrant shall name a date upon which it expires, which date shall be not later than fifteen days after its issue.

(3) Every search warrant shall be executed between 6 a.m. and 9 p.m. standard time, unless the justice by the warrant otherwise authorizes.

Proposed Addition—158(4)

Definition

*(4) In this section and in section 158.1, **"place"** includes a building and a receptacle.*

2002, c. 18, Sched. A, s. 15(3) [Not in force at date of publication.]

Detention of things seized — Time limit for detention — Motion for examination and copying — Motion for release — Appeal where order by justice of the peace

159. (1) Where any thing is seized and brought before a justice, he or she shall by order,

(*a*) detain it or direct it to be detained in the care of a person named in the order; or

(*b*) direct it to be returned,

and the justice may in the order authorize the examination, testing, inspection or reproduction of the thing seized upon such conditions as are reasonably necessary and directed in the order, and may make any other provision as in the opinion of the justice is necessary for its preservation.

Proposed Amendment—159(1)

Order of justice re things seized

159. *(1) When, under paragraph 3 of section 158.2, a thing that has been seized is brought before a justice or a report in respect of it is made to a justice, he or she shall, by order,*

(a) detain the thing or direct it to be detained in the care of a person named in the order; or

(b) direct it to be returned.

2002, c. 18, Sched. A, s. 15(5) [Not in force at date of publication.]

Proposed Amendment—Conditional Amendment—159(1)

On the later of the coming into force of 2002, c. 18, Sched A, s. 15(5) [Not in force at date of publication.] and the day the Good Government Act, 2006 receives Royal Assent [S.O. 2006, c. 19 received Royal Assent June 22, 2006.], subsection 159(1) is replaced by the following:

Order of justice re things seized

(1) When, under paragraph 3 of subsection 158.2(2), a thing that has been seized is brought before a justice or a report in respect of it is made to a justice, he or she shall, by order,

(a) detain the thing or direct it to be detained in the care of a person named in the order; or

(b) direct it to be returned.

2006, c. 19, Sched. B, s. 15(3) [Conditions not yet satisfied.]

Proposed Addition—159(1.1)

Same

(1.1) The justice may, in the order,

(a) authorize the examination, testing, inspection or reproduction of the thing seized, on the conditions that are reasonably necessary and are directed in the order; and

(b) make any other provision that, in his or her opinion, is necessary for the preservation of the thing.

2002, c. 18, Sched. A, s. 15(5) [Not in force at date of publication.]

(2) Nothing shall be detained under an order made under subsection (1) for a period of more than three months after the time of seizure unless, before the expiration of that period,

(*a*) upon motion, a justice is satisfied that having regard to the nature of the investigation, its further detention for a specified period is warranted and he or she so orders; or

(*b*) a proceeding is instituted in which the thing detained may be required.

(3) Upon the motion of the defendant, prosecutor or person having an interest in a thing detained under subsection (1), a justice may make an order for the

examination, testing, inspection or reproduction of any thing detained upon such conditions as are reasonably necessary and directed in the order.

(4) Upon the motion of a person having an interest in a thing detained under subsection (1), and upon notice to the defendant, the person from whom the thing was seized, the person to whom the search warrant was issued and any other person who has an apparent interest in the thing detained, a justice may make an order for the release of any thing detained to the person from whom the thing was seized where it appears that the thing detained is no longer necessary for the purpose of an investigation or proceeding.

(5) Where an order or refusal to make an order under subsection (3) or (4) is made by a justice of the peace, an appeal lies therefrom in the same manner as an appeal from a conviction in a proceeding commenced by means of a certificate.

Examination or seizure of documents where privilege claimed — Opportunity to claim privilege — Examination of documents in custody — Motion to determine privilege — Limitation — Attorney General a party — Private hearing and scrutiny by judge — Order — Release of document where no motion under subs. (4)

160. (1) Where under a search warrant a person is about to examine or seize a document that is in the possession of a lawyer and a solicitor-client privilege is claimed on behalf of a named client in respect of the document, the person shall, without examining or making copies of the document,

(*a*) seize the document and place it, together with any other document seized in respect of which the same claim is made on behalf of the same client, in a package and seal and identify the package; and

(*b*) place the package in the custody of the clerk of the court or, with the consent of the person and the client, in the custody of another person.

(2) No person shall examine or seize a document that is in the possession of a lawyer without giving him or her a reasonable opportunity to claim the privilege under subsection (1).

(3) A judge may, upon the motion made without notice of the lawyer, by order authorize the lawyer to examine or make a copy of the document in the presence of its custodian or the judge, and the order shall contain such provisions as are necessary to ensure that the document is repackaged and resealed without alteration or damage.

(4) Where a document has been seized and placed in custody under subsection (1), the client by or on whose behalf the claim of solicitor-client privilege is made may make a motion to a judge for an order sustaining the privilege and for the return of the document.

(5) A motion under subsection (4) shall be by notice of motion naming a hearing date not later than thirty days after the date on which the document was placed in custody.

(6) The person who seized the document and the Attorney General are parties to a motion under subsection (4) and entitled to at least three days notice thereof.

(7) A motion under subsection (4) shall be heard in private and, for the purposes of the hearing, the judge may examine the document and, if he or she does so, shall cause it to be resealed.

(8) The judge may by order,

(*a*) declare that the solicitor-client privilege exists or does not exist in respect of the document;
(*b*) direct that the document be delivered up to the appropriate person.

(9) Where it appears to a judge upon the motion of the Attorney General or person who seized the document that no motion has been made under subsection (4) within the time limit prescribed by subsection (5), the judge shall order that the document be delivered to the applicant.

Appendix B

Regulations Under the Courts of Justice Act

Rules of the Ontario Court (General Division) and the Ontario Court (Provincial Division) in Appeals Under Section 116 of the Provincial Offences Act — R.R.O. 1990, Reg. 196 [Re-enacted as O. Reg. 723/94]

DEFINITIONS AND INTERPRETATION

Definitions

1. (1) In these rules,
"Act" means the *Provincial Offences Act"*
"appeal court" means the Ontario Court (General Division) or the Ontario Court (Provincial Division), as the case may be, sitting as the appeal court under section 116 of the Act;
"clerk" means the clerk of the Ontario Court (Provincial Division) or the local registrar of the Ontario Court (General Division) to which an appeal is or may be taken under Part VII of the Act;
"file" means file with the clerk;
"judge" means a judge of the Ontario Court (General Division) or the Ontario Court (Provincial Division), as the case may be, sitting as the appeal court under section 116 of the Act.

Application of rules

(2) These rules apply in respect of appeals to the Ontario Court (General Division) or the Ontario Court (Provincial Division) under section 116 of the Act.

General principle

(3) These rules shall be constructed liberally so as to obtain as expeditious a conclusion of every proceeding as is consistent with a just determination of the proceeding.

Matters not provided for

(4) Where matters are not provided for in these rules, the practice shall be determined by analogy to them.

CALCULATION OF TIME

General

2. (1) In the calculation of time under these rules or an order of the court, except where a contrary intention appears.

(*a*) where there is a reference to a number of days between two events, they shall be counted by excluding the day on which the first event happens and including the day on which the second event happens, even if they are described as clear days or the words "at least" are used;
(*b*) where a period of less than seven days is prescribed, holidays shall not be counted;
(*c*) where the time for doing an act under these rules expires on a holiday, the act may be done on the next day that is not a holiday; and
(*d*) service of a document made after 4 p.m. or at any time on a holiday shall be deemed to have been made on the next day that is not a holiday.

Local time

(2) Where a time of day is mentioned in these rules or in any documents in an appeal, the time referred to shall be taken as the time observed locally.

"Holiday"

(3) For the purposes of subsection (1), "holiday" means,
(*a*) any Saturday or Sunday;
(*b*) New Year's Day;
(*c*) Good Friday;
(*d*) Easter Monday;
(*e*) Victoria Day;
(*f*) Canada Day;
(*g*) Civic Holiday;
(*h*) Labour Day;
(*i*) Thanksgiving Day;
(*j*) Remembrance Day;
(*k*) Christmas Day;
(*l*) Boxing Day; and
(*m*) any special holiday proclaimed by the Governor General or the Lieutenant Governor.

Same

(4) Where,
(*a*) New Year's Day, Canada Day or Remembrance Day falls on a Saturday or Sunday, the following Monday is a holiday;
(*b*) Christmas Day falls on a Saturday or Sunday, the following Monday and Tuesday are holidays;
(*c*) Christmas Day falls on a Friday, the following Monday is a holiday.

NOTICE BY MAIL

3. A notice or document given or delivered by mail shall, unless the contrary is shown, be deemed to be given or delivered on the seventh day following the day on which it was mailed.

SUBSTITUTED SERVICE

4. Where, on motion without notice, it appears to a judge that reasonable efforts have been made without success to give or deliver a notice or document in the manner required by these rules or the Act, or that reasonable efforts would not be successful, the judge may make an order for substituted service of the notice or document in such manner as the judge directs or, where necessary in the interests of justice, may dispense with the giving or delivery of the notice or document upon such terms as the judge considers proper in the circumstances.

SERVICE AND FILING OF NOTICE OF APPEAL

Notice of appeal

5. (1) A notice of appeal shall be in Form 1.

Time for service, appeal by defendant

(2) A defendant who appeals shall serve the notice of appeal on the prosecutor and, if the prosecutor is not acting on behalf of the Crown, on the Crown Attorney within 30 days after the date of the decision appealed from.

Time for service, appeal by prosecutor

(3) A prosecutor who appeals shall serve the notice of appeal on the defendant and, if the prosecutor is not acting on behalf of the Crown, on the Crown Attorney within 30 days after the date of the decision appealed from.

Filing

(4) An appellant shall file the notice of appeal with proof of service within five days after service.

Proof of service

(5) Proof of service of the notice of appeal may be made by affidavit.

Admission of service

(6) Where admission of service is endorsed on the notice of appeal, proof need not be made by affidavit.

APPEAL WHERE FINE IMPOSED

6. A defendant who appeals from a decision imposing a fine shall file with the notice of appeal a receipt for payment of the fine issued by the clerk of the court that imposed the fine, unless the clerk is satisfied that an order has been made under subsection 111(2) of the Act and a recognizance has been entered into by the defendant in accordance with the order.

EXTENSION OR ABRIDGMENT OF TIME

Judge's power

7. (1) A judge may extend or abridge the time for bringing an appeal and for doing any other act in connection with an appeal for which a time is prescribed before or after the expiration of the time prescribed.

Notice

(2) A notice of motion to extend or abridge time shall be given to the opposite party, unless otherwise directed by a judge.

TRANSCRIPTS

Certificate

8. (1) An appellant shall file with the notice of appeal a certificate of the clerk of the Ontario Court (Provincial Division) as to transcript of evidence in Form 2.

Filing and delivery of transcript

(2) An appellant shall file and deliver to the respondent,

(*a*) in an appeal against conviction, dismissal, a finding as to ability to conduct a defence or an order under section 161 of the Act, one copy of the transcript of evidence at trial, including reasons for judgment; and

(*b*) in an appeal against conviction and sentence or sentence only, one copy of the transcript of evidence at trial and submissions on sentencing, including reasons for judgment and sentence, if any.

Transcript to Crown Attorney

(3) Where the Crown Attorney has given notice of intervention after receiving notice of appeal, the appellant shall deliver a copy of the transcript of evidence at trial, including reasons for judgment and sentence, if any, to the Crown Attorney.

Time for filing certificate

(4) An appellant who has been issued a provisional legal aid certificate limited to the filing of a notice of appeal and making a motion for release from custody under the *Legal Aid Act* shall file a certificate in Form 2 within one month of filing the notice of appeal.

Deemed abandonment

(5) An appellant referred to in subrule (4) who does not file the certificate within one month of filing the notice of appeal or within such longer period of time as a judge may permit shall be deemed to have abandoned the appeal.

RECOGNIZANCES

9. (1) An order for recognizance and recognizance under section 110 of the Act shall be in Form 3.

(2) An order for recognizance under section 111 of the Act shall be in Form 4.

MOTIONS UNDER ACT OR RULES

Notice of motion

10. (1) A motion provided for by the Act or these rules shall be commenced by a notice of motion.

Time for hearing

(2) There shall be at least three days between service of the notice of motion and the day for hearing the motion.

Time for filing notice

(3) The moving party shall file the notice of motion at least two days before the day for hearing the motion.

Evidence

(4) Evidence on a motion may be given,
(*a*) by affidavit;
(*b*) with the permission of the court, orally; or
(*c*) in the form of a transcript of the examination of a witness.

Power of judge

(5) Upon the hearing of a motion, the justice may receive and base his or her decision on information that the justice considers credible or trustworthy in the circumstances, whether or not other evidence is given.

Hearing where notice not served

(6) A motion may be heard without service of a notice of motion,
(*a*) on consent; or
(*b*) where the motion is made under section 111 or 112 of the Act; or
(*c*) where, having regard to the subject-matter or the circumstances of the motion, it would not be unjust to hear the motion without service of a notice of motion.

Appeal by way of new trial

(7) A person making a motion for an order under section 127 of the Act that an appeal be heard and determined by way of a new trial in the court shall give at least seven days notice of the motion to all other parties to the appeal.

TRANSMISSION OF MATERIAL

s. 115 notice deemed given

11. (1) The clerk of the appeal court shall send a copy of the notice of appeal to the clerk of the Ontario Court (Provincial Division) as the notice required by section 115 of the Act.

Time for transmittal of documents

(2) The clerk of the Ontario Court (Provincial Division) shall transmit the order appealed from and transmit or transfer custody of the other material referred to in section 115 of the Act to the clerk of the appeal court within 10 days after receiving the copy of the notice of appeal.

INTERVENTION OF CROWN ATTORNEY

12. Where a prosecutor is not acting on behalf of the Crown, the Crown Attorney may intervene to act on behalf of the prosecutor or to attend as a party on the appeal.

LISTING OF APPEAL

Appeal list

13. (1) The clerk shall place the appeal on an appeal list for the next sitting of the court at which dates are fixed for hearing appeals as soon as 10 days have elapsed after,

(*a*) the clerk has received the order appealed from and the other material referred to in section 115 of the Act;

(*b*) the appellant has filed a copy of the transcript of evidence at trial, including reasons for judgment or sentence if any; and

(*c*) any other step required by the Act, these rules or the court has been completed.

Notice period

(2) The clerk shall give at least 14 days notice of the date fixed for the hearing of the appeal to the appellant and the respondent and, where the Crown Attorney has filed a notice of intervention, to the Crown Attorney.

Motion under s. 127

(3) Where a motion is made under section 127 of the Act for an order that an appeal be heard and determined by way of a new trial in the court, the clerk shall not place the appeal on an appeal list until the motion has been disposed of and 10 days have elapsed since the disposition of the motion.

DIRECTIONS

14. A party to an appeal may make a motion to the court at any time for directions with respect to the conduct of the appeal.

FACTUMS

Where factum not necessary

15. (1) Unless a judge orders otherwise, a party to an appeal who intends to be present either personally or by counsel at the hearing of the appeal need not file a factum.

Form of factums

(2) Where a factum is requred by order of the court or is filed by a party to an appeal, subrules (3) to (7) apply.

Appellant's factum

(3) An appellant shall prepare an "Appellant's Factum" not exceeding 10 pages in length, excluding the Schedule, and shall file, on or before the date specified in the notice of hearing given under rule 13, one copy of the factum, together with proof of service, on all other parties and persons who have been granted the right to be heard on the appeal.

Same

(4) Except in appeals from sentence only, the appellant's factum shall consist of

(*a*) Part I, entitled "Statement of the Case", containing a statement identifying the appellant, the court in which the proceedings arose, the nature of the charge or charges, the result in that court and the nature of each order to which the appeal relates;
(*b*) Part II, entitled "Summary of the Facts", containing a concise summary of the facts relevant to the issues on the appeal, with such references to the evidence by page and line, or paragraph, as the case may be, as may be necessary;
(*c*) Part III, entitled "Issues and the Law", containing a statement of each issue raised, immediately followed by a concise statement of the law and any authorities relating to that issue;
(*d*) Part IV, entitled "Order Requested", containing a statement of the order that the court is being asked to make; and
(*e*) a Schedule, entitled "Authorities to be Cited", containing a list of the authorities, with citations, to which reference was made in Part III in the order in which they appear in that Part.

Respondent's factum

(5) A respondent shall prepare a "Respondent's Factum" not exceeding 10 pages in length, excluding the Schedule, and shall file, not later than 15 days after receipt of the appellant's factum and not later than 7 days before the date fixed for the hearing of the appeal under rule 13, one copy of the factum, together with proof of service, on all other parties and persons who have been granted the right to be heard on the appeal.

Same

(6) Except in appeals from sentence only, the respondent's factum shall consist of,

(*a*) Part I, entitled "Respondent's Statement as to Facts", containing a statement of the facts in Part II of the appellant's factum that the respondent accepts as correct and those facts with which the respondent disagrees and a concise summary of any additional facts relied on, with such reference to the transcript evidence by page and line or paragraph, as the case may be, as is necessary;
(*b*) Part II, entitled "Response to Appellant's Issues", containing the position of the respondent with respect to each issue raised by the appellant immediately following a concise statement of the law and the authorities relating to that issue;
(*c*) Part III, entitled "Additional Issues", containing a statement of any additional issues raised by the respondent, immediately followed by a concise statement of the law and the authorities relating to those issues;

(*d*) Part IV, entitled "Order Requested", containing a statement of the order that the court will be asked to make; and

(*e*) a Schedule, entitled "Authorities to be Cited", containing a list of the authorities, with citations, referred to in the order in which they appear in Parts II and III.

Paragraphs

(7) The appellant's and the respondent's factum shall be in paragraphs numbered consecutively throughout.

APPEAL IN WRITING

16. An appellant who intends not to be present in person or by counsel at the hearing of the appeal shall file, prior to the date of the hearing,

(*a*) a notice in writing of that intention, unless the appellant has already done so in the notice of appeal; and

(*b*) a statement in writing of the issues and the appellant's arguments on the appeal.

DISMISSAL OF APPEAL

17. The court may dismiss an appeal where the appellant,

(*a*) does not attend in person or by counsel and,

(i) has not indicated in the notice of appeal the appellant's intention not to be present in person or by counsel at the hearing of the appeal,

(ii) has not filed notice in writing of the intention not to be present in person or by counsel at the hearing of the appeal, and

(iii) has not filed a statement in writing of the issues and the appellant's arguments on the appeal;

(*b*) has filed a notice of abandonment;

(*c*) has not filed a transcript of evidence at trial, including reasons for judgment or sentence, if any, within 30 days after receiving notice of completion of the transcript from the clerk of the Ontario Court (Provincial Division);

(*d*) after obtaining an order under subclause 117(1)(*b*)(ii) of the Act for the examination of a witness, has not filed a transcript of the examination within 30 days after receiving notice of completion of the transcription from the other person before whom the witness was examined; or

(*e*) has filed to comply with an order of the court in respect of the appeal.

ABANDONMENT OF APPEALS

Notice of abandonment

18. (1) An appellant who wishes to abandon the appeal may file a notice of abandonment in Form 5.

Signing of notice

(2) The appellant or counsel for the appellant shall sign the notice of abandonment.

Signing by witness

(3) Where the appellant signs the notice of abandonment, the notice must also be signed by another person who witnessed the signing by the appellant.

Affidavit of execution

(4) Where the witness is not counsel for the appellant, the appellant shall file an affidavit of execution by the witness with the notice of abandonment.

Notice to other parties

(5) The clerk shall give a copy of the filed notice of abandonment to each of the other parties to the appeal.

APPEAL RESPECTING RELEASE FROM CUSTODY

Commencing appeal

19. (1) An appeal under section 152 of the Act in respect of release from custody shall be commenced by written notice filed and given to all other parties and, if the Crown Attorney is not a party, to the Crown Attorney.

Grounds for release from custody

(2) On the appeal, the court shall order that the defendant be released from custody pending trial if it is satisfied that the defendant will attend in court for trial.

When order for release takes effect

(3) The court shall provide in the order that the order does not take effect until the defendant,

(*a*) gives an undertaking, either without conditions or with such conditions as the court may order, to attend in court for trial; or

(*b*) enters into a recognizance, with or without sureties, in such amount, with such conditions and before such justice as the court may order either with or without depositing with the justice money or other valuable security specified by the court.

OFFICIAL EXAMINATIONS

Definition, "order"

20. (1) In this rule, "order" means an order under subclause 117(1)(*b*)(ii) of the Act.

Presence of parties, counsel

(2) Except with the consent of the parties or their counsel, the examination of a witness under an order shall take place in the presence of the parties or their counsel.

Tentative appointment

(3) A party who intends to make a motion for an order for the examination of a witness before an official examiner shall obtain a tentative appointment for the examination before making the motion for the order.

Certificate of official examiner

(4) Upon the completion of the examination, the party who made the motion for the order shall file a certificate of the official examiner in Form 6.

Notice of completion of transcript

(5) An official examiner who signs and delivers a certificate in Form 6 shall notify each of the parties to the appeal and the clerk when the transcript of the examination is completed.

SPECIAL COMMISSIONER

Appointment

21. (1) Where the court makes an order under clause 117(1)(*e*) of the Act referring a question to a special commissioner for inquiry and report, the court shall, by order, appoint the special commissioner and fix the date on or before which the inquiry shall be completed and the report shall be filed.

Motion for directions

(2) The special commissioner may make a motion to the court for directions in respect of the inquiry or the report, or both.

Filing of report

(3) Upon completion of the report, the special commissioner,
(*a*) shall file the report, together with one copy for each party to the appeal; and
(*b*) shall give notice of the filing of the report to each party to the appeal.

NOTICE OF DECISION OF COURT

22. Immediately after the disposition of an appeal, the clerk shall give notice of the court's decision, including any written reasons and endorsements,
(*a*) to each party to the appeal who was not present in person or by counsel when the decision was made;
(*b*) to the clerk of the Ontario Court (Provincial Division); and
(*c*) to the Crown Attorney, where a prosecutor is not acting on behalf of the Crown.

TRANSITION

Definition, "preceding rules"

23. (1) In this rule, "preceding rules" means the Rules of the Ontario Court (General Division) and the Ontario Court (Provincial Division) in Appeals under

Section 116 of the *Provincial Offences Act* (Regulation 196 of the Revised Regulations of Ontario, 1990) as they read on the day before these rules come into force.

Application of rules

(2) These rules apply to all appeals, whether commenced before or after these rules come into force, except in respect of steps taken under the preceding rules.

Power of judge

(3) Despite the repeal of the preceding rules and subrule (2), a judge may make an order that an appeal, or a step in the appeal, be conducted under these rules or the preceding rules or make any order that is considered just in order to secure the fair and expeditious conduct of the appeal.

REVOCATION AND COMMENCEMENT

24. (1) Regulation 196 of the Revised Regulations of Ontario, 1990 is revoked.

(2) This Regulation comes into force on December 12, 1994.

Rules of the Ontario Court (Provincial Division) in Appeals Under Section 135 of the Provincial Offences Act — R.R.O. 1990, Reg. 198 [am. O. Reg. 504/93; Re-enacted as O. Reg. 722/94.]

DEFINITIONS AND INTERPRETATION

Definitions

1. (1) In these rules,

"Act" means the *Provincial Offences Act*;

"appeal court" means the Ontario Court (Provincial Division) sitting as the appeal court under sections 135 of the Act;

"clerk" means the clerk of the Ontario Court (Provincial Division);

"file" means file with the clerk;

"judge" means a judge of the Ontario Court (Provincial Division) sitting as the appeal court under section 135 of the Act.

Application of rules

(2) These rules apply in respect of appeals to the Ontario Court (Provincial Division) under section 135 of the Act.

General principle

(3) These rules shall be construed liberally so as to obtain as expeditious a conclusion of every proceeding as is consistent with a just determination of the proceeding.

Matters not provided for

(4) Where matters are not provided for in these rules, the practice shall be determined by analogy to them.

CALCULATION OF TIME

General

2. (1) In the calculation of time under these rules or an order of the court, except where a contrary intention appears,

(*a*) where there is a reference to a number of days between two events, they shall be counted by excluding the day on which the first event happens and including the day on which the second event happens, evey if they are described as clear days or the words "at least" are used;

(*b*) where a period of less than seven days is prescribed, holidays shall not be counted;

(*c*) where the time for doing an act under these rules expires on a holiday, the act may be done on the next day that is not a holiday; and

(*d*) service of a document made after 4 p.m. on or at any time on a holiday shall be deemed to have been made on the next day that is not a holiday.

Local time

(2) Where a time of day is mentioned in these rules or in any documents in an appeal, the time referred to shall be taken as the time observed locally.

"Holiday"

(3) For the purposes of subsection (1), "holiday" means,

(*a*) any Saturday or Sunday;

(*b*) New Year's Day;

(*c*) Good Friday;

(*d*) Easter Monday;

(*e*) Victoria Day;

(*f*) Canada Day;

(*g*) Civic Holiday;

(*h*) Labour Day;

(*i*) Thanksgiving Day;

(*j*) Remembrance Day;

(*k*) Christmas Day;

(*l*) Boxing Day; and

(*m*) any special holiday proclaimed by the Governor General or the Lieutenant Governor.

Same

(4) Where,

(*a*) New Year's Day, Canada Day or Remembrance Day falls on a Saturday or Sunday, the following Monday is a holiday;

(*b*) Christmas Day falls on a Saturday or Sunday, the following Monday and Tuesday are holidays;

(*c*) Christmas Day falls on a Friday, the following Monday is a holiday.

NOTICE BY MAIL

3. A notice or document given or delivered by mail shall, unless the contrary is shown, be deemed to be given or delivered on the seventh day following the day on which it was mailed.

SUBSTITUTED SERVICE

4. Where, on motion without notice, it appears to a judge that reasonable efforts have been made without success to give or deliver a notice or document in the manner required by these rules or the Act, or that reasonable efforts would not be successful, the judge may make an order for substituted service of the notice or document in such manner as the judge directs or, where necessary in the interests of justice, may dispense with the giving or delivery of the notice or document upon such terms as the judge considers proper in the circumstances.

APPEAL WHERE FINE IMPOSED

5. A defendant who appeals from a decision imposing a fine shall file with the notice of appeal a receipt for payment of the fine issued by the clerk of the court that imposed the fine or state in the notice of appeal that the fine has been paid to a municipality responsible for collecting its own parking fines, unless the clerk is satisfied that an order has been made under subsection 111(2) of the Act and a recognizance has been entered into by the defendant in accordance with the order.

FILING OF NOTICE OF APPEAL

Notice of appeal

6. (1) A notice of appeal shall be in Form 1.

Time and place for hearing

(2) Upon the filing of the notice of appeal, the clerk shall set a time and place for the hearing of the appeal in accordance with section 135 of the Act.

Notice to respondent

(3) The clerk shall give the respondent a copy of the filed notice of appeal and a notice of the time and place of the hearing in Form 2.

Timely notice

(4) Notice of the time and place of the hearing shall be given at least 15 days before the day set for the hearing.

Certificate

(5) A certificate of giving a notice under subrule (3) endorsed on the notice by the clerk shall be received in evidence and, in the absence of evidence to the contrary, is proof that the notice was given.

Interpretation

(6) For the purposes of this rule, where the defendant appeals, the prosecutor is the respondent, and vice-versa.

NOTICE TO CROWN ATTORNEY

Copies to Crown Attorney

7. (1) The clerk shall give the Crown Attorney a copy of each notice or document filed with or issued by the clerk in respect of an appeal under these rules.

Intervention of Crown Attorney

(2) Where a prosecutor is not acting on behalf of the Crown, the Crown Attorney may intervene to act on behalf of the prosecutor or to attend as a party on the appeal.

EXTENSION OR ABRIDGMENT OF TIME

Judge's power

8. (1) A judge may extend or abridge the time for bringing an appeal and for doing any other act in connection with an appeal for which a time is prescribed before or after the expiration of the time prescribed.

Notice

(2) A notice of motion to extend or abridge time shall be given to the opposite party, unless otherwise directed by a judge.

TRANSCRIPTS

Transcript not required

9. (1) Unless a judge orders otherwise, a party to an appeal need not provide a transcript of all or any part of the evidence at trial.

Transcripts required

(2) Where the court orders that a transcript of all or any part of the evidence at trial be provided under clause 136(3)(a) of the Act or a party to an appeal files such a transcript, an appellant shall file and deliver to the respondent,

(*a*) in an appeal against conviction or acquittal, one copy of the transcript of evidence at trial, including reasons for judgment; and

(*b*) in an appeal against conviction and sentence or sentence only, one copy of the transcript of evidence at trial and submissions on sentencing, including reasons for judgment and sentence, if any.

Transcript to Crown Attorney

(3) Where the Crown Attorney has given notice of intervention after receiving notice of appeal, the appellant shall deliver a copy of the transcript of evidence at trial, including reasons for judgment and sentence, if any, to the Crown Attorney.

RECOGNIZANCES

10. (1) An order for recognizance and recognizance under section 110 of the Act shall be in Form 3.

(2) An order for recognizance and recognizance under section 111 of the Act shall be in Form 4.

MOTIONS UNDER ACT OR RULES

Notice of motion

11. (1) A motion provided for by the Act or these rules shall be commenced by a notice of motion.

Time of hearing

(2) There shall be at least three days between service of the notice of motion and the day for hearing the motion.

Time for filing notice

(3) The moving party shall file notice of motion at least two days before the day for hearing the motion.

Evidence

(4) Evidence on a motion may be given,
(*a*) by affidavit;
(*b*) with the permission of the court, orally; or
(*c*) in the form of a transcript of the examination of a witness.

Power of judge

(5) Upon the hearing of a motion, the judge may receive and base his or her decision on information that he or she considers credible or trustworthy in the circumstances, whether or not other evidence is given.

Hearing where notice not served

(6) A motion may be heard without service of a notice of motion,
(*a*) on consent;
(*b*) where the motion is made under section 111 or 112 of the Act; or
(*c*) where, having regard to the subject-matter or the circumstances of the motion, it would not be unjust to hear the motion without service of a notice of motion.

DIRECTIONS

12. A party to an appeal may make a motion to the court at any time for directions with respect to the conduct of the appeal.

DISMISSAL OF APPEAL

13. The court may dismiss an appeal where the appellant,

(*a*) does not attend in person or by counsel on the day set by the clerk for the hearing of the appeal;

(*b*) has filed a notice of abandonment;

(*c*) has not filed a transcript of evidence at trial, including reasons for judgment or sentence, if any, within 30 days after receiving notice of completion of the transcript from the clerk of the Ontario Court (Provincial Division); or

(*d*) has failed to comply with an order of the court in respect of the appeal.

ABANDONMENT OF APPEALS

Notice of abandonment

14. (1) An appellant who wishes to abandon the appeal may file a notice of abandonment in Form 5.

Signing of notice

(2) The appellant or counsel for the appellant shall sign the notice of abandonment.

Signing by witness

(3) Where the appellant signs the notice of abandonment, the notice must also be signed by another person who witnessed the signing by the appellant.

Affidavit of execution

(4) Where the witness is not counsel for the appellant, the appellant shall file an affidavit of execution by the witness with the notice of abandonment.

Notice to other parties

(5) The clerk shall give a copy of the filed notice of abandonment to each of the other parties to the appeal.

NOTICE OF DECISION OF COURT

Notice of decision on appeal

15. (1) Immediately after the disposition of an appeal, the clerk shall give notice of the court's decision, including any written reasons and endorsements,

(*a*) to each party to the appeal who was not present in person or by counsel when the decision was made;

(*b*) to the clerk of the Ontario Court (Provincial Division); and

(*c*) to the Crown Attorney, where a prosecutor is not acting on behalf of the Crown.

Deemed receipt of notice of trial

(2) Where the appeal court directs a new trial and sets a date for the trial with the consent of the parties, the defendant is deemed to have received notice of trial.

TRANSITION

Definition, "preceding rules"

16. (1) In this rule, "preceding rules" means the Rules of the Ontario Court (Provincial Division) in Appeals under Section 135 of the *Provincial Offences Act* (Regulation 198 of the Revised Regulations of Ontario, 1990) as they read on the day before these rules come into force.

Application of rules

(2) These rules apply to all appeals, whether commenced before or after these rules come into force, except in respect of steps already taken under the preceding rules.

Power of judge

(3) Despite the repeal of the preceding rules and subrule (2), a judge may make an order that an appeal, or a step in the appeal, be conducted under these rules or the preceding rules or make any order that is considered just in order to secure the fair and expeditious conduct of the appeal.

REVOCATION AND COMMENCEMENT

17. (1) Regulation 198 of the Revised Regulations of Ontario, 1990 and Ontario Regulation 504/93 are revoked.

(2) This Regulation comes into force on December 12, 1994.

Rules of the Ontario Court (Provincial Division) in Provincial Offences Proceedings — R.R.O. 1990, Reg. 200 [am. O. Reg. 505/93; O. Reg. 498/94; O. Reg. 567/00]

1. In these rules, "Act" means the *Provincial Offences Act.*

2. (1) These rules apply to proceedings under the Act and a word or term in the Act has the same meaning in these rules as it has in the Act.

(2) In these rules, any reference to electronic process is a reference to the electronic process in force at the time of the coming into force of the *Provincial Offences Statute Law Amendment Act, 1993.* O. Reg. 498/94, s. 1.

3. These rules shall be construed liberally so as to obtain as expeditious a conclusion of every proceeding as is consistent with a just determination of the proceeding.

4. The following apply to the calculation of a period of time prescribed by the Act, section 205.7 or 205.19 of the *Highway Traffic Act*, these rules or an order of a court:

1. The time shall be calculated by excluding the first day and including the last day of the period.
2. Where a period of less than six days is prescribed, a Saturday or holiday shall not be reckoned.
3. Where the last day of the period of time falls on a Saturday or a holiday, the day next following that is not a Saturday or a holiday shall be deemed to be the last day of the period.

4. Where the days are expressed to be clear days or where the term "at least" is added, the time shall be calculated by excluding both the first day and the last day of the period. O. Reg. 498/94, s. 2; O. Reg. 567/00, s. 1

5. A notice or document given or delivered by mail shall, unless the contrary is shown, be deemed to be given or delivered on the seventh day following the day on which it was mailed.

6. For the purpose of proceedings under Part I or II of the Act, the amount of fine set by the court for an offence is such amount as may be set by the Chief Judge of the Ontario Court (Provincial Division).

7. (1) An application provided for by the Act or these rules shall be commenced by notice of application.

(2) A motion provided for by the Act or these rules shall be commenced by notice of motion.

(3) There shall be at least three days between the giving of notice of application or notice of motion and the day for hearing the application or motion.

(4) An applicant or moving party shall file notice of application or notice of motion at least two days before the day for hearing the application or motion.

(5) Evidence on an application or motion may be given,
(*a*) by affidavit;
(*b*) with the permission of the court, orally; or
(*c*) in the form of a transcript of the examination of a witness.

(6) Upon the hearing of an application or motion and whether or not other evidence is given on the application or motion, the justice may receive and base his or her decision upon information the justice considers credible or trustworthy in the circumstances.

(7) An application or motion may be heard without notice,
(*a*) on consent; or
(*b*) where, having regard to the subject-matter or the circumstances of the application or motion, it would not be unjust to hear the application or motion without notice.

(8) Subrules (2) to (5) do not apply in respect of a motion under section 66 of the Act.

8. (1) Where a certificate of parking infraction has been issued in respect of a parking infraction under a municipal by-law without a reference to the number of the by-law that creates the offence, the number of the by-law shall be affixed or appended to the court filing document when the certificate is filed in the office of the court.

(2) Where a certificate of parking infraction has been issued alleging a parking infraction against the defendant as owner of a vehicle, evidence of the ownership of the vehicle shall be affixed or appended to the court filing document when the certificate is filed in the office of the court.

(3) A certificate of parking infraction shall be affixed or appended to the court filing document when the certificate is filed in the office of the court.

(4) Where a defendant delivers a parking infraction notice or notice of impending conviction in respect of an alleged parking infraction under a municipal

by-law and gives notice of intention to appear in court for the purpose of entering a plea and having a trial of the matter, the parking infraction notice or notice of impending conviction shall be affixed or appended to the court filing document when the certificate of parking infraction is filed in the office of the court.

(5) Where a defendant files a notice of intention to appear under subsection 17.1(3) or 18.1.1(3) of the Act, the notice of intention to appear shall be affixed or appended to the court filing document when the certificate of parking infraction is filed in the office of the court.

(6) In this rule and subrule 22(2), "court filing document" means a document approved by the clerk of the court. O. Reg. 498/94, s. 3.

9. (1) A provincial offences officer who files a certificate of offence in the office of the court shall file with the certificate of offence a certificate control list, in the form that shall be supplied by the clerk of the court, with the certificate recorded on the list.

(2) A provincial offences officer who files a certificate of parking infraction in the office of the court shall file with it a certificate control list in the form approved by the clerk of the court, with the certificate recorded on the list.

(3) A single certificate control list may be filed with as many certificates of offence as can be accounted for on the certificate control list.

(4) A single certificate control list may be filed with as many certificates of parking infractions as can be accounted for on the certificate control list.

(5) The clerk of the court shall endorse on the certificate control list a receipt for the certificates of offence or certificates of parking infraction filed with the certificate control list.

(6) The clerk of the court shall, on request, give a copy of the receipt to the provincial offences officer who filed the certificate control list.

(7) Subrules (1) to (6) do not apply if a certificate of offence or a certificate of parking infraction is filed in an electronic format. O. Reg. 498/94, s. 4.

10. A facsimile signature of the person designated by the regulations is sufficient authentication of the certificate requesting a conviction under subsection 18.2(1.1) of the Act. O. Reg. 505/93, s. 1; O. Reg. 498/94, s. 5.

11. (1) The clerk of the court shall not accept for filing a certificate of offence more than seven days after the day on which the offence notice or summons was served unless the time is extended by the court.

(2) No certificate of offence, certificate of parking infraction or certificate requesting a conviction shall be accepted for filing by direct electronic transmission after the last day prescribed for its filing, unless the time is extended by the court. O. Reg. 498/94, s. 6.

12. (1) The clerk of the court shall endorse the date of filing in every certificate of offence, certificate of parking infraction or certificate requesting conviction filed in the office of the court, except any such certificate filed in an electronic format.

(2) The clerk of the court shall ensure that the date of filing is indicated on any document filed in an electronic format.

(3) A certificate of offence, certificate of parking infraction or certificate requesting a conviction filed by direct electronic transmission shall be deemed to be filed the day on which the transmission concludes, unless the contrary is shown. O. Reg. 505/93, s. 2; O. Reg. 498/94, s. 7.

12.1 [Revoked O. Reg. 498/94, s. 8.]

13. (1) On the delivery of an offence notice under section 5 of the Act, a parking infraction notice under subsection 17(1) of the Act or a notice of impending conviction under subsection 18.1(1) of the Act, giving notice of intention to appear in court for the purpose of entering a plea and having a trial of the matter, the clerk of the court shall, where proceedings have been commenced, set a day and time for trial.

(1.1) On the filing of a notice of intention to appear under section 5.1 of the Act, the clerk of the court shall, where proceedings have been commenced, set a day and time for trial.

(2) Where a parking infraction notice issued in respect of an alleged parking infraction under a municipal by-law is received under subsection 17(1) of the Act or a notice of impending conviction for such an infraction is received under subsection 18.1.1(1) of the Act, the clerk of the court shall give notice of the time and place of trial to the defendant and the prosecutor as soon as practicable after the prosecutor has filed the certificate of parking infraction in the office of the court, together with the corresponding parking infraction notice or notice of impending conviction.

(2.1) Where a notice of intention to appear is filed under subsection 17.1(3) or 18.1.1(3) of the Act, the clerk of the court shall give notice of the time and place of trial to the defendant and prosecutor as soon as practicable after the prosecutor has filed the certificate of parking infraction in the office of the court together with the notice of intention to appear.

(3) The clerk of the court shall give notice of the trial to the defendant and prosecutor at least seven days before the day set for trial.

(4) Where a parking infraction is alleged against the defendant as owner of a vehicle, notice of the trial shall be given to the person identified as the holder of the permit, as defined in section 6 of the *Highway Traffic Act*, in the evidence of the ownership of the vehicle affixed or appended to the certificate of parking infraction.

(5) A certificate as to the giving of a notice of trial endorsed on the notice of trial by the clerk of the court shall be received in evidence and, in the absence of evidence to the contrary, is proof of the giving of the notice stated in the certificate.

(6) Where a defendant files a notice of intention to appear under section 5.1 of the Act and it appears that the certificate of offence has not been filed, the clerk of the court shall,

(*a*) provide the defendant with a receipt for the notice; and

(*b*) as soon as practicable after the filing of the certificate of offence, set a day and time for trial and issue the notice of trial. O. Reg. 505/93, s. 4; O. Reg. 498/94, s. 9.

14. (1) A defendant who attends at the time and place specified in an offence notice for the purpose of taking steps under subsection 7(1) of the Act shall give the offence notice to the office of the court specified in the notice.

(2) The court shall give to a defendant a receipt for an offence notice delivered to the court in accordance with subrule (1).

15. (1) The following matters shall be dealt with only in court:

1. Quashing a proceeding, except under section 9, 18.3 or 18.5 of the Act or under section 205.7 or 205.19 of the *Highway Traffic Act.*
2. Amending an information, a certificate of offence or a certificate of parking infraction.

(2) A justice may dispose of an application under section 18.3 of the Act on the basis of the parking infraction notice and the form of application presented by the applicant.

(3) A justice may dispose of an application under section 18.5 of the Act on the basis of the form of application presented by the applicant, together with any oral submission the applicant wishes to make or the justice wishes to hear.

(4) A justice may dispose of an application under section 19 of the Act on the basis of the notice of fine and due date and the affidavit of the applicant. O. Reg. 505/93, s. 5; O. Reg. 498/94, s. 10; O. Reg. 567/00, s. 2

16. A justice shall not quash a proceeding or amend a certificate of offence in respect of a defendant who is appearing before the justice for the purposes of section 7 of the Act.

17. Where a defendant appears before a justice under section 7 of the Act and it appears that the certificate of offence has not been filed in the office of the court, the justice may receive the plea of guilty and submissions of the defendant and specify the amount of fine the justice will impose and the time the justice will allow for payment when the certificate of offence is filed and a conviction is entered.

18. Where a defendant appears before a justice under section 7 of the Act and the justice is of the opinion that the certificate of offence is so defective on its face so that it cannot be cured under section 33, 34, 35 or 36 of the Act, the justice shall refuse to accept the plea, shall inform the defendant of the reason for the refusal and shall inform the defendant of the provisions of section 5 or 5.1 of the Act as applicable. O. Reg. 498/94, s. 11.

19. Money paid to the office of the court by a defendant who was served with an offence notice shall be refunded to the defendant if the certificate of offence is not filed in the office of the court named therein within seven days after the day on which the offence notice was served or within such extension of time as may be granted by the court.

20. Where notice is given to the clerk by the prosecutor that the prosecutor does not intend to file a certificate requesting conviction or a certificate of parking infraction that has been issued in respect of a parking infraction under an Act of the Legislature or under a regulation made under the authority of an Act, the prosecutor shall furnish the clerk with the name and address of the person to whom the parking infraction notice was issued and money paid to the office of the court in respect of the alleged parking infraction shall be refunded to that person. O. Reg. 505/93, s. 6.

21. Every justice shall keep a daily docket, electronically or in the form supplied by the clerk of the court, and shall record the disposition of every proceeding or matter under Part I or II of the Act dealt with by the justice. O. Reg. 498/94, s. 12.

22. (1) A justice acting under section 7 of the Act who imposes a fine that is less than the set fine or less than the minimum fine prescribed for the offence by the provision that creates the penalty shall endorse on the certificate of offence or the information, as the case may be, the decision and the reasons for the decision.

(1.1) A justice who quashes a proceeding under section 9 or 9.1 of the Act or under section 205.7, 205.11 or 205.19 of the *Highway Traffic Act* shall endorse on the certificate of offence or the information, as the case may be, the decision and the reasons for the decision.

(2) A justice who quashes a proceeding under section 18.4 of the Act shall endorse on the court filing document to which the certificate of parking infraction is affixed or appended the decision and the reasons for the decision.

(2.1) A justice who strikes out a conviction under section 18.3 or 18.5 of the Act shall endorse on the form of application the decision and the reasons for the decision.

(3) In addition to recording the decision on a daily docket, a justice referred to in subrule (1) or (1.1) shall complete a separate report, in the form that shall be supplied by the clerk of the court, of the decision and the reasons for the decision.

(4) A completed report mentioned in subrule (3) forms part of and shall be kept with the records of the court maintained by the clerk of the court. O. Reg. 505/93, s. 7; O. Reg. 498/94, s. 13; O. Reg. 567/00, s. 3

22.1 A justice acting under section 9 of the Act or under section 205.7 of the *Highway Traffic Act* may examine by electronic means a certificate of offence that has been filed in an electronic format and may indicate his or her disposition of the proceeding by electronic means. O. Reg. 498/94, s. 14.

23. Upon payment of a fine, the administrative officer of the entity receiving the fine shall, upon request, issue to the defendant a receipt for the payment. O. Reg. 505/93, s. 8.

24. [Revoked O. Reg. 498/94, s. 15.].

25. A justice who issues a warrant of committal under subsection 69(14) of the Act shall enter the reasons for the warrant in the records of the court. O. Reg. 498/94, s. 16.

26. Where a person is sentenced to a term of imprisonment and a warrant of committal is issued for custody of the person to commence, under subsection 63(2) of the Act, on a day that is later than the day of sentencing, the clerk of the court, as soon as practicable after the warrant is issued,

(*a*) shall cause to be given or delivered to the person a notice stating the warrant has been issued and specifying the place where and the time within which the person is to surrender into custody; and

(*b*) shall deliver the warrant to the individual who is to accept the custody of the person.

27. (1) The following oath is prescribed for the purpose of subsection 84(1) of the Act:

I, ...

do swear (or solemnly affirm) that I am capable of translating and will translate to the best of my skill and ability from

....
.... to ....
(name of language) (name of language)
.... to ....
(name of language) (name of language)
in this proceeding.
SO HELP ME GOD. (Omit this line in an affirmation).

(2) The following oath is prescribed for the purpose of subsection 84(2) of the Act:

I, ...
do swear (or solemnly affirm) that I am capable of translating and will translate to the best of my skill and ability
from .... to ....
(name of language) (name of language)
.... to ....
(name of language) (name of language)
in proceedings under the *Provincial Offences Act*.
SO HELP ME GOD. (Omit this line in an affirmation).

28. (1) The clerk of the court who receives notice from the clerk of an appeal court that a notice of appeal has been filed shall transmit the order appealed from and transmit or transfer custody of all other material referred to in section 133 of the Act to the clerk of the appeal court within ten days after receiving the notice, to the extent that the clerk of the court receiving notice has the order or the other material in his or her possession.

(1.1) The clerk of the court receiving notice shall direct that any electronic document that has not been previously printed for the purpose of disposing of the charge and that is required as part of an appeal record be printed so as to create an original record, unless the appeal court requests that the document be transmitted to it in an electronic format.

(2) In an appeal from an order made under Part II, if the clerk of the court receiving notice does not have the order or the other material in his or her possession, the clerk may request and the municipality shall provide to the clerk the certificate of parking infraction and proof of ownership of the motor vehicle relating to the prosecution of the matter giving rise to the appeal. O. Reg. 505/93, s. 9; O. Reg. 498/94, s. 17.

29. Where a transcript of evidence at trial, including reasons for judgment or sentence, is requested from the clerk of the court for the purpose of an appeal, the clerk,

(*a*) shall complete and deliver to the person making the request a certificate of preparation of transcript in Form 2 of Regulation 196 of Revised Regulations of Ontario, 1990;

(*b*) shall ensure that the transcript is prepared with reasonable diligence;

(*c*) shall obtain and attach to the transcript a certificate by the person who prepared the transcript that it is an accurate transcription of the evidence and reasons recorded at trial; and

(*d*) shall notify,

(i) the appellant,

(ii) the clerk of the court in which the appeal is taken, and

(iii) if the Crown Attorney is not the appellant or respondent, the Crown Attorney, when the transcript has been completed.

30. The clerk of the court who receives notice of the decision of an appeal court on an appeal from a decision of the court shall give the notice and any written reasons or endorsement included with the notice to the justice whose decision was appealed from.

31. (1) Where, upon an appeal, the appeal court has directed a new trial, upon motion by the prosecutor without notice a justice shall issue a summons to the defendant.

(2) Where a justice issues a summons under subrule (1), the clerk of the court shall, as soon as is practicable, give notice to the prosecutor of the time and place of the trial.

(3) Where the appeal court has directed a new trial and sets a date for the trial with the consent of the parties to the appeal, the defendant shall be deemed to have received notice of trial, and subrules (1) and (2) do not apply. O. Reg. 498/94, s. 18.

32. (1) An affidavit of service of an offence notice or summons shall be in Form 101.

(2) An affidavit in support of a request under section 11 or 19 of the Act or section 205.13 or 205.23 of the *Highway Traffic Act* shall be in Form 102.

(3) A certificate under section 11 of the Act or section 205.13 or 205.23 of the *Highway Traffic Act* shall be in Form 103.

(4) A summons under section 22 of the Act shall be in Form 104.

(5) An information under section 23 of the Act shall be in Form 105.

(6) A summons under section 24 of the Act shall be in Form 106.

(7) A warrant for arrest under section 24 of the Act shall be in Form 107.

(8) A notice of cancellation of summons under section 24 of the Act shall be in Form 108.

(9) A summons under section 39 of the Act shall be in Form 109.

(10) A warrant under subsection 40(1) of the Act shall be in Form 110.

(11) A warrant under subsection 40(2) of the Act shall be in Form 111.

(12) A recognizance by witness under section 40 of the Act shall be in Form 112.

(13) A warrant under subsection 40(10) of the Act shall be in Form 113.

(14) An order under subsection 40(6) of the Act shall be in Form 114.

(15) An order under section 41 of the Act shall be in Form 115.

(16) A certificate under section 42 of the Act shall be in Form 116.

(17) An order to attend for examination under section 44 of the Act shall be in Form 117.

(18) A warrant to take a defendant into custody under section 44 of the Act shall be in Form 118.

(19) A certificate of execution of a warrant issued under subsection 44(6) of the Act shall be in Form 119.

(20) A summons under section 51 of the Act shall be in Form 120.

(21) An order of dismissal under section 53 of the Act shall be in Form 121.

(22) A summons to a defendant under section 54 of the Act shall be in Form 122.

(23) A warrant under section 54 of the Act shall be in Form 123.

(24) A warrant under subsection 63(2) of the Act shall be in Form 124.

(25) A motion under subsection 66(6) of the Act shall be in Form 125.

(26) An order under subsection 66(6) of the Act extending time for payment of a fine shall be in Form 126.

(27) A certificate of default under section 68 of the Act shall be in Form 127.

(28) [Revoked O. Reg. 498/94, s. 19.]

(29) [Revoked O. Reg. 498/94, s. 19.]

(30) [Revoked O. Reg. 498/94, s. 19.]

(31) An undertaking by a defendant to appear shall be in Form 131.

(32) A probation order under section 72 of the Act shall be in Form 132.

(33) A summons to a defendant where a new trial is ordered by an appeal court shall be in Form 133.

(34) A recognizance under subsection 149(2) of the Act shall be in Form 134.

(35) A recognizance under section 150 of the Act shall be in Form 135.

(36) An order for detention of a defendant under section 150 of the Act shall be in Form 136.

(37) A warrant under section 155 of the Act for the arrest of a defendant shall be in Form 137.

(38) A certificate of arrest under section 155 of the Act shall be in Form 138.

(39) A certificate under subsection 157(1) of the Act as to failure to comply with a condition of a recognizance shall be in Form 139.

(40) An information to obtain a search warrant under section 158 of the Act shall be in Form 140.

(41) A search warrant under section 158 of the Act shall be in Form 141.

(42) A statement under section 161 of the Act shall be in Form 142.

(43) A warrant remanding,
(*a*) a witness under subsection 40(6) of the Act; or
(*b*) a defendant under subsection 150(4) of the Act, shall be in Form 143.

(44) An order for the release of a defendant under subsection 150(2) of the Act shall be in Form 144.

(45) An order for the release of a person in custody under subsection 40(9) of the Act shall be in Form 145.

(46) A warrant of committal the form of which is not otherwise specified in these rules shall be in Form 146.

(47) An order the form of which is not otherwise specified in these rules shall be in Form 147.

(48) A recognizance under subsection 149(3) of the Act shall be in Form 148.

(49) [Revoked O. Reg. 498/94, s. 19.]

(50) An application under section 18.3 of the Act shall be in Form 150.

(51) An application under section 18.5 of the Act shall be in Form 151.

(52) An application under subsection 19(2) of the Act shall be in Form 152.

(53) An order under subsection 69(21) of the Act shall be in Form 153. O. Reg. 505/93, s. 10; O. Reg. 498/94, s. 19; O. Reg. 567/00, s. 4.

Appendix C

Forms

Notice of Motion

Ministry of the Attorney General
Ministère du Procureur général
Ontario

NOTICE OF MOTION
AVIS DE MOTION

BETWEEN / *ENTRE* .... Prosecutor / *Poursuivant*

and / *et*

.... Defendant / *Défendeur*

TAKE NOTICE that an application will be made by the ....
SACHEZ QU'UNE requête sera déposée par (prosecutor/defendant) / *(poursuivant/défendeur)*

on / *le* ...., yr / *an* ...., before the Ontario Court of Justice / *devant la Cour de justice de l'Ontario*

at / *à* ....

in the following matter: / *en ce qui concerne l'affaire suivant :*

....

....

....

for an Order as follows: / *Pour une ordonnance comme suit :*

....

....

....

....

....

....

And further take notice that is support of this application will be read the affidavit of ....
Sachez aussi qu'à l'appui de cette requête sera lu l'affidavit de

......................., and such other and further evidence as may be required.
ainsi que d'autres preuves qui s'avéreront nécessaires.

Dated this / *Fait le* ...day of / *jour de* ...., yr / *an* ....

at / *à* ....

Signed / *Signature* ....

Address / *Adresse* ....

☐ defendant/prosecutor / *défendeur/poursuivant*

☐ counsel for defendant/prosecutor / *avocat du défendeur/poursuivant*

☐ Agent for defendant/prosecutor / *mandataire du défendeur/poursuivant*

TO / À :
Prosecutor (or Defendant) and the Clerk of the Court
Poursuivant (ou défendeur) et au greffier de la Cour

FOR INFORMATION ON ACCESS TO ONTARIO COURTS FOR PERSONS WITH DISABILITIES CALL 1-800-387-4456 TORONTO AREA 326-0111

POUR PLUS DE RENSEIGNEMENTS SUR L'ACCÈS DES PERSONNES HANDICAPÉES AUX TRIBUNAUX DE L'ONTARIO, COMPOSEZ LE 1-800-387-4456 RÉGION DE TORONTO 326-0111

CD 0007 (Rev. 05/99)

General Form for Affidavit

Ministry of the Attorney General | Ministère du Procureur général

Ontario

GENERAL FORM FOR AFFIDAVIT
FORMULE GÉNÉRALE D'AFFIDAVIT

I, ...
Je soussigné(e),
of ....
de
make oath and say as follows:
déclare sous serment que:

....

....

....

....

....

....

....

....
(signature)

Sworn by the said ....
Déclaré sous serment par
before me, ...
devant moi
at..
dans le/la
on the ... day of ...., yr ....
le *jour de* *an*

....
A commissioner, etc./Commissaire, etc.

CD 0006 (rev 10/99)

Notice of Intention to Appear (Form 7)

NOTICE OF INTENTION TO APPEAR
AVIS D'INTENTION DE COMPARAÎTRE

Ontario Court Of Justice
Cour de justice de l'Ontario
PROVINCE OF ONTARIO
PROVINCE DE L'ONTARIO

Form / *Formule* 7
Provincial Offences Act
Loi sur les infractions provinciales
Reg. / *Règl.* 950

TAKE NOTICE THAT I ....
VEUILLEZ PRENDRE AVIS QUE JE, SOUSSIGNÉ(E) (defendant's name / *nom du défendeur/de la défenderesse*)

....
Current address / *adresse actuelle* Street / *rue* Apt. / *app.*

....
Municipality / *municipalité* Province Postal Code/ *code postal*

....
Offence number / *numéro de l'infraction* Offence date / *date de l'infraction*

wish to give notice of my intention to appear in court to enter a plea of not guilty at the time and place set for the trial respecting the charge set out in the Offence Notice or Parking Infraction Notice / *désire aviser de mon intention de comparaître devant le tribunal pour inscrire un plaidoyer de non-culpabilité à l'heure et au lieu prévus pour le procès en réponse à l'accusation énoncée dans l'avis d'infraction ou l'avis d'infraction de stationnement*

FOR ANY OFFENCE EXCEPT s.s. 144(18.1) OF THE HTA COMPLETE THIS SECTION:
POUR TOUTE INFRACTION NON VISÉE AU PARAGRAPHE 144 (18.1) DU CODE DE LA ROUTE, REMPLIR CETTE SECTION :

I intend to challenge the Provincial Offences Officer's evidence. I request that the officer attend the trial.
J'ai l'intention de contester la preuve de l'agent des infractions provinciales. Je demande que l'agent assiste au procès.

☐ No / *Non* ☐ Yes / *Oui*

Note:
If you have been charged with an offence under s.s. 144(18.1) of the *Highway Traffic Act* (red light running/owner), s. 205.20 of the *Highway Traffic Act* provides that you must apply to the justice at trial if you wish to compel the attendance of the Provincial Offences Officer who issued the Certificate of Offence or who certified the photographs to be tendered at your trial.

Remarque :
Si vous avez été accusé(e) d'une infraction visée au paragraphe 144 (18.1) du Code de la route *(passage au feu rouge/propriétaire), l'article 205.20 du* Code de la route *prévoit que vous devez vous adresser au juge du procès si vous désirez obtenir la comparution de l'agent des infractions provinciales qui a délivré le procès-verbal d'infraction ou qui a certifié les photos qui seront présentées en preuve lors de votre procès.*

☐ I intend to appear in court to enter a plea at the time and place set for the trial and I wish that it be held in the English language

☐ *J'ai l'intention de comparaître devant le tribunal pour inscrire un plaidoyer à l'heure et au lieu prévus pour le procès et je désire que le procès se déroule en français.*

I request a .... language interpreter for the trial.
(leave blank if inapplicable)

Je demande l'aide d'un interprète de langue .... *pour le procès.*
(À remplir s'il y a lieu)

Note: If you **fail to notify** the court office of **address changes** you may not receive important notices *e.g.*, your Notice of Trial. You may be convicted in your absence if you do not attend the trial.

Remarque *: Si vous **omettez de prévenir** le greffe du tribunal de **tout changement d'adresse**, vous pourriez ne pas recevoir d'importants avis (par ex., votre avis de procès). Vous pourriez être déclaré(e) coupable en votre absence si vous n'assistez pas au procès.*

....
(signature of defendant or representative / *signature du défendeur/de la défenderesse ou du représentant/de la représentante*)

.... 20 ......
date

Representative's Name & Address/ *nom et adresse du représentant/de la représentante*

....
Name/ *nom*

....
Current address / *adresse actuelle* *Street / rue* *Apt./ app.*

....
Municipality / *municipalité* Province Postal Code/ *code postal*

Disclosure Request Form

Brampton

Legal Services

Request Date: ____________________

THIS FORM HAS BEEN DEVELOPED TO EXPEDITE DISCLOSURE OF YOUR CASE.

Please complete the information required below and return this form to:

Prosecutors' Office
Ontario Court of Justice
5 Ray Lawson Blvd.
Brampton, ON L6Y 5L7

INQUIRIES: (905) 450-7211 (voice)
(905) 450-4368 (fax)

YOU MUST HAVE A COURT DATE PRIOR TO REQUESTING DISCLOSURE. PLEASE BE ADVISED THAT YOUR DISCLOSURE WILL TAKE FOUR TO SIX WEEKS TO OBTAIN.

IF YOU DO NOT RECEIVE DISCLOSURE ON YOUR ORIGINAL COURT DATE & THE MATTER IS ADJOURNED FOR LACK OF DISCLOSURE, IT IS YOUR RESPONSIBILITY TO RE-REQUEST IT WITH THE NEW COURT DATE.

NAME OF DEFENDANT: ____________________

OFFICER IN CHARGE: Peel Regional Police
- Name ____________________
- Badge # ____________________
- Division ____________________
- Offence Notice # ____________________

OFFENCE DATE: ____________________

COURT DATE/TIME/COURTROOM #: ____________________

CHARGE (S): ____________________

PARTIES REQUESTING DISCLOSURE: ____________________

ADDRESS (if required): ____________________

____

TELEPHONE # ____________________ FAX # ____________________

Ontario Court of Justice, Prosecutions, 5 Ray Lawson Blvd., Brampton, ON L6Y 5L7 Tel: 905-450-7211 Fax: 905-874-2692 www.brampton.ca TTY 905-874-2130

THE CORPORATION OF THE CITY OF BRAMPTON

Request for Disclosure

To Staff Sergeant: Request Made As Of: January 10, 2003

Department:

Re Constable: Badge:

REQUEST FOR DISCLOSURE

Defendant:

Offence Date: November 29, 2002 - P.O.N.

Charge: Careless Driving - HTA

Court Date: **May 5, 2003 at 10:30 a.m. – Courtroom #18**

The City of Brampton Prosecutors' Office has received a request for disclosure in the above-mentioned charge. Please have the officer prepare and forward a copy of the accident report, a full copy of their notes, and any witness statements in respect to this charge to the attention of . This should be sent to 50 Kennedy Road South, Ontario Court of Justice, Prosecutors' Office via your Peel Regional Police courier.

If the notes are illegible they will have to be type written.

Please have the officer comply with this request by:

Respectfully Submitted,

Ontario Court of Justice, Prosecutors' Office
50 Kennedy Road South
(905) 450-7211 (Voice)
(905) 450-4368 (Fax)
@city.brampton.on.ca

PLEASE RETURN A COPY OF THIS MEMO WITH THE DISCLOSURE MATERIALS.

Disclosure Facsimile Message Form

FACSIMILE MESSAGE

THE CORPORATION OF THE CITY OF BRAMPTON
2 Wellington Street West, 6th Floor, Brampton, Ontario L6Y 4R2
Telephone: (905) 874-2675

FROM: **SENT:** **2/5/03**

Disclosure Clerk
From my FAX No.:

Number of Pages (including cover sheet):

If there are any problems with this transmission, please call
at (905) 450-7211

TO:

FAX:

SUBJECT:

MESSAGE: As per your request, please find enclosed disclosure material for the above noted individual.

RECEIVER'S SIGNATURE: ______________________________

This facsimile transmission is confidential, may contain legally privileged information (which privilege is expressly claimed and not waived), and is intended for the review of only the individual or party to whom it is addressed, and for no one else. If you are not the intended recipient, you are hereby notified that any dissemination, distribution, or copying of this facsimile transmission is strictly prohibited.

If you have received this facsimile transmission in error, or you are not the intended recipient, please notify us immediately by calling (905) 450-7211. We would also request that you either destroy the facsimile transmission or return it to us by mail.

Request for Provincial Offences Disclosure

Name of Accused: ______________________________

Telephone Number Where You Can Be Reached: ______________________________

Ticket Number: ______________________________

		Section #	Statute
Charges:	(1)	____________	______________________
	(2)	____________	______________________
	(3)	____________	______________________

(Continue below If Required)

Investigating Force: London P.D. ( ) Strathroy P.D. ( )

O.P.P. ____________ ( ) Other ____________ ( )
(Detachment) (Please identify)

Next Court Date: ______________________________

Today's Date: ______________________________

Signature of Defendant: ______________________________ OR

Signature of Counsel/Student/Agent: ______________________________

Name of Law Firm: ____________ Telephone Number: ____________

YOU ARE RESPONSIBLE FOR
PICKING UP YOUR DISCLOSURE.
PLEASE ALLOW 10 WORKING DAYS.

MISSISSAUGA

PROVINCIAL OFFENCES ACT PART 1 CHARGES

DISCLOSURE REQUEST

Please complete the information required below upon receiving a trial date and return this form to the Prosecution Office, Central Library, 950 Burnhamthorpe Rd. West, Mississauga ON L5B 3B4 or fax to 905-615-4504. Once disclosure becomes available it will be forwarded to you by fax transmission or you will be contacted regarding pick-up of this material. Your co-operation and assistance is appreciated.

PLEASE NOTE: REPLACEMENT OF ANY DISCLOSURE MATERIAL PREVIOUSLY PROVIDED WILL BE SUBJECT TO A FEE IN ACCORDANCE WITH THE CITY OF MISSISSAUGA GENERAL FEES AND CHARGES BY-LAW NO. 0539-2004.

Prosecution Office Phone: 905-615-4088 Fax: 905-615-4504

DEFENDANT: ______________________________

CHARGES: ______________________________

WAS A COLLISION INVOLVED: YES ______ **NO** ______

OFFENCE NO: ____________ **OFFENCE DATE:** ____________

TRIAL DATE: ________ **TIME:** ________ **COURT RM:** ________

OFFICERS BADGE NO: PEEL __________ **OPP** __________

DATE REQUESTED: __________ **REQUESTED BY:** __________

ADDRESS

____

PHONE NO: ______________ **FAX NO:** ______________

Regional
NIAGARA

PROVINCIAL OFFENCES COURT

TO: Nancy A. Macdonald Duncan
Regional Prosecutor
Court House
4635 Queen Street, P.O. Box 840
Niagara Falls, Ontario, L2E 6V6

Tel: (905) 371-8988
Cel: (905) 933-6435
Fax: (905) 371-9855

FROM: ______________________

____

____

____

DATE: ______________________

DEFENDANT: ______________________

COURT DATE: ______________________

OFFENCE DATE: ______________________

PON: ______________________

OFFICER: ______________________

CHARGES: ______________________

Faxing Disclosure Materials Procedures

June 3, 2002

To Whom It May Concern:

<u>RE: Faxing out Disclosure Materials – A New Procedure</u>

Please be advised that as of June 3, 2002 the City of Brampton Prosecutors' office will be implementing a new procedure when faxing out disclosure. In order to ensure that your office receives all disclosure documents in our possession we will be adding that a signature line to our fax cover sheet. Upon receiving your disclosure material, we ask that you sign the bottom of our cover sheet and fax it back to our office thus indicating that you have received the number of pages indemnified on the cover sheet.

This new procedure will ensure you are receiving all required documents and ensure there were no problems with the transmission. If our office does not receive a signed copy of the fax cover sheet the service of faxing will be discontinued and we will ask that you pick up your disclosure material in the future.

Our office provides the option of faxing out disclosure in order to make the process more convenient for everyone. If you have any questions please do not hesitate to contact our office at (905) 450-7211 and by facsimile at (905) 450-4368.

Yours truly,

City of Brampton Prosecutor's Office

Probation Order (s. 72)

PROBATION ORDER
ORDONNANCE DE PROBATION

Under Section 72 of the *Provincial Offences Act*
Aux termes de l'article 72 de la Loi sur les infractions provinciales

ONTARIO COURT OF JUSTICE
COUR DE JUSTICE DE L'ONTARIO
PROVINCE OF ONTARIO
PROVINCE DE L'ONTARIO

Form / *Formule* 132
Courts of Justice Act
Loi sur les tribunaux judiciaires
R.R.O. / *R.R.O.* 1990
O. Reg. / *Régl. de l'Ont.* 200

Whereas ____________________ hereinafter called the Defendant
Attendu que ____________________ *ci-après appelé le défendeur*

was convicted of the offence of / *a été reconnu coupable d'avoir commis l'infraction suivant*

contrary to ____________________ section ____________
par dérogation à ____________________ *article* ____________

by the Ontario Court of Justice at **5 Ray Lawson Boulevard**
devant la Cour de justice de l'Ontario au(à la)

on the ______ day of ____________, yr. ______ in a proceeding commenced by information.
le ______ *jour de* ____________ *an* ______ *à la suite d'une poursuite intentée par voie de dénonciation.*

And whereas on the ______ day of ____________, yr. ______, the court
Et attendu que ______ *jour de* ____________ *an* ______ *le tribunal*
(check applicable box / *cocher ce qui s'applique ici*)

☐ suspended the passing of sentence on the Defendant and directed the Defendant to comply with the conditions set out below.
a suspendu le prononcé de la peine imposée au défendeur et ordonné que celui-ci conforme aux conditions énumérées ci-dessous.

☐ in addition to / *en plus de*
- ☐ fining the Defendant / *lui imposer une amende*
- ☐ sentencing the Defendant to imprisonment / *le condamner à une peine d'emprisonnement*

directed that the Defendant comply with the conditions set out below.
a ordonné que celui-ci conforme aux conditions énumérées ci-dessous.

☐ imposed upon the Defendant a sentence of imprisonment that did not exceed ninety days, ordered that the sentence be served intermittently and directed that the Defendant comply with the conditions set out below at all times when the Defendant is not in confinement under that sentence.
a imposée au défendeur une peine d'emprisonnement d'une durée que n'excède pas quatre-vingt-dix jours, a ordonné que la peine soit purgée de façon intermittente et a ordonné que le défendeur se conforme aux conditions ci-dessous pendant tout le temps qu'il n'est pas détenu aux termes de la condamnation prononcée contre lui.

Therefore, it is ordered that for the period of ____________________ commencing
À ces causes, ordre est donné que pour la période de ____________________ *qui commence*
(check applicable box / *cocher ce que s'applique ici*)

☐ from the date of this order,
à compter de la date de cette ordonnance,

☐ from the date of the Defendant's release from custody,
à compter de la date à laquelle le défendeur a été remis en liberté,

the Defendant shall comply with the following conditions:
le défendeur doit se conformer aux conditions suivantes :

1. The Defendant shall not commit the same offence or any related or similar offence, or any offence under a statute of Canada or Ontario or any other province of Canada that is punishable by imprisonment.
Le défendeur ne doit pas commettre la même infraction, toute infraction connexe ou semblable ou toute infraction qui, aux termes d'une loi du Canada, de l'Ontario ou de toute autre province du Canada, est punissable d'une peine d'emprisonnement.

2. The Defendant shall appear before the court as and when required.
Le défendeur doit comparaître devant le tribunal de la façon prescrite et au moment où il est enjoint de le faire.

POA 0132 CSD (rev. 11/03) (posted / *affichée* 03/01/05)

3. The Defendant shall notify the court of any change in the Defendant's address.
Le défendeur doit aviser le tribunal de tout changement d'adresse.

And, in addition, the Defendant / *Et le défendeur doit de plus*
(set out and number additional conditions separately / *énoncer et numéroter les conditions supplémentaires séparément*)

Ordered at **Brampton, Ontario**
Ordonnance rendue à

this ________ day of ____________________, yr. __________
ce *jour de* *an*

____
Judge or Justice of the Peace in and for the Province of Ontario
Juge ou juge de paix et pour la province de l'Ontario

I certify that the Defendant was given a copy of this probation order on the ______ day of ____________________, yr. ______
Je certifie qu'une copie de cette ordonnance de probation a été remise au défendeur le *jour de* *an*

☐ by personal service
par voie de signification personnelle

☐ by sending it to the Defendant by mail to
par courrier à

the Defendant's last known address appearing on the records of the court.
la dernière adresse du défendeur qui est donnée dans les archives du tribunal.

____
Clerk / *Greffier*

NOTE: Sections 73 and 75 of the *Provincial Offences Act* is as follows:

73 (1) When order comes into force – A probation order comes into force.
(a) on the dale on which the order is made; or
(b) where the defendant is sentenced to imprisonment other than a sentence to be served intermittently, upon the expiration of that sentence.

(2) Continuation in force – Subject to section 75, where a defendant who is bound by a probation order is convicted of an offence or is imprisoned in default of payment of a fine, the order continues in force except in so far as the sentence or imprisonment renders it impossible for the defendant to comply for the time being with the order.

75 Breach of probation order – Where a defendant who is bound by a probation order is convicted of an offence constituting a breach of condition of the order and,
(a) the time within which the defendant may appeal or make a motion for leave to appeal against that conviction has expired and defendant has not taken an appeal or made a motion for leave to appeal;
(b) the defendant has taken an appeal of made a motion for leave to appeal against the conviction and the appeal of motion for leave has been dismissed or abandoned; or
(c) the defendant has given written notice to the court that convicted him/her that the defendant elects not to appeal,

or where the defendant otherwise wilfully fails or refuses to comply with the order, the defendant is guilty of an offence and upon conviction the court may,
(d) impose a fine of not more than $1,000 or imprisonment for a term of not more than thirty days, or both, an din lieu of or in addition to the penalty, continue the probation order with such changes or additions and for such extended term, not exceeding an additional year, as the court considers reasonable; or

(e) where the justice presiding is the justice who made the original order, in lieu or imposing the penalty under clause (d), revoke the probation order and impose the sentence the passing of which was suspended upon the making of the probation order.

***REMARQUE** : Les articles 73 et 75 Loi sur les infractions provinciales se lisent comme suit :*

73 1) Une ordonnance de probation entre en vigueur
(a) à la date de son émission; ou
(b) à l'expiration de la peine lorsque le défendeur est condamné à purger la peine d'emprisonnement autrement que d'une façon intermittente.

2) Sous réserve de l'article 75, lorsqu'un défendeur, sous le coup d'une ordonnance de probation, est reconnu coupable d'une infraction ou est emprisonné pour défaut de paiement d'une amende, l'ordonnance demeure en vigueur, sauf dans la mesure où la peine ou l'emprisonnement l'empêchent de se conformer aux dispositions de l'ordonnance.

75 Lorsqu'un défendeur qui est sous le coup d'une ordonnance de probation est reconnu coupable d'une infraction qui constitue une violation de conditions de l'ordonnance et
(a) que le délai durant lequel il peut interjeter appel de cette condamnation ou demander la permission de la porter en appel est expiré et qu'il n'a pas interjeté appel ou demandé la permission d'en appeler;
(b) qu'il a interjeté appel de cette condamnation ou qu'il a demandé la permission de la porter en appel et que l'appel ou la permission d'en appeler a été rejeté ou qu'il a abandonné son recours; ou
(c) qu'il a donné un avis écrit au tribunal qui l'a reconnu coupable, de son choix de ne pas interjeter appel,

ou, lorsque le défendeur, d'une autre façon fait sciemment défaut ou refuse de se conformer à l'ordonnance, il est coupable d'une infraction, et le tribunal peut, après avoir reconnu sa culpabilité,
(d) imposer une amende d'au plus 1 000 dollars ou un emprisonnement pour une période d'au plus trente jours ou les deux à la fois et, au lieu de la peine ou en plus de celle-ci, maintenir en vigueur l'ordonnance de probation pour une période n'excédant pas une année supplémentaire, en lui apportant les modifications ou les additions que le tribunal estime raisonnable; ou
(e) lorsque le juge qui préside le tribunal est celui qui a émis l'ordonnance originale, annuler l'ordonnance de probation et imposer la peine qui a été suspendue lors de l'émission de l'ordonnance de probation, au lieu d'imposer la peine prévue aux termes de l'alinéa d)

POA 0132 CSD (rev 11/03) (posted / *affichée* 03/01/05)

Motion for Extension of Time to Pay Fine (subs. 66(6))

MOTION UNDER SUBSECTION 66 (6) OF THE PROVINCIAL OFFENCES ACT
FOR EXTENSION OF TIME TO PAY FINE
REQUÊTE PRÉSENTÉE AUX TERMES DU PARAGRAPHE 66 (6) DE LA LOI SUR INFRACTIONS PROVINCIALES
EN VUE D'OBTENIR UNE PROROGATION DU DÉLAI POUR ACQUITTER LE PAIEMENT D'UNE AMENDE

ONTARIO COURT
OF JUSTICE
PROVINCE OF ONTARIO
COUR DE JUSTICE
DE L'ONTARIO
PROVINCE DE L'ONTARIO

Form 125
Formule 125
Courts of Justice Act
Loi sur les tribunaux judiciaires
O. Reg. / *Régl. O.* 200/90

(PLEASE PRINT / *LETTRES MOULÉES S.V.P.*)

1. I / *Je soussigné(e),* ....

of / *de* ....
(occupation / *profession*)

was convicted in Ontario Court of Justice / *ai été déclaré coupable devant la Cour de justice de l'Ontario*

at / *à* .... on the / *le* ...... day of / *jour de* ...., yr/*an* ....

of the offence of / *d'avoir commis l'infraction suivante* ....

contrary to / *par dérogation à* .... section / *article* ....

and was sentenced to pay a fine of $.................. (including cost and Victim Fine Surcharge)
et j'ai été condamné à verser une amende de *$ (y compris les frais et la suramende compensatoire).*

2. I was given / *J'ai obtenu un délai de* .... days/months to pay this amount / *jours (ou mois) pour acquitter ce montant.*

3. I have paid / *J'ai versé* $.................. *$* in satisfaction of the above amount / *pour qu'ils soient affectés au paiement du montant ci-dessus.*

4. I am unable to pay this amount within the time given for payment for the following reasons:
Il ne m'est pas possible d'acquitter le montant imposé dans le délai qui m'est accordé pour les raisons suivantes :

....

....

5. I hereby apply for an extension of time for payment until
Je formule cette requête en vue d'obtenir une prorogation du délai de paiement jusqu'au

the .... day of / *jour de* ...., yr / *an* ....

6. I am / *Je suis âgé de* .... years of age / *ans.*

7. I am / *Je* (check one / *cochez l'un ou l'autre, selon le cas*)
☐ employed / *possède un emploi*
☐ unemployed / *suis sans emploi*

8. (check one) (*cochez l'un ou l'autre selon le cas*)
☐ This is my first application for an extension
Je demande une prorogation du délai de paiement pour la première fois
☐ I previously obtained / J'ai déjà obtenu .... extension(s) of time for payment, the last of which expired / will expire upon / *prorogation(s) du délai de paiement dont la dernière s'est terminée (ou doit se terminer)*

the / *le* .... day of / *jour de* ...., yr / *an* ....

Date at / *Fait à* ....

this / *ce* .... day of / *jour de* ...., yr / *an* .... ______________________
(signature)

CD 0809 (Rev. 05/99)

Order Extending Time for Payment

ORDER EXTENDING TIME FOR PAYMENT
ORDONNANCE EN VUE D'OBTENIR UNE PROROGATION DU DÉLAI DE PAIEMENT
Under Section 66 of the Provincial Offences Act
aux termes de l'article 66 de la Loi sur les infractions provinciales

ONTARIO COURT
OF JUSTICE
PROVINCE OF ONTARIO
COUR DE JUSTICE
DE L'ONTARIO
PROVINCE DE L'ONTARIO

Form 126
Formule 126
Courts of Justice Act
Loi sur les tribunaux judiciaires
O. Reg. / *Régl. O.* 498/94

Upon reading the attached motion of
À la lecture de la requête ci-jointe de

dated the / *qui porte la date du* . . . . . . .day of / *jour de* . . . . yr / *an* . . . .

it is hereby ordered that the time for payment of the fine (including cost and Victim Surcharge) mentioned therein
j'ordonne, par le présentes, que le délai pour acquitter l'amende (y compris les frais et la suramende compensatoire) dont il est question dans la requête

(check appropriate box / cochez la cas approprlée)

A ☐ Is extended to the. . . . . day of. . . . . ,yr / an. . . . .
soit prorogé jusqu'au

B ☐ Is extended to the . . . . day of. . . . . , yr / an. to allow
soit prorogé jusqu'au *pour permettre*
for the following periodic payments / *les paiements périodiques suivants :*

. . . .

. . . .

. . . .

☐ Is not extended for the following reasons:
ne soit pas prorogé pour les raisons suivantes :

. . . .

. . . .

. . . .

. . . .

Ordered at / *Ordonnance rendue à*

this / *ce* . . . . day of / *jour de* . . . .

yr / *an* . . . .

If extension granted, Defendant's current address / *Si la prorogation est accordée, indiquer l'adresse actuelle du défendeur.*

. . . .

. . . .

. . . .

____
Justice of the Peace in and for the Province of Ontario
Juge de paix dans et pour la province de l'Ontario

CD 0809 (Rev. 05/99)

Record of Reopening Application (ss. 11, 19)

ONTARIO COURT
OF JUSTICE
PROVINCE OF ONTARIO
COUR DE JUSTICE
DE L'ONTARIO
PROVINCE DE L'ONTARIO

RECORD OF REOPENING APPLICATION
(SECTIONS 11, 19 OF THE *PROVINCIAL OFFENCES ACT* AND 205.13 OF THE *HIGHWAY TRAFFIC ACT*)
DOSSIER DE RÉOUVERTURE D'UNE DEMANDE
(ARTICLES 11 ET 19 DE LA LOI SUR LES INFRACTIONS PROVINCIALES *ET ARTICLE 205.13* DU CODE DE LA ROUTE)

____
OFFENCE NUMBER / NUMÉRO D'INFRACTION

Defendant's Name / *Nom du défendeur* ______________________

Current Address / *Adresse actuelle* ______________________

On the ______ day of ________, yr. _____, an application was made by the defendant/agent to reopen a conviction made
Le , *le défendeur/représentant a fait une demande en vue de la réouverture*

without a hearing on the ______ day of ________, yr. ______ .
de la déclaration de culpabilité faite sans audience, le

The following notice were sent/delivered to the defendant or agent:
Les avis suivants ont été envoyés/livrés au défendeur ou au représentant :

	Yes / *Oui*	No / *Non*	Unknown / *N.A.*
Offence Notice/Parking Infraction Notice *Avis d'infraction/Avis d'infraction de stationnement*	☐	☐	☐
Did the Provincial Offences Officer certify service? *L'agent des infractions provinciales a-t-il confirmé la signification?*	☐	☐	☐
Notice of Impending Conviction *Avis de déclaration de culpabilité imminente*	☐	☐	☐
Notice of Trial *Avis de procès*	☐	☐	☐
Notice of Fine and Due Date *Avis d'amende et de date d'échéance*	☐	☐	☐
Was a Notice of Intention to Appear filed? *Un avis d'intention de comparaître a-t-il été dépose?*	☐	☐	☐
Was a trial date set for the offence? *Une date de procès a-t-elle été fixée?*	☐	☐	☐
Was the defendant or agent present at trial? *Le défendeur ou le représenant a-t-il comparu au procès?*	☐	☐	☐

ORDER OF THE JUSTICE / ORDONNANCE DU JUGE

☐ Application deniied / *Demande rejetée* ______________________
☐ Conviction struck out, plea of guilty accepted and sentence imposed
Déclaration de culpabilité annulée, plaidoyer de culpabilité accepté et peine imposée
☐ Conviction struck out and Notice of Trial given to defendant/agent
Déclaration de culpabilité annulée et Avis de procès donné au défendeur/représentant
☐ Other / *Autre*

____
____
____

______________________ Justice of the Peace in and for the Province of Ontario / *Juge de paix dans et pour la province de l'Ontario*

______________________ Date

CD 0819 (rev. 11/99)

Affidavit in Support of Request for Reopening

Affidavit in Support of a Request for Reopening Form 102 / *Formule 102*
Affidavit à l'appui d'une demande de réouverture

(Under section 11 or subsection 19(1) of the *Provincial Offences Act* or section 205.13 or section 205.23 of the *Highway Traffic Act*)
(En vertu de l'article 11 ou du paragraphe 19(1) de la Loi sur les infractions provinciales *ou de l'article 205.13 ou de l'article 205.23 du* Code de la route)

ONTARIO COURT OF JUSTICE
COUR DE JUSTICE DE L'ONTARIO

PROVINCE OF ONTARIO
PROVINCE DE L'ONTARIO

I, ...
Je soussigné(e), (name / *nom*)

of ....
de (address / *adresse*)

make oath/affirm and say as follows:
déclare sous serment et affirme ce qui suit :

1. I was convicted without a hearing on the .... day of .... yr. ...., of the offence of
J'ai été reconnu(e) coupable sans la tenue d'une audience le *jour de* *an* *de l'infraction de*

....

Contrary to .... Section ....
contrairement à la/au *article*

2. (a) I was unable to appear at my hearing through no fault of my own because:
Je n'ai pu comparaître à mon audience, sans faute de ma part, parce que :

....
(state reason / *donner la raison*)

....

....

or/ou

(b) a notice or document relating to the offence was not delivered to me, namely:
un avis ou un document concernant l'infraction ne m'a pas été livré, notamment :

....
(identify document / *préciser quel document*)

....

....

3. The conviction first came to my attention on the .... day of ......, yr. ......
J'ai pris connaissance de la déclaration de culpabilité pour la première fois le *jour de* *an*

Sworn/affirmed before me at......................
Fait sous serment/affirmé devant moi à

this .... day of ....
le *jour de*

yr. ....
an

....
A Commissioner, etc./*Commissaire, etc.* (Signature of defendant/*Signature du défendeur/de la défenderesse*)

NOTE: Section 86 of the Provincial Offences Act provides: Every person who makes an assertion of fact in a statement or entry in a document or form for use under this Act knowing that the assertion is false is guilty of an offence and on conviction is liable to a fine of not more than $2,000.

Remarque : Selon l'article 86 de la Loi sur les infractions provinciales, «Est coupable d'une infraction et passible, sur déclaration de culpabilité, d'une amende d'au plus 2 000 $, quiconque affirme un fait dans une déclaration ou l'inscrit dans un document ou une formule dont la présente loi prévoit l'usage, et sait que cette affirmation est fausse».

FOR INFORMATION ON ACCESS TO ONTARIO COURTS FOR PERSONS WITH DISABILITIES, CALL 1-800-387-4456 TORONTO AREA 326-0111

POUR PLUS DE RENSEIGNEMENTS SUR L'ACCÈS DES PERSONNES HANDICAPÉES AUX TRIBUNAUX DE L'ONTARIO, COMPOSEZ LE 1-800-387-4456 RÉGION DE TORONTO 326-0111

CD 0801 (rev. 05/00)

Certificate of Striking Out Conviction

CERTIFICATE OF STRIKING OUT CONVICTION

(SECTION 11 OR 19 OF THE *PROVINCIAL OFFENCES ACT* OR SECTION 205.13 OR SECTION 205.23 OF THE *HIGHWAY TRAFFIC ACT*)

CERTIFICAT D'ANNULATION DE DÉCLARATION DE CULPABILITÉ

(ARTICLE 11 OU 19 DE LA LOI SUR LES INFRACTIONS PROVINCIALES *OU ARTICLES 205.13 OU ARTICLE 205.23 DU* CODE DE LA ROUTE*)*

Form 103 / *Formule 103*

TO: (Defendant) / *AU/À LA : (Défendeur/défenderesse)*

______________________ Offence Number / *Numéro d'infraction* ______________

______________________ Offence Date / *Date d'infraction* ______________

______________________ Statute / *Loi* ______________

______________________ Section / *Article* ______________

I certify that the conviction entered on the ________ day of ________, yr. ________, against the defendant in respect of
J'atteste que la déclaration de culpabilité, enregistrée le ________ *jour de* ________ *en* ________ *contre le défendeur ou la défenderesse susmentionné(e), en ce qui*

the offence described above was struck out by me on the ________ day of ________, yr. ________ .
concerne l'infraction décrite ci-dessus, a été annulée par moi le ________ *jour de* ________ *an* ________

____
Justice of the Peace in and for the Province of Ontario
Juge de paix dans et pour la province de l'Ontario

CD 0827 (rev. 05/00)

Notice of Appeal [Part I and Part II]

ONTARIO COURT OF JUSTICE
PROVINCE OF ONTARIO
COUR DE JUSTICE DE L'ONTARIO
PROVINCE DE L'ONTARIO

NOTICE OF APPEAL
AVIS D'APPEL

Parts I and II under Section 135 of the Provincial Offences Act
Parties I et II, aux termes de l'article 135 de la Loi sur les infractions provinciales

Form 1
Formule 1
Courts of Justice Act
Loi sur les tribunaux judiciaires
O. Reg. 722/94
Régl. O. 722/94

1. Ontario Court of Justice at / *Cour de justice de l'Ontario à* ....

2. Appellant is / *L'appelant est*

☐ Defendant / *le défendeur* ☐ Prosecutor / *le poursuivant* ☐ Attorney General / *le procureur général*

3. Name of appellant: / *Nom de l'appelant:* ....

Address for service: / *Adresse où les significations peuvent être faites:* ....

4. Counsel for appellant / *Avocat de l'appelant*

Name / *Nom* ....

Address for service: / *Adresse où les significations peuvent être faites:* ....

5. Name of respondent (if known) / *Nom de l'intimé (s'il est connu)* ....

Address for service: / *Adresse où les significations peuvent être faites :* ....

6. Counsel for respondent (if known): / *Avocat de l'intimé (s'il connu) :* ....

Address for service: / *Adresse où les significations peuvent être faites :* ....

7. Decision of Ontario Court of Justice: / *Décision de la Cour de justice de l'Ontario :*
(include name of Judge or Justice of the Peace appealed from, if known / *(Inscrire le nom du juge ou du juge de paix dont la décision est portée en appel, s'il est connu)*

....

8. Date of decision: / *Date de la décision :* ....

9. The appellant appeals against: / *L'appelant interjette appel :*

☐ Conviction / *de la déclaration de culpabilité* ☐ Dismissal / *du rejet de l'accusation* ☐ Sentence / *de la sentence*

10. If the appellant is in custody, place where held: / *Si l'appelant est sous garde, lieu de détention :* ....

11. (a) Description of offence[1]: / *Description de l'infraction[1] :* ....

(b) Certificate Number (if known): / *Numéro du procès verbal (s'il est connu) :* ....

[1] for example, speeding / *par exemple, excès de vitesse*

FOR INFORMATION ON ACCESS TO ONTARIO COURTS FOR PERSONS WITH DISABILITIES, CALL 1-800-387-4456 TORONTO AREA 326-0111
POUR PLUS DE RENSEIGNEMENTS SUR L'ACCÈS DES PERSONNES HANDICAPÉES AUX TRIBUNAUX DE L'ONTARIO, COMPOSEZ LE 1-800-387-4456 RÉGION DE TORONTO 326-0111

CD 0201 (rev 04/99)

12 (1) Statute[2] / *Loi*[2] : ....

13 Date of offence / *Date de l'infraction* : ....

14 Plea at trial: / *Plaidoyer au procès* :

The plea entered was: / *Le plaidoyer inscrit* :

(check one / cocher la case appropriée) ☐ Guilty / *coupable* ☐ Not guilty / *non coupable* ☐ Not known / *non connu*

15 The appellant wants the appeal court to: / *L'appelant désire que le tribunal d'appel* :
(check one / cocher la case appropriée)

☐ Find the defendant not guilty / *Déclare le défendeur non coupable*
☐ Find the defendant guilty / *Déclare le défendeur coupable*
☐ Order a new trial / *Ordonne la tenue d'un nouveau procès*
☐ Change the sentence / *Modifie la sentence*
☐ Other: / *Autre* : *(specify/préciser)*

....

....

....

16 The grounds of appeal are: / *Les motifs d'appel sont les suivants* : ....

....

Complete No. 17 for *Provincial Offences Act*, Part II, Parking Offences where the municipality is collecting its own parking fines.
Remplir le N° 17 dans le cas des infractions de stationnement visées par la partie II de la* Loi sur les infractions provinciales*, lorsque la municipalité perçoit ses propres amendes de stationnement.

17 The fine has been paid in full at .... on ....
L'amende a été payée intégralement à/au (municipality/*municipalité*) *le* (date)

18 Date: ....

19 Signature of appellant or counsel or agent:
Signature de l'appelant ou de son avocat ou représentant : ....

NOTES
A If appellant's address for service is that of the appellant's counsel, state counsel's full address and add appellant's own full address.
B Please notify the clerk of the court in writing immediately of any change of address. The court will communicate with you by mail at the address shown by you in this notice unless you notify the court of a change in your address.
C This notice of appeal must be filed with the clerk of the Ontario Court of Justice at the location where the decision appealed from was made.

Sections 111 and 112 of the *Provincial Offences Act* are as follows:
111. (1) A notice of appeal by a defendant shall not be accepted for filing if the defendant has not paid in full the fine imposed by the decision appealed from.
(2) A judge may waive compliance with subsection (1) and order that the appellant enter into a recognizance to appear on the appeal, and the recognizance shall be in such amount, with or without sureties, as the judge directs.
112. The filing of a notice of appeal does not stay the conviction unless a judge so orders.

REMARQUES :
A Si l'adresse fournie par l'appelant comme étant l'endroit où les significations peuvent lui être faites est celle de son avocat, donner l'adresse au complet de l'avocat et ajouter au complet l'adresse personnelle de l'appelant.
B Veuillez informer immédiatement par écrit le greffier du tribunal de tout changement d'adresse. Le tribunal s'adressera à vous par courrier à l'adresse que vous aurez donnée dans cet avis à moins que vous n'avisiez le tribunal que celle-ci a été changée.
C Cet avis d'appel doit être déposé auprès du greffier de la Cour de justice de l'Ontario dans la localité où l'appel a été interjeté.

Les articles 111 et 112 de la Loi sur les infractions provinciales *se lisent comme suit* :
111. (1) l'avis d'appel d'un défendeur n'est pas accepté pour dépôt s'il n'a pas payé intégralement l'amende imposée par la décision portée en appel.
(2) Un juge d'appel peut dispenser l'appelant de se conformer au paragraphe (1) et lui ordonner de consentir un engagement à comparaître en appel. Le juge décide du montant de l'engagement, avec ou sans caution.
112. Le dépôt d'un avis d'appel ne suspend pas la déclaration de culpabilité à moins qu'un juge d'appel ne l'ordonne.

---

[2] for example, *Highway Traffic Act* / *par exemple,* Code de la route

CO 0201 (rev. 04/99)

Notice of Appeal (Form 1) [Part III]

ONTARIO COURT OF JUSTICE
PROVINCE OF ONTARIO
COUR DE JUSTICE DE L'ONTARIO
PROVINCE DE L'ONTARIO

NOTICE OF APPEAL
Under Section 116 of the *Provincial Offences Act*
AVIS D'APPEL INTERJETÉ
En vertu de l'article 116 de la Loi sur les infractions provinciales

Form 1 PART III
Formule 1
Court of Justice Act
Loi sur les tribunaux judiciaires
O. Reg. 723/94
Règl. de l'Ont. 723/94

(Strike out inapplicable words / *Rayer ce qui ne s'applique pas*)

1. Superior Court of Justice or Ontario Court of Justice at ....
Cour supérieure de justice ou Cour de justice de l'Ontario à
....

2. Appellant is / *L'appelant(e) est*
☐ Defendant / *le défendeur (la défenderesse)* ☐ Prosecutor / *le poursuivant*
☐ Attorney General / *le procureur général*

3. Name of appellant: / *Nom de l'appelant(e) :* ....
Address for service: / *Domicile élu :* ....
....

4. Counsel for appellant: / *Avocat(e) de l'appelant(e) :* Name: / *Nom :* ....
Address for service: / *Domicile élu :* ....
....

5. Name of respondent (if known): / *Nom de l'intimé(e) (s'il est connu) :* ....
Address for service: / *Domicile élu :* ....
....

6. Counsel for respondent (if known): / *Avocat(e) de l'intimé(e) (s'il est connu) :* ....
Address for service: / *Domicile élu :* ....
....

7. Decision of Ontario Court of Justice: / *Décision rendue par la Cour de justice de l'Ontario :*
(include name of Judge or Justice of Peace appealed from, if known)
(inscrire le nom du juge ou du juge de paix dont la décision est portée en appel, s'il est connu) :
....
....

8. Date of decision: / *Date de la décision :* ....

9. The appellant appeals against: / *L'appelant(e) interjette appel :*
☐ conviction / *de la déclaration de culpabilité*
☐ dismissal / *du rejet de l'accusation*
☐ finding as to ability to conduct a defense / *de la conclusion quant à la capacité du défendeur (de la défenderesse) d'assurer sa défense*
☐ sentence / *de la sentence*
☐ order (s. 161 of the *P.O.A.* / *de l'ordonnance (art. 161 de la* L.I.P.)

by the Ontario Court of Justice / *de la Cour de justice de l'Ontario*

at / *à/au* ....
(address of court / *adresse du tribunal*)

[illegible] 1-800-387-4456 [illegible] 326-0111
[illegible] 1-800-387-4456 [illegible] 326-0111

CD 0301 (rev 03/00)

10. If defendant is in custody, place where held: / *Si l'appelant(e) est sous garde, lieu de détention :*..................................

....

11. (a) Description of offence[1]: / *Description de l'infraction[1] :* ....

(b) Information Number (if known) / *Numéro de la dénonciation (s'il est connu)* ....

12. (1) Statute[2]: / *Loi[2] :* ....

(2) Section[3] / *Article[3] :* ....

13. Date of offence: / *Date de l'infraction :* ....

14. Please at trial. / *Plaidoyer au procès :*..

15. The grounds for appeal are: / *Moyens d'appel :*
(specify the question of law or issue where the appeal is from conviction or acquittal or finding as to ability to conduct a defence or specify the ground for appeal against sentence / *préciser la question de droit ou la question en litige lorsqu'il est interjeté appel de la déclaration de culpabilité, de l'acquittement ou de la conclusion quant à la capacité du défendeur (de la défenderesse) d'assurer sa défense, ou préciser les moyens d'appel contre la sentence)*

1. ....

2. ....

16. In support of this appeal, the appellant relies upon the following:
À l'appui du présent appel, l'appelant(e) se fonde sur les documents suivants :
(set out documents such as transcript, etc. upon which the appellant relies)
(indiquer les documents, tels que les transcriptions, sur lesquels se fonde l'appelant(e))

1. ....

2. ....

17. The relief sought is: / *Mesure de redressement demandée :* ....

18. The appellant intends : / *Intention de l'appelant(e) :*

☐ to be present in person or by counsel and to present the issues and the appellant's arguments orally.
comparaître en personne ou par l'entremise d'un(e) avocat(e) et débattre les questions en litige et présenter ses arguments oralement.

☐ not to be present in person or by counsel and to present the issues and the appellant's arguments in writing.
ne comparaître ni en personne ni par l'entremise d'un(e) avocat(e) et débattre les questions en litige et présenter ses arguments par écrit.

19. Does the appellant intend to make a motion for an order that the appeal be heard by way of new trial in the appeal court?
L'appelant(e) a-t-il(elle) l'intention de présenter une motion en vue d'obtenir une ordonnance prévoyant la tenue de l'appel sous forme d'un nouveau procès devant le tribunal d'appel?

☐ Yes / *oui* ☐ No / *non*

20. Date:..

21. Signature of appellant or counsel: / *Signature de l'appelant(e) ou de son avocat(e) :* ....

NOTES:

1. If appellant's address for service is that of the appellant's counsel, state counsel's full address and add appellant's own full address.
2. Please notify the clerk of the court in writing immediately of any change of address. The court will communicate with you by mail at the address shown by you in this notice unless you notify the court of a change in your address.
3. This notice of appeal must be filed with the local registrar of the Superior Court of Justice or Ontario Court of Justice.

REMARQUES :

1. *Si le domicile élu de l'appelant(e) est celui de son avocat(e), indiquer l'adresse au complet de l'avocat(e) de même que l'adresse au complet de l'appelant(e) lui-même(elle-même).*
2. *En cas de changement d'adresse, en aviser immédiatement le greffier du tribunal par écrit. Si le tribunal n'est pas avisé, il communiquera avec vous par courrier à l'adresse indiquée au présent avis.*
3. *Le présent avis d'appel doit être déposé auprès du greffier local de la Cour supérieure de justice ou de la Cour de justice de l'Ontario.*

[1] for example, careless driving / *par exemple, conduite imprudente*

[2] for example, *Highway Traffic Act* / *par exemple, Code de la route*

[3] for example, Section 130 / *par exemple, article 130*

CO 0301 (rev 03/00)

Order for Transcript

Ministry of the Attorney General

Order for Transcript

Title of Proceeding

Date of Trial or Hearing

Name of Court

Date Transcript ordered

I require ____________ (No. of copies) copy/ies of the transcript of the evidence taken in the above matter, and upon being advised of the completion of the transcript, I undertake to pay the standard fee prescribed.

In the event I desire to cance this order, I will do so by written communication to the reporter involved and undertake to pay the standard fee for the work done up to date of receipt of written communication by the reporter.

Signature

Name of Firm

Address

Telephone Number

Date Order Received		Date Transcript		Number of Pages	Number of Copies
at Office	by Reporter	Completed	Delivered		

Form 2211 (06/90)

Notice of Time and Place of Hearing of Appeal (s. 135)

ONTARIO COURT OF JUSTICE
PROVINCE OF ONTARIO
COUR DE JUSTICE DE L'ONTARIO
PROVINCE DE L'ONTARIO

NOTICE OF TIME AND PLACE OF HEARING OF APPEAL
AVIS DE L'HEURE, DE LA DATE ET DU LIEU DE L'AUDITION DE L'APPEL
Under Section 135 of the *Provincial Offences Act*
Interjeté en vertu de l'article 135 de la Loi sur les infractions provinciales

Form 2
Formule 2
Courts of Justice Act
Loi sur les tribunaux judiciaires
O. Reg. 722/94
Règl. O. 722/94

To/*Destinataires* : ...., appellant/*appelant*

....
(address/*adresse*)

and/*et*

...., respondent/*intimé*

....
(address/*adresse*)

Take notice that the appeal in respect of the/*Avis vous est donné que l'appel relatif à* ....

....

in the Ontario Court of Justice on/*interjeté devant la Cour de justice de l'Ontario le* ...., yr./*an* ....

in respect of the charge that/*relativement à l'accusation selon laquelle* ....
(name/*nom*)

of/*de* ....

on or about/*le ou vers le* ...., yr./*an* ....

at/*à* ....

did commit the offence(s) of/*a commis l'infraction (les infractions) suivante(s)*..

....

....

....
(set out charges/*indiquer les accusations*)

contrary to/*en violation de l'article* ....section/*article* ....

will be heard in the Ontario Court of Justice at/*sera entendu devant la Cour de justice de l'Ontario à/au*

....

on/*le* ...., yr./*an*..............., at/*à* .... M
(*heure*)

Given at/*Fait à* ....

on/*le*......................................, yr./*an* ....

____
Clerk / *Greffier*

FOR INFORMATION ON ACCESS TO ONTARIO COURTS FOR PERSONS WITH DISABILITIES, CALL 1-800-387-4456 TORONTO AREA 326-0111

POUR PLUS DE RENSEIGNEMENTS SUR L'ACCÈS DES PERSONNES HANDICAPÉES AUX TRIBUNAUX DE L'ONTARIO, COMPOSEZ LE 1-800-387-4456 RÉGION DE TORONTO 326-0111

CD 0202 (rev 10/99)

Appendix D

List of Provincial Offences Courts in Ontario

Barrie Provincial Offences Court
56 Mulcaster St.
Barrie, ON L4M 4T5
Tel: 705-739-4291
Fax: 705-739-4292

Brampton Provincial Offences Court
5 Ray Lawson Blvd.
Brampton, ON L6Y 5L7
Tel: 905-450-4770
E-mail:
provincialoffencescourt@brampton.ca

Brantford Provincial Offences Court
102 Wellington Square
Brantford, ON N3T 5R7
Tel: 519-751-9100
Fax: 519-751-0404

Burlington Provincial Offences Court
2051 Plains Rd. E.
Burlington, ON L7R 5A5
Tel: 905-637-1274
Fax: 905-637-5919

Caledon Provincial Offences Court
6311 Old Church Rd.
Caledon, ON L7C 1J6
Tel: 905-584-2273
Fax: 905-584-2861
TF: 1-800-303-2546

Cambridge Provincial Offences Court
152 Main Street
Cambridge, ON N1R 6R1
Tel: 519-740-5796
Fax: 519-622-4081

Cayuga Provincial Offences Court
45 Munsee St. North, P.O. Box 220
Cayuga, ON N0A 1E0
Tel: 905-772-3327
Fax: 905-772-5810

Elmvale Provincial Offences Court
(No Office Staff at this Location, Contact Barrie Provincial Offences Court for Admin Services)
L0L 1P0

Knox Building
35 Queen St. West
Elmvale, ON L0L 1P0
Tel: 705-739-4291
Fax: 705-739-4292

Fort Erie Provincial Offences Court
(Satellite Court)
200 Jarvis St.
Fort Erie, ON L2A 2S5
Tel: 905-871-8811
Niagara Falls Office: 905-371-9855 (Inquiries)

Hamilton Provincial Offences Court
John Sopinka Courthouse
45 Main Street East, Suite 408
Hamilton, ON L8N 2B7
Tel: 905-540-5592
Fax: 905-540-5730

Guelph Provincial Offences Court
55 Wyndham Street N.
Old Quebec Street (mall), Suite 215
Guelph, ON N1H 7T8
Tel.: 519-826-0762
Fax: 519-826-6814
Email: courtservices@caguelph.ca

Huron County Provincial Offences Court
1 Courthouse Square
Goderich, ON N7A 1M2
Tel: 519-524-8394
Fax: 519-524-2044

Kenora Provincial Offences Court
1 Main St. South
Kenora, ON P9N 3X2
Tel: 807-467-2984
Fax: 807-467-8530
Email: poa@kenora.ca

Kingston Provincial Offences Court
Macdonald Cartier Building
279 Wellington St.
Kingston, ON K7K 6E1
Tel: 613-547-8557
Fax: 613-547-8558

Kitchener Provincial Offences Court
77 Queen St. North
Kitchener, ON N2H 2H1
Tel: 519-745-9446
Fax: 519-745-0520

Leeds and Grenville Provincial Offences Court
32A Wall Street
Brockville, ON K6V 4R9
Tel: 613-342-2357
Fax: 613-342-8891
Email: poa@uclg.on.ca

Lindsay Provincial Offences Court
440 Kent St. West, Lower Level
Lindsay, ON K9V 5P2
Tel: 705-324-3962

London Provincial Offences Court
824 Dundas St.
London, ON N5W 5R1
Tel: 519-661-1882
Fax: 519-661-1944

Milton Provincial Offences Court
100 Nipissing Rd.
Milton, ON L9T 5B2
Tel: 905-876-2025
Fax: 905-876-0586

Mississauga Provincial Offences Court
950 Burnhamthorpe Road W.
Mississauaga, ON L5C 3B4
Tel: 905-615-4500

Napanee Provincial Offences Court
County Memorial Building
41 Dundas St. E.
Napanee, ON
Tel: 613-354-4883
Fax: 613-354-3112

Newmarket Provincial Offences Court
Ontario Court of Justice
465 Davis Drive, Suite 200
Newmarket, ON L3Y 7T9
Tel: 905-898-0425
TF: 1-877-331-3309

Niagara Falls Provincial Offences Court
4635 Queen Street, P.O. Box 840
Niagara Falls, ON L2E 6V6
Tel: 905-371-8988
Fax: 905-371-9855
TF: 1-866-278-8303

Norfolk County Provincial Offences Court
The Court House, Suite 402
50 Frederick Hobson VC Drive
Simcoe, ON N3Y 4L5
Tel: 519-428-2494
Fax: 519-428-4291

Northumberland County Provincial Offences Court
860 William St. Upper Level
Cobourg, ON K9A 3A9
Tel: 905-372-3329
TF: 1-800-354-7050
Fax: 905-372-6529

Oakville Provincial Offences Court
(courtrooms not available here)
1225 Trafalgar Rd., PO Box 206
Oakville, ON L6J 5A2
Tel: 905-338-4394
Fax: 905-338-4257

Orangeville Provincial Offences Court
10 Louisa Street
Orangeville, ON L9W 3P9
Tel: 519-941-5808
Fax: 519-940-3865

Orillia Provincial Offences Court
575 West St. South
Orillia, ON L3V 7N6
Tel: 705-326-2960
Fax: 705-326-3613

Ottawa Provincial Offences Court
100 Constellation Cres., 1st Floor
Nepean, ON K2G 6J8
Tel: 613-580-2665
TF: 1-800-724-2913
Fax: 613-580-2664

Owen Sound Provincial Offences Court
595, 9th Avenue East
Owen Sound, ON N4K 3E3
Tel: 519-376-2205 ext. 260
Email: poa@greycounty.on.ca

Penetanguishene Provincial Offences Court
(No Office Staff at this Location, Contact Barrie Provincial Offences Court for Admin Services)
Town Hall, 10 Robert Street West
Penetanguishene, ON
Tel: 705-739-4291
Fax: 705-739-4292

Peterborough Provincial Offences Court
99 Simcoe St.
Peterborough, ON K9H 2H3
Tel: 705-742-7777 ext. 2099
Fax: 705-743-9292

Prince Edward County Provincial Offences Court
#1, 67 King Street
Picton, ON
Tel: 613-476-2148

Richmond Hill Provincial Offences Court
Ontario Court of Justice
50 High Tech Rd.
Richmond Hill, ON L4B 4N7
Tel: 905-762-2105
TF: 1-866-758-0750

Sarnia Provincial Offences Court
Lambton Shared Services Centre, 2nd Floor
Bayside Mall
150 N. Christina Street Suite Y01A
Sarnia, ON N7T 7W5
Tel: 519-344-8880
Fax: 519-344-9379

Stratford, Perth County Court House, Provincial Offences Court
1 Huron Street
Stratford, ON, N5A 5S4
Tel: 1-519-271-0531

St. Catharines Provincial Offences Court
POA, 71 King St
St. Catharines, ON L2R 3H7
Tel: 905-687-6590
Fax: 905-687-6614

Toronto Court Services
(Administrative Services only at this location)
137 Edward St., 2nd Floor
Toronto, ON M5G 2P8
Tel: 416-338-7320 (General Inquiries)
Fax: 416-338-7388
Email: poacourt@toronto.ca

Toronto East Provincial Offences Court
1530 Markham Rd., Main Floor
Scarborough, ON M1B 3G4
Tel: 416-338-7320 (General Inquiries)

Toronto South Provincial Offences Court
Old City Hall
60 Queen Street West
Toronto, ON M5H 2M3
Tel.: 416-338-7320 (General Inquiry)

Toronto West Provincial Offences Court
York Civic Centre
2700 Eglinton Ave W.
Toronto, ON M6M 1V1
Tel: 416-338-7320 (General Inquiries)

Walkerton Provincial Offences Court
215 Cayley Street
Walkerton , ON N0G 2V0
Tel: 519-376-2205 ext. 260
Email: poa@greycounty.ca

Welland Provincial Offences Court
3 Cross St.
Welland, ON L3B 5X6
Tel: 905-734-6387
Fax: 905-734-7816
TF: 1-800-756-9477

Whitby Provincial Offences Court
605 Rossland Rd. E.,
P.O. Box 740
Whitby, ON L1N 0B3
Phone: 905-668-3130
Fax: 905-668-3166
Email: courts.poa@durham.ca

Windsor Provincial Offences Court
251 Goyeau St., Ste 300
Windsor, ON N9A 6V2
Tel: 519-255-6555
Fax: 519-255-6556

Woodstock Provincial Offences Court
Oxford County Court House
Courtroom # 4
415 Hunter Street
Woodstock, ON N4S 4G6
Tel: 519-539-9800 Ext. 3043

Index